DEEP WOUNDS, DEEP HEALING

Deep Wounds
Deep Healing

Discovering the Vital Link between
Spiritual Warfare and Inner Healing

Charles H. Kraft

with Ellen Kearney
and Mark H. White

Servant Publications
Ann Arbor, Michigan

Vine Books is an imprint of Servant Publications
especially designed to serve evangelical Christians.

The names and characterizations in this book drawn from the author's
personal experience are rendered pseudonymously and as fictional com-
posites. Any similarity between the names and characterizations of these
individuals and real people is unintended and purely coincidental.

Scripture texts used in this work, unless otherwise indicated, are taken
from *The Good News Bible: The Bible in Today's English Version;* copyright
© 1976 for Old Testament, American Bible Society, New York; copyright © 1966, 1971, and 1976 for New Testament, American Bible
Society, New York. The Scripture texts are cited by permission of the
copyright owner.

Published by Servant Publications
P.O. Box 8617
Ann Arbor, Michigan 48107

Cover design by Gerald L. Gawronski/ The Look

97   10 9 8 7 6 5 4

Printed in the United States of America

ISBN 0-89283-784-5

Library of Congress Cataloging-in-Publication Data
Kraft, Charles H.
    Deep wounds, deep healing : discovering the vital link between
spiritual warfare and inner healing / Charles H. Kraft : with Ellen
Kearney and Mark H. White.
        p. cm.
    Includes bibliographical references.
    ISBN 0-89283-784-5
    1. Spiritual healing. 2. Pastoral counseling. 3. Prayer—Christi-
anity. I. Kearney, Ellen. II. White, Mark H. III. Title.
BT732.5.K73   1993
253.5—dc20   93-29660

Contents

Introduction

THE SUBJECT of inner or, as I prefer to refer to it, *deep-level healing* is confusing for many within the Christian community. For those accustomed to prayer for healing, the confusion often lies in the fact that, though the healing comes through prayer, it seldom happens immediately, as Jesus' healings seemed to. If it takes several sessions, it doesn't seem like "real" prayer ministry. It seems more like psychological counseling. Inner healing doesn't seem to offer the quick results we are used to when physical healing is the object.

"Why," I am frequently asked, "doesn't healing come immediately when we pray, like it did with Jesus?" I don't know the answer to this question. What I do know is that prayer for deep-level healing frequently leads to the greatest freedom, aside from salvation, that I've ever seen. Release from bondage to such things as anger, depression, unforgiveness, and low self-esteem are but some of the results of this type of prayer ministry. And the transformation the Holy Spirit accomplishes in a person when he sets that person free from these inner torments is incredible.

There are, however, at least two further sources of this confusion: 1) the anti-psychology movement within American Christianity, typified by the activities of Dave Hunt, Martin and Deidre Bobgan, and Don Matzat; and 2) the kinds of questions raised by those who are pro-psychology concerning whether counseling can be effectively done by nonprofessionals.

The anti-psychology movement sees a close relationship between the methods of psychologists (some of which are used in inner healing) and those used by New Age and other occult practitioners. As I have pointed out in my book, *Christianity With Power,*[1] though Hunt and others do well to warn Christians of the danger of getting entangled with the occult, their opposition to Christian psychology and inner healing is based on a wrong assumption. *Their assumption is that, since certain techniques are used by the Enemy, the techniques themselves are infected and, therefore, wrong for Christians.* What they fail to recognize is that these techniques, though used by the followers of Satan, have been put in the universe by God to be used for his purposes. The problem is, therefore, not in the techniques but in the power behind the techniques. When psychological insights and techniques are empowered by Satan, the process in which they are used is wrong. *When, however, insight and technique is empowered by God, the process is right.*

A second problem with the anti-psychology movement is that it is crippled by Western rationalism. This group is unable to get beyond the influence of the eighteenth-century philosophical movement called "The Enlightenment," a movement, by the way, that was anything but Christian. This is a perspective that has elevated human reason to preeminence among human characteristics and that has badly infected both Western society and Western Christianity. This group is, therefore, afraid of emotion or anything else that explores reality outside the rigidly rationalistic tradition of its type of Christianity. In *Christianity With Power,* I have discussed the problems such a tradition raises for those who seek to be biblical in experiencing God's presence and power.

Having said that, I do not want to be perceived as uncritically endorsing all that is done by psychologists and those involved in inner healing. I have my own set of criticisms of both. Even Christian psychologists, for example, often use their techniques without consciously claiming the power God has authorized us to use when we minister to people (Lk 9:1). Furthermore, there are those in inner healing who use guided imagery to take people on flights of fancy away from the truth rather than toward it. These justify some of Hunt's claims that guided imagery opens people up to the Enemy's deceit. Untruth and deceit are never right in God's work—not because the psychological techniques are wrong, but because those techniques have been used to deceive rather than to discover the truth.

A view that is more balanced than either the anti-psychology perspective or the overprofessional attitude of the psychological establishment is that of Siang-Yang Tan, a Christian professional psychologist who has written a definitive book entitled *Lay Counseling: Equipping Christians for a Helping Ministry*. He and Gary Collins, another Christian professional, see counseling broadly as "a caring relationship in which one person tries to help another deal more effectively with the stresses of life."[2] They describe lay counselors as "individuals who lack the training, education, experience, or credentials to be professional counselors, but who nevertheless are involved in helping people cope with personal problems."[3]

Tan, Collins, and others within the psychological community see the amount of emotional brokenness in our world increasing to such an extent that there are far more in need of help than can possibly be tended to by professionals. They see, then, a tremendous need for nonprofessionals to participate in the tasks of getting people emotionally well. As a Christian and an advocate of lay counseling, therefore, Tan argues that there is a biblical basis for Christians to be involved in lay counseling.

Deep-level healing is a form of lay counseling that Tan and other Christian psychologists approve of. Though we who practice this form of counseling are seldom highly trained in psychological technique, we look to psychology for as much help as we can get from it. But we also seek to work in the power of God, believing that *the ideal combination is the power of God empowering the best techniques humans have been able to discover for dealing with deep-level problems.*

This is the perspective we take here. We live in an emotionally damaged and damaging world. And rationalistic Christianity, unfortunately, often contributes to the damage. So, often, does a secular approach to counseling, whether employed by non-Christians or by Christians. Many in our churches can see the damage happening and many are experiencing it firsthand, but they don't know what to do about it. Christians today seem to know little about how to do what the Father sent Jesus to do (Jn 20:21) by working with him to set captives free (Lk 4:18). Contrary to what the anti-psychology contingent is saying, merely bringing people to Christ for salvation and then quoting a few Scripture verses concerning God's attitude toward their problems is not succeeding in bringing people to the freedom Jesus promised. Indeed, many of God's children seem to live their lives in the Enemy's prisoner of war camps. Behind the scenes, then, the Enemy is actively engaged in keeping us either ignorant of or bickering about how to bring healing.

This book is dedicated to increasing our ability to help set captives free. It attempts to be biblical, balanced, and comprehensive. It is based on more than a decade of my own experience, plus a good bit of experience on the part of several colleagues.

I want to thank several of these colleagues for their assistance. My highest gratitude goes to the two whose names are on the title page: Ellen Kearney and Mark H. White. Drawing from their own experiences in ministry, each of them helped greatly in writing portions of this book and in finding examples to illustrate the principles. In addition, they searched the literature to find pertinent quotes and revised various sections of the manuscript as needed.

Others to whom I am grateful for assistance of various kinds include: Barbara Sturgis, Nancy Thomas, Tracy Jashinski, Jeanie Connell, Marti Browne, Molly Sutherland-Dodd, Gary Hixson and the many whose books I have profited from. I also thank my wife, Marguerite, for putting up with the pressures that come from having a husband in ministry and writing.

Finally, I am deeply grateful to Dave Came, managing editor of Servant Publications, for his assistance and personal interest in the book and especially for his patience with me when I missed deadlines. Thanks also to Ann Spangler and Beth Feia of Servant

Publications and Dr. David King for invaluable help with chapter eleven, as well as to Paul Witte for compiling the index.

Biblical quotations are from the Good News translation, unless otherwise indicated. Standard abbreviations are used for the others: NIV (*New International Version*), LB (*The Living Bible*), PHILLIPS (J.B. Phillips' *New Testament in Modern English*), NKJV (*New King James Version*), NEB (*New English Bible*).

Part One

An Introduction to Deep-Level Healing

1

It's about Freedom

The preacher was expounding on Philippians 3:13b, "Forgetting those things that are behind..." He had connected that verse with 2 Corinthians 5:17, "If anyone is in Christ, he is a new creature. Old things are passed away, behold, all things have become new." With enthusiasm, as if debating with someone who disagreed, he emphasized his main point, that once a person has accepted Christ as personal Savior, the past is gone, all things have become new. So, he contended, we are not to look back but to forge ahead in our new life in Christ, just as if the past hadn't happened at all. Nothing from the past can affect our present lives, he said, for Jesus took care of all of it at conversion. Though most of the audience listened without betraying what they were thinking, a few shifted position in their seats after that last remark.

The preacher was particularly disturbed over the increasing number of Christians who go to psychologists. "Christians do not need psychologists," he thundered, "the Bible is the only therapy we need! Jesus never took people back through their past experiences to find out what their parents and others did to them to cause them to be messed up. All we need to do is admit our sins, confess them, and be done with the past!"

As the preacher continued his diatribe, I grew increasingly

embarrassed for the hurting ones in the audience. I could not ignore the fact that research has shown that at least 40 percent of the women, plus a fair percentage of the men, in an audience such as this would have experienced some kind of abuse early in life, be it physical or sexual. Would these people recognize that the preacher was wrong? Or would they heap more condemnation on themselves, feeling that there was something wrong with them spiritually, since they were not finding it possible to dismiss the past? Though I did not take a poll, I suspect that many in the congregation left church that morning feeling very guilty and spiritually condemned because they didn't have the victory over the past the preacher had promised them in Christ.

How were they to know that the preacher was misusing his text? The text in context is referring to the *good* things Paul had accomplished—the "medals" he had won in the race of life. He's saying that unless he puts those accomplishments behind him and bends all his efforts to winning the present race, he will not make it to the finish line. *It's the victories, not the defeats, we are to forget,* lest we glory in them and lose the next race. The Bible never tells us to ignore or bury past pain.

Unfortunately, many of those sitting in the congregation that Sunday morning found themselves among the captives Jesus came to free. They had come to Christ but were still prisoners of war in the conflict between God and Satan, many through no fault of their own. And the preacher was only making their captivity worse. Though they had survived abuse of some sort, they still lived with the pain of the memories. Now they were being subjected to a kind of spiritual abuse.

PEOPLE NEED FREEDOM

People are hurting. Just as in Jesus' day, we have been beaten up by Satan. He attacks us from the inside. He attacks us from the outside. Spiritually, our relationship with God is often far from ideal. That closeness with our Creator, for whom we are made, often eludes us. Likewise, the relationship with ourselves is often negative. As I talk to people about their self-image, I find that the vast majority of them at least dislike, if not hate, this person they are supposed to love. And our relationships with others are often warped as well. For many, the list of those they dislike, envy, harbor anger toward, or even hate is much longer than the list of those they genuinely care about.

And most of us have assumed the fault was totally ours. We've known about our sin nature and, assuming it was the only factor, have blamed ourselves for the whole mess. Because our basic assumptions were not those of Jesus, we've usually not seen the Enemy's hand in our affairs. Not that our problems are all his fault—they're not. We've given him plenty to work with. And we have to take full responsibility for doing something about our failures.

But Jesus didn't blame the hurting. He never condemned or blamed those who were ill or demonized. He treated them as victims. Even those who had sinned, he saw as more worthy of pity than of punishment. Note the way he treated the woman caught in adultery (Jn 8:1-11), the Samaritan woman (Jn 4:1-42), and Peter after his denials (Jn 21:15-19, see below). Jesus seemed to see such people as those who had stumbled, had even been overpowered, rather than as those who had rebelled. His part, then, was to free them from the Enemy.

David A. Seamands points out that "God understood what it meant to be a human being. But because of the incarnation, His ultimate identification with us in the sufferings and death of Christ, God now fully knows and understands, not simply from factual omniscience but from actual experience."[1]

Note, though, that Jesus never advised people to "stuff" their hurts. In his kingdom people are not simply to put bad things out of their minds. Rather, they are to face them. As with sin, so with abuse and other disagreeable experiences, in the kingdom we are to face our pain squarely and deal with it honestly. These things have happened to us. They are a part of our history. We are not to deny them. We must admit the experiences and any unacceptable reactions to them. Then, by giving our old attitudes to God, we receive the "rest" he promised us when we come to him with our burdens (Mt 11:28).

We are told to deal honestly with our sin by admitting it to God (1 Jn 1:9), thereby allowing him to add it to the load Jesus carried to the cross. John and Paula Sandford tell us that "human free will is so precious to our Lord that He will not let the efficacy of the cross be applied to us without our consent."[2] We've learned how to do this and to receive the sweet release that comes from God's forgiveness. But Jesus also died to take away the pain of the broken-hearted (Is 61:1-3): "The Sovereign Lord has filled me with his spirit. He has chosen me and sent me to bring good news to the poor, to heal the broken-hearted, to announce release to captives and freedom to those in prison. He has sent me to proclaim that the time has come when the Lord will save his people and defeat their enemies. He has sent me to comfort all who mourn, to give to those who mourn in Zion joy and gladness instead of grief, a song of praise instead of sorrow." These are the verses Jesus quoted when announcing why he had come (Lk 4:18-19).

Whether the people Jesus ministered to were victims of spiritual abuse or of a more direct attack by the Enemy, Jesus came to "proclaim liberty to the captives" and to set them free (Lk 4:18-19). He does this in a spiritual sense when people receive him as Savior. But he offers more. Jesus desires that we be as free from the influence of Satan as he himself was. He said of himself that Satan had "no power over [him]," "no rights over [him]" (Jn 14:30b NEB).

In perhaps Jesus' finest invitation, he says, "Come to me, all of you who are weary and overburdened, and I will give you rest! Put on my yoke and learn from me. For I am gentle and humble in heart and you will find rest for your souls. For my yoke is easy and my burden is light" (Mt 11:28-30 PHILLIPS).

Jesus invites his people to freedom. But many of them don't seem to experience this freedom. Saved yes, free no. He left us peace (Jn 14:27), but we remain troubled. Jesus went around blessing, healing, delivering, and forgiving. He brought peace and freedom to people being battered by the Enemy. He brought them freedom for now as well as for eternity. And he gave to his disciples

(Lk 9:1-2), and through them to us (Mt 28:20), the authority and power to bring such complete freedom to our contemporaries.

A HURTING DISCIPLE

The rehabilitation of Peter, recorded in John 21:15-19, is an excellent example of how Jesus brings freedom from the past. Peter was born again. His spirit was headed for heaven. But he had responded badly to temptation, denying three times vehemently that he was a follower of his Lord and best friend. As Jesus had predicted, the Enemy had "sifted" him like wheat (Lk 22:31) and Peter had failed. Peter was so overwhelmed by guilt and remorse that he could not forgive himself or even seek the Lord's forgiveness. Indeed, he had opted out of kingdom work and chosen to return to fishing (Jn 21:3).

Matthew's account tells us that once the rooster had crowed, Peter realized what he had done and "went out and wept bitterly" (Mt 26:75b). Though he was sorry and the Lord was ready to forgive and accept him, it appears that Peter could not receive it. So Jesus, after the resurrection, made a special point to resolve this. Taking Peter aside, Jesus questioned him about his love. Three times Jesus asked Peter if he loved him and three times Peter said yes. Each time, Jesus recommissioned Peter to the work of feeding and tending the Lord's flock.

It is not coincidental that Jesus asked the question and gave the commission three times, for he knew Peter needed to be freed from the belief that his mistake meant that he did not love and could not serve the Lord. Just as it was a three-fold denial, it had to be a three-fold restoration in order to be complete.

Jesus, in a very tender way, took Peter back to the past. He did not try to get Peter to deny or forget that horrible evening. Rather, Jesus gently healed the memory so that what had been a gaping, open wound was turned into a healed scar. Some pain remained—enough to challenge Peter to faithful service to the end of his days. But the fear of the memory left, as did the pain of his guilt. This is a form of memory healing we will discuss further. The principles of deep-level healing are found in this and many other passages throughout the Bible. We can draw from them in our ministry.

SURFACE- AND DEEP-HEALING

I have come to believe that God wants to be given the opportunity to heal everyone.[3] And he usually chooses to do so with human assistance. Our records show that Jesus always combined healing, including casting out of demons, with the communication of the gospel. Furthermore, he never turned anyone down who came to him for healing. On nearly every occasion when he refers to how his followers are to communicate the gospel, he specifies that healing and casting out of demons is to be included (see Mt 10:7-8; Mk 3:14-15; 16:15-18; Lk 9:1-2; 10:8-9, etc.). "As the Father sent me, so I send you," he says in John 20:21. Presumably, then, we are to behave like Jesus behaved, to love as he loved, to communicate what and how he communicated, and to heal as he healed. He promised, "Whoever believes in me will do what I do— yes, he will do even greater things, because I am going to the Father" (Jn 14:12b).

Certainly his early followers understood him this way. They went everywhere proclaiming the kingdom in word and deed, including healing, (see Acts 3:6-8; 5:12-15; 6:8; 8:4-7, 13; 10:36-41; 14:8-10, etc.). All through the history of the church, then, there have been people who understood that following Jesus means bringing healing to others. In our day even many of us who were brought up in Western rationalistic Christianity are discovering that God still heals when we minister in authority in Jesus' name.

But healing is not the main issue, love is. Jesus, with all the power of the universe at his disposal, chose to use that power in the service of love. God heals because he loves, not simply because he wants to show his power. Indeed, when people came to Jesus seeking miracles for their own sake, he declined (Mt 12:38-39). When hurting people came, however, he felt compassion toward them and healed them (Mt 9:36; 14:14).

Most of the healings we read about in Scripture seem to be physical healings. These are what I call "surface-level healings." However, when God does a work on the surface, we can be sure there is also something deeper going on. Jesus makes this explicit to the paralyzed man of Capernaum when he states, "Your sins are forgiven" (Mt 9:2b). Yet, with the man born blind (Jn 9), Jesus assures his disciples that his problem was *not* the result of sin. With regard to the woman who had been stooped over for eighteen years, then, Jesus points to the fact that she had been in captivity to Satan (Lk 13:16).

The key principle here is that problems that seem to be simply surface-level usually have deeper roots. Typical is the woman who came to me complaining of stiffness in her shoulders and neck. I asked my usual questions, "When did it start?" and "What else was going on in your life at that time?" She told me it started a year or so ago during a messy divorce in which her former husband blamed her for the events leading up to the divorce. Under the guidance of the Holy Spirit, she was able to forgive both herself and her husband. And the physical problem disappeared—without our even praying for it.

On another occasion, I was ministering to a woman I'll call Ellie who had hurt her leg badly playing volleyball. At the time, the doctor who repaired the injury considered the problem routine. But when she returned to him two weeks after the accident, he was amazed to find that her condition was even worse than it had been before. As she explained this to me, I suspected that there must be something in her system that was weakening it, something that would not let healing take place as it should.

So we went back into her early life to see if there was anything there that might relate to her present problem. We discovered a history of abuse resulting in a large amount of self-condemnation and a very damaged self-image. So we spent the next three hours working on these attitudes and their roots through the kind of deep-level healing process we will describe later. As God broke through to her in event after event, she was able to forgive those who had hurt her and to come to a new understanding of who she is in Christ. Not only did her attitude toward herself change, her leg grew strong enough so that she was able to leave the church without using her crutches! And this happened without our even praying for her physical condition. Once the emotional damage was healed, her body was strengthened and God repaired the remaining physical damage.

The point is, apparent surface-level problems are usually connected with something deeper in the person's life. Indeed, we have often found that if we simply pray for a physical problem, without dealing with deeper issues, one of two things happens: either the person is not healed at all, or the problem goes away immediately but soon comes back to stay until the deeper issues are dealt with. Jesus wants to heal the person at whatever level there is a need.

I like to picture surface- and deep-level healing as follows. (Demonization may be, but is not necessarily, attached to either surface- or deep-level problems.)

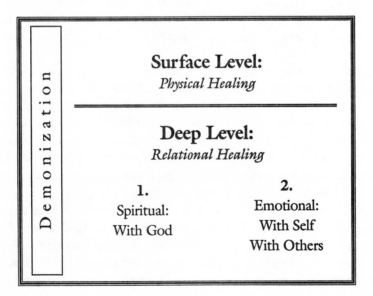

Demonization

Surface Level:
Physical Healing

Deep Level:
Relational Healing

1.
Spiritual:
With God

2.
Emotional:
With Self
With Others

HINDRANCES TO FREEDOM

1. Worldview. The apostle Paul points out that all humans have imperfect sight and partial knowledge: "What we see now is like a dim image in a mirror; then we shall see face-to-face. What I know now is only partial; then it will be complete—as complete as God's knowledge of me" (1 Cor 13:12).

God has, Paul says, a more complete view than we do. God's view may be referred to as *REALITY* in capital letters. This is how things actually are. Only God sees things that way. The view from our end I label *reality* in small letters. This is perceptual reality, a limited and sin-infected view that comes with our humanness.

What Paul is talking about is the fact that, though God's *REALITY* does exist, it is beyond our seeing and knowing. Part of that *REALITY* is presented to us in the Bible. But even the Bible is subject to human interpretation. And all interpretation is done in terms of our *reality*. We see even the Bible as "a dim image in a mirror," and know even the biblical revelation of God and his works in the partial way we know the rest of *REALITY*.

The study of human cultures helps us to understand that as we grow up, we learn the assumptions believed by the adults of our society. We call these assumptions our worldview. On the basis of these assumptions, we interpret all we see of *REALITY*. All that we think we know, then, we know in relation to these assumptions.

There are at least three kinds of basic assumptions: 1) those concerning what to believe or not believe; 2) those concerning what to value or not to value; 3) those concerning what to commit oneself to or against. Ever since the eighteenth-century "Enlightenment" movement, Western Christianity has participated in the rationalism, materialism, and humanism of the surrounding secular society. We, like secularists, have learned to focus on the material world and to largely ignore spiritual reality, even though we are theoretically committed to a biblical view of invisible beings and power. Our concern for power is largely the same as that of non-Christians—focused on human power over the material universe. It is usually only slightly altered in the direction of the primary concern of biblical peoples (and of most contemporary non-Western societies) for spiritual power. We practice, therefore, a largely powerless Christianity in which such beings as Satan, demons, and angels seem more mythical than real.

Most Western Christians would even view God as fairly distant and not very active in human affairs. For this reason we find it difficult to believe that God works today as he did in scriptural times to bring people to the freedom he has promised. We have been infected by assumptions that lead us to believe that what we can see and touch, especially if it is endorsed by science, is real, while things that cannot be touched are either not real or not important. We have also learned to assume that God is not really involved in anything that can be explained scientifically.

For example, we may give God credit for an amazing healing from cancer that the doctors cannot explain, but doubt that he is involved when the same or a lesser healing takes place after medicine or surgery has been used. Likewise, we may agree that Satan influenced Hitler, but not believe Satan was involved in the latest difficulty we have had with health or our automobile.

We have become innocent victims of a worldview that makes it difficult to believe much of the Bible and to see God's hand in events. If we are to participate in deep-level healing, therefore (either as bringers or receivers of healing), we need to open up to a more scriptural view of God's presence, power, and willingness to heal. To do this, we must reject any view of God that holds that he doesn't want to heal. We must stand against feelings of inadequacy, fear of opening up to spiritual things, and the unwillingness to risk, and the fear of being labeled a weird "faith healer."

Though I believe we need to maintain a healthy skepticism such as that of Thomas, we need to fight any tendency to follow the example of the Pharisees who refused to believe no matter how much proof they saw. If we are to change, we must be willing to risk new experiences with God. If we do, we will find ourselves changing in our understanding of God's love, power, and willingness to do wonderful things in our lives. I recommend that you read the record of my own changes in these areas in my book, *Christianity With Power*.[4]

2. Failure to see the war. Once we have pierced through the worldview problem, we can see in the Scriptures that there is a cosmic war going on between the kingdom of God and that of Satan. This war rages both in the air and on the ground. As humans, whether or not we like it, we are constantly influenced by the war. Peter saw this when he said, "Your enemy, the Devil, roams round like a roaring lion, looking for someone to devour" (1 Pt 5:8b).

Satan is a created being, perhaps at the level of an archangel, who appears to have rebelled against God (Ez 28; Is 14). Though Satan has been led as a captive in Jesus' victory parade and publicly humiliated (Col 2:15), he still has great power and authority in the world. We are told that "the whole world is under the rule of the Evil One" (1 Jn 5:19b) and that he is "the ruler of the spiritual powers in space, the spirit who now controls the people who disobey God" (Eph 2:2b). Jesus called him "the ruler of this world" (Jn 14:30b) and didn't dispute his claim that the power and wealth of the world "has been handed over to me, and I can give it to anyone I choose" (Lk 4:6b).

Satan has other powers that serve him. They are called by such names as demons, evil spirits, unclean spirits, fallen angels, principalities, powers, rulers, and authorities. As the prince in charge, it seems that Satan has a great deal of control over the "systems" of this world (for example, governments, media, academic activity, philosophers, etc.). As a result, they war against us. Satan also takes advantage of our sinful human nature ("the flesh") which is already hostile toward the things of God (Gal 5:16,17).

Jesus, however, brought a more powerful kingdom. He came to earth "behind Enemy lines" to establish his kingdom in the domain occupied by the Enemy. Jesus constantly spoke about the kingdom. Through it, he set about "to destroy what the Devil had done" (1 Jn 3:8b). The Gospels record, then, a selection of the events in which he bested his adversary. He took him on one-on-one in the temptations (Lk 4:1-13). He then declared war on the oppressor, stating that his purpose was to "proclaim liberty to the captives and... to set free the oppressed" (Lk 4:18b). Jesus took ground from Satan over and over again in healings (for example, Lk 4:38-39), casting out of demons (for example, Mt 12:28), forgiving sins (for example, Lk 5:19-20), calming weather (Lk 8:22-25), raising the dead (Lk 7:11-17; Jn 11:1-44) and then once and for all through his own death and resurrection.

George Eldon Ladd asserts, "... the Kingdom of God, which belongs to the age of the future when Christ comes in glory, has already penetrated This Age. Satan is not yet destroyed as he will be when he is cast into the lake of fire. Satan is not yet bound as he will be during the Millennium of the abyss. Yet God's Kingdom is active; God is attacking the Kingdom of Satan."[5]

Jesus' kingdom is both now and "not yet." When we look at the "back of the Book" we see that the victory is assured. But for reasons we don't understand, the Enemy has not yet been locked up. And there are still casualties, as there were during the Second World War between the time when the Allied forces landed at Normandy in June 1944 and the German surrender in May 1945. The culmination of the kingdom will take place when he returns (1 Cor 15:23-26; Rev 19:11-16).

Until then, we are to serve Jesus by extending his kingdom. He sends us into the world just as the Father sent him into the world (Jn 20:21). Just as he received the Holy Spirit at his baptism (Lk 3:21-22) and began to do mighty works, so we are to receive the same "gift" (Acts 2:38) and, as he promised, to do in our world what he did in his (Jn 14:12). As Jesus worked, not in his own power (Jn 5:19), but only with that of the Holy Spirit (Acts 10:38), so we are to imitate his dependence. We are to accept our commission and to extend his kingdom with the authority and power Jesus gave his disciples (Lk 9:1-2), and then commanded them to pass on to their followers (Mt 28:20). We, like they, are to be filled with the Holy Spirit (Acts 1:4-8) and to do the works of Jesus.

Thus the war between the kingdom of God and that of Satan is to be waged. And freedom from the Enemy's captivity is the major theme (Lk 4:18-19). Deep-level healing accomplished through partnership between the Holy Spirit and God's people is an important part of winning this war.

3. Habits. A third hindrance to freedom lies in the habitual reactions of those receiving ministry. As we grow, we develop ways of responding to the various situations we encounter. These reactions come automatically and are very difficult to control. They need to be probed in ministry to discover the roots that need to be healed.

To get at them, we need to ask questions such as: How does the person handle disappointment? Imperfection in self or others? Anger? What, then, in the person's experience would seem to predict such reactions? Special attention should be given to any difficulties in the person's relating to self, others, or God.

Unforgiveness is the most frequent block to freedom and the cause of much difficulty for those who come for ministry. The habit of holding things against self, others, and God results in the unforgiving person being bound up in captivity to the Enemy. This is why Jesus had so much to say about the necessity of forgiving. Seamands calls forgiveness "the most therapeutic fact in all of life."[6] See further treatments of this most important problem in chapters seven and nine.

Captivity to certain strong negative emotions frequently signals spiritual as well as emotional problems. These include anger, hate, fear, rejection, shame, guilt, depression, anxiety, and the like. Though damaging habits in the emotional area seem to be the most frequent symptoms among Christians who come for deep-level healing, habits in "spiritual" activities such as worship, Bible study, and prayer often also emerge as problem areas. Such problems will usually provide clues concerning inner healing issues.

A wrong view of God is quite common among those who have been severely mistreated—especially those abused by parents or other authority figures. Survivors of abusive situations tend to ascribe the characteristics of the abuser to God or blame God for allowing them to be hurt without helping them. Underlying attitudes of this sort emerge in the form of fear of God or anger toward God. Even a tendency to overspiritualize often masks a poor attitude toward God.

When people know or suspect that there will be unpleasant memories or feelings to deal with, their habit will probably be to try to avoid doing so. Our place is to help them tread the path of truth. We serve a God who delights in the truth and gives us the courage and power to face it, no matter how frightening that prospect may be. Our Enemy, the Devil, however, seeks to keep people captive through fear of facing the truth. The person coming for ministry is often in difficulty at least partly because of an inability to face the truth of some past or present situation. As Jesus points out, though, experiencing the truth is the path to freedom (Jn 8:32).

Ignoring or bypassing things allows them to fester and creates a point of attack for the Enemy. Being honest with oneself and with God is the only way to get through all of the emotional garbage that has piled up over the years. Helping people with such issues must, however, be done carefully and lovingly, lest they go away with an added burden of guilt on top of their already heavy load.

Part of what the person will have to face is sin. As humans, we are, of course, habitual sinners. As the comic-strip character Pogo has said, "We have met the enemy—and they is us!" The sin, however, is less likely to be rebellion than a reaction to abuse that, though quite normal when the abuse happened, became sinful when the person held onto it. We can certainly sympathize with victims when they react in anger, resentment, and even hatefulness to their abusers. But even "victims" need to take responsibility for any of their reactions that have led them into sin. When people allow themselves to "wallow" in such attitudes, they soon find themselves harboring unforgiveness. And unforgiveness is a serious sin, against which we are warned continually (see Mt 6:14-15).

All sin must, of course, be admitted and confessed to the Lord. And his promise of forgiveness is sure (1 Jn 1:9). But hurting people need to be led very gently to deal with any sinfulness of their natural reactions. I have found it usually advisable, for example, to lead them to forgive without ever mentioning that unforgiveness is a sin. I prefer, rather, to focus on the freedom Jesus offers to those who want release from attitudes such as unforgiveness, anger, resentment, desire for revenge, and the like. People receive freedom and forgiveness simultaneously when such attitudes are given to the Lord.

Receiving such freedom and forgiveness is, however, often difficult for people who have long lived with self-condemnation. And Satan is always ready to pour false guilt on people, even after they have been forgiven by God. Once a person has confessed a sin or given up a sinful attitude, therefore, it is often very healing when we use the authority given us in John 20:23 to pronounce them forgiven.

Ministry will proceed much more rapidly and successfully as people are able to fully realize their position in Christ. In spite of the fact that we are called kings and priests (Rv 1:6; 5:10), children of God (1 Jn 3:1), heirs of God and joint heirs with Christ (Rom 8:14-17; Gal 4:6-7), a wrong view of who we are in Christ is the legacy of many evangelical traditions. And, as Seamands puts it, "Satan's greatest psychological weapon is a gut-level feeling of inferiority, inadequacy, and low self-worth... Low self-esteem paralyzes our potential, destroys our dreams, ruins our relationships, and sabotages our Christian service.[7] I like to refer to such theological positions as "Worm Theologies." Such belief systems have Christians looking at themselves continually as lowly, depraved, and unworthy to be in relationship with God. See chapter eight for more on this important topic.

4. Lack of intimacy. As the Second Adam, Jesus demonstrated the intimacy with the Father that Adam, Eve, and all their descendents were meant to experience. He constantly attended to what the Father was saying. Thus he could claim, "I say only what the Father has instructed me to say" (Jn 8:28b). He was lining himself up with what the Father was doing. Thus he could say, "the Son... does only what he sees his Father doing. What the Father does, the Son also does" (Jn 5:19b). He lived in absolute dependence on the Father, affirming by life as well as by word, "By myself I can do nothing. As I hear from God, I judge, and my judgment is true because I do not live to please myself but to do the will of the Father who sent me" (Jn 5:30 PHILLIPS).

Staying close to the Father was a day-by-day priority for Jesus. To make sure he kept on track, he regularly spent time alone with the Father. Over and over again we read that Jesus withdrew "to a solitary place" (Mt 14:13b NIV) to be alone with the Father.

Whether we are seeking freedom or seeking to bring freedom to others, maintaining intimacy with Jesus is a crucial requirement. Deep-level healing is about good relationships, first with God, then with self and others. Moving close to God, then, is a primary aim of ministry. To bring this about, satanic interference in prayer, worship, and Bible study often has to be overcome through dealing with internal emotional and spiritual "garbage."

As for those of us who seek to minister to others, intimacy with Jesus as our source of power becomes our lifeline. The Sandfords emphasize this when they point out, "Our spirit finds nurture from its source, from God. It is personal devotion and corporate worship which are the first basis of nurture of our spirit. The Holy Spirit is by design the power of our life. 'It is the Spirit who gives us life...' (Jn 6:63a)."[8]

Every time I minister, I am acutely aware of the fact that I am not the healer. Healing doesn't happen because I am gifted. *People are touched, healed, and delivered because God himself is there, doing what he likes to do.* Whatever happens, therefore, is not by *my* strength or power, but by *his* Spirit (Zec 4:6). And this depends on the extent to which I maintain that closeness with the Source of strength and power.

Living in such intimacy is not, however, the mysterious thing many people make it out to be. It doesn't necessarily involve a lot of religious ritual. People often ask me, "How do you prepare for a ministry session?" The truth is, I seldom go to great lengths to prepare for any given session. I try to stay prepared constantly, because I never know when I'll be called on to help someone. I frequently have to be ready on the spur of the moment in restaurants, while visiting other people, during or after class, in my office, and even over the telephone. In fact, I probably minister more in situations with no preparation time than in those before which I have had time to fast and pray. So I try to always be prepared by staying close to Jesus.

Though our power comes from the indwelling Holy Spirit, I believe our spiritual authority flows directly from our intimacy with Jesus. We dare not ignore this very important facet of ministry, either for ourselves or for those we minister to. We should, therefore, do our best to imitate Jesus' approach to maintaining intimacy with the Father. Though he was a Son, he worked at the Father-Son relationship by regularly spending time with the Father. So should we.

For Further Reading

At the end of each chapter, we are including references we have found helpful in other books to assist those who would like further information on the particular subject. Usually page numbers of relevant sections in the books are cited. Please refer to the bibliography for complete source information on the books listed.

Neil Anderson, *Victory Over the Darkness*, 37-50.

Charles H. Kraft, *Christianity with Power*.

John and Paula Sandford, *The Transformation of the Inner Man*, 95-106.

David A. Seamands, *Healing of Memories*, 33-41; *Putting Away Childish Things*, 72-87; *Healing Grace*, 25-39.

2

What Is Deep-Level Healing?

PAUL'S STORY

Paul came to me feeling a keen sense of discouragement and defeat. He was in his early thirties and had been a Christian for ten years. He felt that his life before conversion was fairly normal except for a few excursions into sexual sins. His childhood, he said, had been fairly uneventful, except that he had had quite a temper and felt that the frequency of masturbation during adolescence might have been excessive. He also mentioned that he had developed quite a collection of *Playboy* and *Penthouse* magazines during his teenage years.

Soon after Paul accepted Christ, he had met a young woman whom he described as "a wonderful person, just right for me." He had expected his conversion, plus his marriage, to bring both his temper and his lustful thoughts under control. But they hadn't. In fact, a major part of his concern was over the way he acted when he got angry at his wife. He seemed to completely lose control. Each time that happened, then, he was filled with guilt and remorse, too ashamed of himself even to ask his wife for forgiveness. So he lived, worked, and worshiped with a fake smile on his face and a deep sense of defeat in his heart.

To start our ministry session I prayed, asking the Lord to be present in love and power and forbidding the Enemy to have any influence on what we did or said. I asked the Holy Spirit to give us the words to say, the thoughts to think, and the right things to do to bring freedom to his child.

Since problems such as temper and lust have roots, I felt led to take Paul back to conception by using the faith picturing exercise I call "back-to-the-womb" and describe in chapter six. Since problems such as Paul described are usually rooted in early life experiences, this approach enables many people to discover root experiences they never knew were there.

Without at this point getting into the details of that exercise, as Paul saw and felt himself in his mother's womb, he became aware of an intense feeling of anger. He described the baby's feelings with terms such as angry, upset, feeling unwanted, and rejected. And as these feelings came, Paul remembered that his mother had once shouted at him in a fit of rage that he had caused her trouble ever since his conception and that she never wanted to have him. At that point I asked Paul if his mother blew up like that very often. He said, "No," but that she was a very unhappy woman, perhaps hiding anger and dissatisfaction. He had never heard details, but what he had heard concerning her early life led him to believe it had been hard. Since he was the oldest child, I asked if he had been conceived before his parents got married. He had.

I spoke of the hands of God forming Paul in his mother's womb (Ps 139:13, 15) and asked Paul if he could picture that. I wanted him to know that God was with him in those very early days and that, as with Jeremiah (1:5), the Father had planned him and chosen him before birth. Granted that his parents did not want him to be conceived, I asked Paul if he thought Jesus had made a mistake in allowing the conception. He agreed with me that his conception was neither a mistake nor unanticipated. On that basis, then, I invited him to choose to go with God's will rather than with his parents'.

This he did. Then, identifying again with the preborn baby, he forgave his parents for not wanting him. As he did this, the feelings he was having as a baby changed dramatically. The anger, resentment, heaviness, and darkness were replaced by light, lightness, and anticipation of being born. As we went through the remaining months of gestation, then, Paul found a new sense of self-acceptance emerging and growing excitement about coming into the world.

There was more to do, but the success of this experience provided a firm basis on which to build a new self-image, a new closeness to his wife, and a new relationship with his parents. He discovered that his anger at his mother had broadened as he grew up into anger at women in general. He confessed that his early sexual adventures, some of his masturbation, and even some of his experiences with his wife had been at least partly motivated by an angry desire to humiliate women. Forgiving his mother, then, released him from the roots of his captivity to such a motivation. Paul still had quite a number of habits and habitual reactions to revise even after the roots were gone, but these were and are manageable with little or no help from others.

There is a new smile on Paul's face and a new intimacy with Jesus, with his wife, and with his family. There is also a newfound acceptance of himself. He loves the freedom and is active now in helping others in the same way he has been helped (2 Cor 1:4).

DEFINING DEEP-LEVEL HEALING

People often ask, "What is the difference between deep-level healing and professional counseling?" My answer is that the two approaches should be seen as more complementary than radically different. Like professional counseling, deep-level healing involves a great deal of counseling. Since most of us do not have professional credentials, however, we would have to be classified as lay counselors. But deep-level healing is not simply counseling, at least in the secular sense, since it involves praying as a major component of the process. We believe that God has given us as Christians the privilege of working in his power. We should not, therefore, work only in human power when we counsel.

Deep-level healing is, however, often most effective when the counselee also goes to a professional counselor; though we seek to empower human technique with prayer, professional counselors usually have more techniques at their disposal. In addition, professionals have a wider and broader knowledge of the workings of the human psyche to draw from. They can, therefore, often help their clients in many ways not ordinarily a part of the "repertoire" of the one who works in deep-level healing. The ideal would be for one trained in the field of psychology to also work in the power of prayer.

The professionals whose counselees come to me often tell me that many times when clients work with me, they seem to experience "spurts" toward health. These spurts, then, provide them with new thresholds from which to work with the professional. As we pray together, the power of the Holy Spirit often enables the person to jump to a new level of wellness that then becomes the new level from which the slower process of working with the professional counselor continues.

Though it is true that deep-level healing can push things faster, it is sometimes the case that faster is not better. Recently, in working with clients with multiple personalities, I have found that working in the power of the Spirit has opened up too many things at the same time. I have, therefore, taken the advice of the professional counselors to 1) work only on problems they are also working on and 2) not to push things too fast. When too much is being worked on at the same time, the client can get confused and the process so disorganized that progress is minimal at best.

With this in mind, let's consider some of the current definitions of deep-level or inner healing. David Seamands, one of the pioneers in the development of inner healing, sees it as "a form of Christian counseling and prayer which focuses the healing power of the Spirit on certain types of emotional/spiritual problems. It is *one* and *only one* of such ministries; and should never be made the *one and only* form, for such overemphasis leads to exaggeration and misuse."[1]

Two other pioneers in the field, John and Paula Sandford, in their book *Transformation of the Inner Man*, see such ministry as aimed at the transformation of the inner being of a person, a ministry to the inner person.

One of my favorite definitions is that of Betty Tapscott: "Inner healing is the healing of the inner [person]: the mind, the emotions, the painful memories, the dreams. It is the process through prayer whereby we are set free from resentment, rejection, self-pity, depression, guilt, fear, sorrow, hatred, inferiority, condemnation, or worthlessness, etc."[2]

I would add to this definition that it encompasses the healing of the spirit as well. The more I minister to people, the more I find wounding that appears to go deeper than the mind or emotions. Certain types of circumstances and abuse (such as rejection by parents or Satanic Ritual Abuse) seem to affect the very core of the person—the spirit. The Sandfords have dealt with this topic at length in their book *Healing the Wounded Spirit.* They have described various types of injury that the human spirit can sustain and how the Holy Spirit works through inner healing to set captives free.

In my recently published book entitled *Defeating Dark Angels,* I have defined deep-level healing as:

> a ministry in the power of the Holy Spirit aimed at bringing healing to the whole person. Since the majority of human ailments are closely tied to damage in the emotional and spiritual areas, inner healing focuses there. It seeks to bring the power of Christ to bear on the roots from which such damage springs. Since these are often in the memories carried unconsciously by those who come for help, inner healing involves a special focus on what is sometimes called "the healing of the memories." Specific problems often encountered are unforgiveness, anger, bitterness, rejection, low self-esteem, fear, worry, sexual issues and the like.[3]

Most of us could identify with several of the problems in this list. And many of us could add to the list. As humans we often experience deep levels of brokenness. We continually face the influences of our fallen nature and the fallenness of the world around us. Our Enemy, Satan, constantly uses the society in which we live (what 1 John 2:15-16 refers to as "the world") and the human nature we carry with us (our "flesh") to make things difficult for us. But our Lord has provided the means by which we can move into the freedom Jesus promised in Luke 4:18-19.

Actually, human brokenness often serves as the launching pad for two very important dimensions of Jesus' desire to bring freedom to his people. First of all, pain—whether physical, emotional, or spiritual—is often what God uses to alert people to their need for ministry. When people are in pain, they are usually much more willing to let the Lord come close and help. Most of those who come to us for deep-level healing come with a sense of desperation. They often have tried other approaches to resolving their problems but found those efforts unsuccessful. Indeed, they may have lived for quite a while with significant suffering. At last they are reaching toward the source of all healing—Jesus.

Jamey came with just such a motivation. His stomach had been troubling him for nearly two years. He had undergone a number of medical tests and had even gone to a psychologist for several months. To no effect. About all he had discovered was that the stomach got worse whenever his parents came to visit. After asking God to lead us, I felt led to ask about Jamey's relationship with his parents.

At first Jamey claimed that he and his parents had always gotten along well. He spoke fondly of how his dad had coached his Little League team and had always attended his basketball and baseball games as he went through grade school, junior and senior high. I asked if he remembered any stomach problems during those growing up years. He thought for awhile. Then suddenly, as if by revelation, memories he had not consciously thought of for years came back. "Though it wasn't as intense then as it is now," he said, "I remember feeling a knot in my stomach before every game, especially when my father was present." As I probed, then, Jamey told me of a father who never seemed to be satisfied with anything Jamey did, whether in athletics or in any other area of life. He remembered the terror he felt at the thought that he might fail either in athletics or in his studies. He remembered the same feeling of terror as his wedding date approached and later as each of their three children were born. Worse yet, it was now becoming obvious to him that his stomach problem got worse every time he became anxious about his wife's reactions to things he planned to do.

During the next hour or so, we were able to help Jamey understand the roots of several of his father's problems and their effects on him. His father had been deeply frustrated in his early life. He failed often and was seldom recognized or complimented even when he did well. Living in intense guilt over his past life, he pushed his son to succeed but could generate no warmth or even acceptance for him when he did. Fortunately, Jamey usually succeeded very well, so he rarely experienced his father's wrath. Before any given event, however, his imagination held him captive to what he felt might happen if he let his father down.

Jamey was able to see both his father and himself as victims and to allow Jesus to soften his heart toward his father, himself, and his wife. He was then able to forgive all three, including himself. He was also able to admit his anger at God and to forgive God for allowing all this to happen. (The concept of releasing your anger against God and then the need to forgive him is controversial and will be clarified later in the book.) As the Holy Spirit dealt with issue after issue by allowing Jamey to picture Jesus in several of the most memorable events involved, his stomach pain became less and less. When it was completely gone, we knew we had gone far enough for that session. Though there were other things to deal with in later sessions, the stomach problem and the emotional captivity it signaled have never come back. Jamey was free!

Though this type of freedom is frequently the result of deep-level ministry, there is usually an even more important benefit. Over and over again, people report that the physical or emotional healing they receive is overshadowed by the deepening that occurs in their relationship with the Lord as a result of the time in ministry. They find that God has used their desperation, brought on by the pain, as a means of bringing them closer to him.

The second benefit that can come out of the healing of brokenness is that the recipient often develops a heart for such ministry to others. Many of the ministry team members with whom I work have moved from experiencing healing themselves to a compassionate ministry to others. This is in keeping with 2 Corinthians 1:4 which says: "[God] helps us in all our troubles, so that we are able to help others who have all kinds of troubles, using the same help that we ourselves have received from God."

The fact that we have received help from God is a powerful motivator to help others who are hurting. Those who have themselves been healed of deep hurts are amazingly effective in ministry, even when their own healing is still incomplete. Out of our pain and the healing we are receiving, we can offer hope to others that their struggle will be worth it.

DEEP-LEVEL HEALING IS ABOUT WHOLE PEOPLE

There are two senses in which deep-level healing is about whole people. First, it aims to make people who are hurting whole again. This entire book deals with that subject. This section, however, focuses on wholeness in the second sense—the fact that we need to deal with the whole person when we seek to bring about deep-level healing.

People are not simply a collection of various parts. Each part of us is intricately connected to many other parts so that all function together. Though, for the sake of analysis, we can speak about body, mind, emotions, personality, and will, in real life all of these come as a unit in any given person. They do not function separately and should not be dealt with in isolation from each other as is usually done by health professionals. If we have physical pain, we are likely to go to a medical doctor who simply treats the physical problem as if it were divorced from the rest of our being. Or, if we have an emotional or psychological difficulty, we go to a psychologist who treats that part of us. For spiritual problems, then, we may go to a pastor or other spiritual advisor.

Such approaches to treatment are usually inadequate. Even medical doctors admit that more than 80 percent of physical illnesses spring from emotional problems. "A doctor who works in a mental hospital in Tennessee put it this way, 'Half of my patients could go home in a week if they knew they were forgiven'."[4] Yet medical training seldom enables a doctor to deal in any meaningful way with a person's emotions. He or she has learned simply to function as a body mechanic. Likewise, though some psychologists suggest that many emotional difficulties are rooted in spiritual problems, they are seldom able to help in that area. And, sadly, psychological training programs in Christian institutions tend to give the impression that it is illegitimate to combine prayer counseling with professional counseling.

But people are integrated and, when they hurt, usually need healing in more than one part of them. As Rita Bennett has said, "Your soul—intellect, will, emotions, memories, subconscious, personality, creativity, motivations—has the potential for total peace, but there may be wounds, some very deep, not yet healed. Each of us will need further healing during our lifetime.[5]

Our rule, then, is to deal with the whole person and to seek to bring healing at the deepest level necessary. In this sense, deep-level healing is more comprehensive than any of the usual secular models of healing. It is also more personal and more focused on love. For we believe that healing is about loving people. It is absolutely essential in our practice of ministry that people go away feeling they have been loved.

As mentioned above, many times people come for ministry with physical problems that disappear after some emotional or spiritual issue is dealt with. A short discussion of the physical problem usually reveals a deeper problem in the emotional, spiritual, or relational area. When, then, we deal with the deeper area, the presenting problem usually dissolves. There are, however, times when the presenting problem remains but the person has received a deeper healing through the touch of the Holy Spirit and the love of another person. Often, the person receives healing for things that were never even mentioned, either in place of what was in focus or in addition to it.

Judy's experience illustrates this principle. She had suffered with back pain for six years and had received prayer for that problem from my colleague Dr. Peter Wagner, who is greatly gifted in dealing with physical problems. When this was unsuccessful, he sent her to me to see if there might be a deeper issue to deal with. As is my custom, I asked her what was going on in her life when the pain started. Judy revealed that she had been four months pregnant, the same point at which she had miscarried in her previous pregnancy. So we worked with her through the loss of the earlier child by using a faith picturing technique that will be described in chapter six. In this way, we worked through the pain of the miscarriage, enabling Judy to release both her damaged emotions and her baby to Jesus. She was immediately released from her back pain and, as a bonus, was later healed of some other physical problems through prayer with Dr. Wagner.

HOW DEEP-LEVEL HEALING RELATES TO OTHER TYPES OF HEALING

We start with the assertion that there is only one Healer in the universe, God. Just as all life has its source in God, I believe all healing has its source in him, even when that healing is mediated by unbelievers. I believe that no conception is simply the result of the physical process of sexual intercourse. God is involved in every one. He is the only one who can give life. In the same way, only God can repair those parts of the life process that have gone off track. As with most of the other things God does in the world, however, he usually uses human instruments to bring about healing.

As mentioned in chapter one, our Western worldview pressures us to dichotomize between what humans do and what God does. If we can explain something like healing in terms of "natural" human activities, such as the use of medicine, surgery, or human counseling, we usually assume that God was not involved. This is, however, untrue. In reality, God is involved in every facet of human experience whether or not we recognize his presence. It is he who makes the medicine work. It is he who makes a surgical procedure effective. These processes do not simply work automatically. God is in everything that really helps people, even if the vehicle is medicine or people, and even if we can explain the human part of the process scientifically.

Deep-level healing is one of the approaches to healing that God is pleased to work with. But there are at least four others.

1. One of the most obvious approaches to healing is *physical medicine*. It is God who has given us doctors and medicine. He works with doctors and the physical processes they have learned to use, whether or not the doctors acknowledge him. He uses their skills even if they don't pray or give him credit for their successes. They work more effectively, however, when they have the power of prayer behind them.

We believe in doctors and medicine and advise those who come to us to use their services to the fullest. We tell those who have been put on medicine by a doctor to keep taking that medicine until the doctor decides it is no longer necessary. Given our inability to know for certain what God is doing in the healing process, it is very unwise for people to stop taking medicine after they have been prayed for in hopes that they have been healed. The doctor who prescribed the medicine is the one who has the authority to cancel it. Jesus followed such a principle when he told the healed leper to go show himself to the priest who alone was authorized to pronounce him clean (Mt 8:2-4).

There is one problem that needs to be watched, however. People often respect the opinions of doctors so much that they take their diagnoses as gospel truth. A negative diagnosis given by a doctor, then, often takes on the status of a curse. Such a diagnosis needs to be seen as an opinion, not as a prediction. And any tendency to let a diagnosis determine the future, as would a curse, needs to be rejected.

2. Psychologists, psychiatrists, and counselors are used by God to heal. They specialize in dealing with emotional and mental problems, problems that even medical doctors admit underlie most of the physical problems they treat.

We believe in psychological counseling and, as stated above, recommend that our clients get competent help from such professionals, in addition to the help they get from us. Some recent studies are, however, calling into question the value of much psychological counseling. It appears that psychologists and psychiatrists, though good at analyzing people's problems, are often not very effective at bringing about improvement. Many clients seem to receive very little help.[6]

My assessment of the situation is that professional counselors are usually good at technique but limited by at least three major problems. 1) Human motivation and power, especially if both have to be supplied by the client, are seldom enough to bring about the necessary changes. 2) The spiritual nature of humans is usually neglected at best and denied at worst. Yet sickness of the human spirit is often at the root of the problems presented. 3) The limitations of a fifty-minute appointment are severe; seldom is their time enough to really come to grips with any given set of problems before the time is up.

Concerning this last point, Seamands concludes, "Because the prayer session is so important, it is essential that it be planned properly. The session requires unhurried time and an unpressured schedule. This means that it should not simply be an hour worked into a regular counseling schedule. It should not be subject to clock-watching by anyone."[7]

We find that working for two to three hours at a time is much more productive than working for one hour. "One of the chief obstacles to healing is our obsession with the immediate. The 'itch for the instantaneous' pervades much of our Christian thinking.... We have become impatient and frustrated with things that take time."[8]

I wish that more Christian psychologists would learn the ideal combination: proven technique empowered by prayer. Of course, in spite of prayer, many people do not get motivated enough to do their part to move toward healing. And there are enough complexities in dealing with the human psyche that even the best techniques do not assure healing for everyone. But good technique with the empowerment of prayer is infinitely better than technique without such specific empowerment by God.

3. *Pastoral counseling* **is often used by God.** God has given many pastors the ability to help greatly. Yet, though it is in emotional and spiritual areas that most people need help, many pastors do not have the skills or training to deal with them. Pastoral training programs in seminaries and Bible schools usually focus almost "people skills." Some pastors do develop counseling gifts, but they often do not know and use the authority Jesus gives, along with the empowering of the Holy Spirit, to heal as effectively as they might.

Nevertheless, those involved in pastoral counseling who minister in the authority of Jesus and the empowerment of the Holy Spirit often work in ways quite similar to what we are recommending. They are our closest relatives among the various healing communities.

4. A fourth type of healing ministry we relate to is what is called *deliverance.* A deliverance ministry specializes in casting out demons. Unfortunately, many deliverance ministries lead people to think that once the demons are gone, their problems are over. Such is seldom the case, however, since *the real problems are the things the demons are attached to, not the demons themselves.*

In deep-level healing we get to cast out lots of demons. But we recognize that *demons are like rats. And rats go for "garbage."* "Garbage" is the term I use to refer to the spiritual or emotional problems to which demons attach themselves. In order to live in a person, demons need to have a legal right. That right is provided when there are things in the person's past or present life to which demons can attach. When that is taken away, the demons usually go quietly.

Most deliverance ministries focus more on the rats than on the garbage. What often occurs, then, is a big fight to expel the demons. But even though the demons are gone, there is often a considerable amount of garbage left. And the person continues to experience most of the same problems. Deep-level healing deals with the root problems (the garbage), whether or not demons are involved. This usually results in dealing with the demons toward the end of the ministry, after they have been weakened through loss of the things they were attached to. They then usually go very easily, without a fight. For more on dealing with demons, see chapter twelve and my book *Defeating Dark Angels*.

DISTINGUISHING FACTORS IN DEEP-LEVEL HEALING

To summarize and amplify what we have said above, I'd like to point to four distinguishing features of deep-level healing.

1. **Deep-level healing is *prayer ministry*.** Though much of what we do involves counseling, the context in which the counsel is given is prayer. We seek to imitate Jesus by first listening to what God is saying and then working in his authority to do only what he wants us to do (Jn 5:30).

We have to be careful not to get caught up in technique. We dare not make the "Moses mistake." When God told Moses to get water from a rock the second time (Nm 20:7-12), instead of listening to God and doing what he commanded, Moses did what he had done on the previous occasion. On this occasion, God told Moses to speak to the rock (v. 8), not to strike it with his rod. But, remembering what he had done previously (Ex 17:5-6), Moses struck the rock and incurred God's anger. To avoid this mistake, *we need to be careful to listen for God's instructions for this occasion, not simply to do what worked last time.* Then and only then can we pray with the confidence and authority we need to bring the healing God intends.

Prayer ministry endeavors to utilize the gifts of the Holy Spirit to their fullest. For this reason it is good to work in teams, where God's gifts will flow through more people.

2. Deep-level healing is *holistic*. Our aim is to get the person well at the deepest level necessary. Usually this requires dealing with several aspects of the person: body, spirit, emotions, mind, or will.

This is not easy. It demands that we learn as much as possible about all areas of personhood and about how each area impacts the other areas. It is unlikely, therefore, that those ministering deep-level healing will be as expert in any given area as those who have specialized in those areas. In many ways, then, we are generalists rather than specialists. Yet we find ourselves constantly being consulted by specialists for advice on problems that they recognize as relating to areas of a client's experience outside their area of expertise.

For example, I and several of my colleagues in deep-healing ministry have recently been consulted by professional psychologists who found they were "over their heads" in attempting to deal with problems related to multiple personality disorder and demonization. In some of these cases, we understood both problems better than the professionals did, largely due to the fact that we are more holistic in our approach.

3. Deep-level healing *employs power wrapped in love*. The most important mark of Christians is that they are called to be signs or instruments of God's *love* (Jn 13:34-35). Jesus certainly demonstrated the use of God's power in serving the cause of love. *Jesus healed because he loved.* Over and over, the Gospels record that Jesus ministered to the needs of people because he felt pity or compassion for them (for example, Mt 9:36; 14:14; 15:32; 20:34).

Though deep-level healers seek to minister in the gifts of the Spirit, *we are just as concerned to exhibit the fruits of the Spirit.* We find that people who experience the love of Christ through our ministry are blessed, whether or not they receive the healing they seek. One man for whom we saw little visible change remarked, "I've *never* been prayed for like that before," to register the fact that something amazing, though intangible, had happened inside him. And a recent conversation with him, several years after that event, indicates that important growth has happened since that date stemming, as best we can discern, from the fact that he felt incredibly loved as he was prayed for.

4. The deep-level healing approach *freely borrows and uses insights from any legitimate source.* Perhaps because we are not established as professionals with turf to protect, we can be eclectic in seeking insight. We seek whatever spiritual insight God has given to any of his people, whether or not they claim to do inner healing. But we also are open to whatever insight God has given to professionals, whether Christian or non-Christian.

We seek to be discerning with regard to the insights and techniques we use, however. We commit ourselves to use only those compatible with scriptural principles and to use them only under the power and guidance of the Holy Spirit. And there are dangers. For example, we make considerable use of what I call "faith picturing" (visualization). But New Age people also make extensive use of this technique, but under the power of the Enemy. As we will see in the chapter on technique (chapter six), this God-given ability can be used in ways that glorify him or can be used in ways that are not pleasing to him.

For Further Reading

Charles H. Kraft, *Defeating Dark Angels,* 139-56.

John and Mark Sandford, *A Comprehensive Guide to Deliverance and Inner Healing,* 49-85.

John and Paula Sandford, *The Transformation of the Inner Man,* 103-201.

3

Who Needs Deep-Level Healing?

JULIE'S STORY

Emotionally, Julie was a woman who had been deeply scarred. She was now in her thirties, but continued to carry heavy emotional wounds from childhood days. Julie's father was an alcoholic during most of her growing-up years. Julie remembers instances when she and her mother would have to go out at night "looking for Daddy" trying to find out what he was up to and when or if he was ever coming home. This greatly reduced Julie's sense of stability in the home.

The lack of stability was compounded by the shame she felt as friends and relatives would ask pointed and painful questions about her father. These questions had few easy answers.

Unfortunately, but understandably, Julie's mother did not handle these questions by telling the truth. She chose instead to cover the truth about Julie's father with lies made up to protect herself and the children from the shame he was causing. She, of course, needed an ally, so she encouraged Julie, who was the oldest of her siblings, to lie about her father to people who would call him on the phone or who wanted to know how he was doing.

Although she had a strong sense of the truth, Julie found that she frequently faced great pressure within herself to lie about other things as well. For the most part, Julie remained strong against this temptation. But being the oldest, Julie felt a strong sense of responsibility for what was going on in the family. As her mother's lying became more frequent, she vowed that when she grew up she would never lie again. This vow, however, gave the Enemy a grip on Julie.

On the one hand, she fought the temptation to lie but, on the other, she was frequently forced by her feelings of responsibility and duty toward her mother to fudge on the truth. The result was a high level of confusion. It was the frustration over temptation, doubt, and confusion that pushed Julie to seek prayer ministry.

We found in one of the first sessions that a spirit of lying had entered Julie some twenty years earlier while she was being pressured to lie about her father. This accusing spirit had been feeding on the confusion in Julie. When she lied, the spirit made her feel guilty, yet when she got in a tight spot in areas of life not related to her father's problems, the same spirit pushed her to lie her way out of it. The spirit even prompted her to make the vow, increasing her guilt whenever she broke it by lying. Julie felt that others disbelieved her when she was telling the truth. One of her secret fears was that if she were ever falsely accused of a crime in a court of law, the jury would find her to be guilty.

Through the deep-level healing of some of Julie's childhood memories, the sin of lying was confessed and forgiven by God at its entry point. Julie was able to take responsibility for her sin but also to recognize and renounce the influence the lying spirit had gained in her life. These two choices released Julie from a large part of the self-condemnation she felt over her problems. She then had to release herself from the responsibility she felt both for her family and for the vow she had taken. When she gave both of these to Jesus, we were able to cast out the demon, releasing her from that pressure. From then on, she has often had to claim the victories we won with her by resisting the feelings of responsibility and guilt whenever they have started to return.

Though the process was more difficult than this recounting of it may indicate, it is exciting now, several months later, to see Julie with greater freedom to enjoy the honesty and truth that come with the Christian life. She is able both to be truthful and to enter more fully into trusting relationships. She is also able to joyfully use her spiritual gifts in ministering to others. Julie is largely free from even the temptation to lie. She is also free from the self-condemnation and confusion that so characterized her life previous to this time of ministry.

TWO KINDS OF PEOPLE NEED DEEP-LEVEL HEALING

There are basically two kinds of people for whom deep-level healing is appropriate: sinners and victims. Those who have knowingly or unknowingly committed sin need freedom from the internal damage that sin has produced and continues to produce. Once we have come to Christ as Savior, of course, the sin problem is dealt with for eternity. The problem facing many of the redeemed, however, is the need for freedom from the present effects of that sin. *Jesus came to release prisoners as much from present captivity as from future damnation.*

The second kind of people needing deep healing are those who have been sinned against, those who have become the victims of other people's sinning. Jesus paid special attention to those in this category in his day. For reasons we don't understand, God allows people to hurt other people. These hurts, then, stimulate reactions (see chapter seven) that, if they are not tended to, eat away at the inner beings of the wounded ones in such a way that they cause many more problems than the original hurt did.

This chapter will be devoted to dealing with these two types of problems. First, the sin problem.

THE ENEMY'S GRIP THROUGH SIN

Sin is a major issue in deep-level healing. In some sense, all of the problems we deal with are sin-related. Either the person who comes for help has sinned or someone has sinned against her or him. Though it is no sin to be sinned against, the reaction to such abuse may easily become sin. When hurt, it is normal to get angry. Such anger is not a sin in and of itself (Eph 4:26). But it may become sin if we allow it to spawn such things as resentment, hate, unforgiveness, and bitterness. If we wallow in such negativity, our reactions become sinful, even if they started out simply as normal, natural reactions to difficult situations. See chapter seven for more on reactions.

There are also outright sins that have to be dealt with. When someone has taken a life through abortion or has committed adultery or has lied or stolen, confession of such acts to God according to 1 John 1:9 is a must if the person is to be freed by Jesus.

We had been attempting for two-and-a-half hours to get Bob free from a rather tenacious demon. He had shared with us several details of a very difficult love-hate relationship with his father, a pastor whose ministry in recent years had faltered.

We helped Bob to deal with the anger and unforgiveness he felt toward his father. Since sin is often taken as an accusation, it is my habit to avoid using that term, though I usually ask the person if he or she has confessed all known sin. Early in the session, I had asked Bob this question, and his answer was that he thought he had. So we were surprised when he blurted out, "I've never admitted this to anybody. I committed adultery in my father's church! It was after this that the church started going downhill." A simple confession of this fact to God, then, brought forgiveness and enabled us to get rid of the demon.

When ministering to people, we should always look for any such obvious sins. *It is, however, very important how we probe.* It is easy to be unloving in searching for sin in the lives of people who have been abused. They are already sensitive and, if we are not careful, may read more into even our most innocent attempts to probe in this area than we intend.

DEALING WITH SIN

The issue of personal responsibility is a crucial, yet sensitive one (see chapter seven). Some who minister focus their attention almost entirely on the moral failings of the client and concentrate most of their efforts toward healing through more righteous living. *Though any moral failings must be dealt with thoroughly and the need to live a righteous life should be emphasized, all too often focusing on such matters compounds the problem rather than bringing healing.* People who are hurting often have an incredible ability to collect more hurt and to add it to what they are already carrying. When, then, we label a reaction such as unforgiveness or anger as sin, the hurting person usually turns in on him or herself, heaping on much greater condemnation and making ministry all the more difficult.

Sin is an important issue. Nowhere in Scripture do we find permission to blame others, the world, or Satan for our problems. Julie, in the case described at the opening of this chapter, could not blame the demon or her parents for the fact that she regularly lied, even though they exerted strong pressure on her. She had to take responsibility for her own sin. Each of us must give an account for our actions and reactions. However, there is more to healing than the recognition of sin. Most of the people we work with have been deeply hurt and, because of this, have chosen unhealthy ways to deal with their pain. Though we do need to address their wrong reactions, jumping on the sin issue will usually either submerge people under a greater load of shame and guilt than they came with or induce them to raise their defenses higher.

The Samaritan woman (Jn 4) and the woman caught in the act of adultery (Jn 8) were both sinners. But they already knew that; they had condemned themselves and had borne the condemnation of others. It is significant that Jesus did not focus on their sins. Self-condemned people aren't helped when we focus on their failures. Instead, the Master showed them acceptance and love, gently leading them along the path to forgiveness.

Though we dare not be soft on sin, it is not our job to convict people of sin. Even Jesus himself refused to do that (Jn 3:17). Instead, he saw his mission as bringing release to people (Lk 4:18-19). The task of convicting people belongs to the Holy Spirit (Jn 16:8). We, like Jesus, are to be agents of God's reconciliation (2 Cor 5:20) and as such are called to minister love and restoration.

Our job is to free people from guilt, not to heap more on them. This often involves helping the people to whom we minister to accept the forgiveness aleady granted them by the Lord.

I find that most of those who come to me are already in the position of the woman caught committing adultery (Jn 8). They are keenly aware of their sins and, in fact, have usually confessed them to God over and over again without feeling released. Guilt and self-condemnation weigh so heavily on these people that they often cannot even believe that God will forgive them. Any additional hint of condemnation only drives them deeper into hopelessness. The most helpful and healing approach is to follow the path Jesus used with Peter (Jn 21) and with the adulteress (Jn 8). He focused not on their sins but on God's willingness to accept them back.

CONFESSION AND REPENTANCE

When there is a sin issue, it is frequently necessary to lead people to confess the sin and repent of it. One of God's rules of the universe is that unconfessed, unrepented sin puts people into captivity. David ran afoul of this rule and states, "When I did not confess my sins, I was worn out from crying all day long. Day and night you punished me, Lord; my strength was completely drained, as moisture is dried up by the summer heat. Then I confessed my sins to you; I did not conceal my wrongdoings. I decided to confess them to you, and you forgave all my sins" (Ps 32:3-5).

Confession and repentence are powerful and necessary prerequisites to deep-level healing. Confession is threefold: confession to oneself; confession to God; and, sometimes, confession to others. Confession is the opposite of denial. Denial of sin produces a self-inflicted wound. Such wounds enslave us to the Enemy.

Denying that we have sinned not only makes God a liar (1 Jn 1:10), it is self-deception and self-deceit (1 Jn 1:8). Healing and freedom, however, require a relationship with ourselves that is honest and true. If we are to be free, we need to be able to recognize our sin quickly, resist the temptation to deny it, and take it to God in confession and repentance. The first step is to confess the sin to oneself.

Confession to oneself must be followed by confession to God. Because of Christ's death and resurrection, God is able to release us from captivity to our sin and the Enemy who lurks behind it. Confession to God needs to be specific so that specific forgiveness and healing can replace the sin in our lives. If we receive God's mercy and forgiveness, the area that was wounded now is healed, or at least well on its way toward healing. We can then move on to the next level of the process.

Though most of our sins are between us and God, those that involve other persons may need to be confessed to them as well. Asking forgiveness from those we have offended, though difficult, is another requirement for freedom. Our unforgiveness of another person restricts that person's freedom and their unforgiveness toward us restricts ours. We need, then, to confess to and repent before those we have hurt to free both ourselves and them.

In addition, there is often benefit when we confess our sins to and receive prayer from a small group of Christians who are close to us. In speaking of healing and forgiveness, James (5:16b) commands us to "confess your sins to one another and pray for one another, so that you will be healed." God has established the members of his body to function as a single unit with one another (1 Cor 12:12-31). When one member is hurting, all of the members are hurting. We need to help carry one another's burdens, thus fulfilling the law of Christ (Gal 6:2). The Sandfords tell us, "The very purpose of our being here on earth is that right here, in the body, we may be loved to life in a way Heaven could not provide. God designed that we should find His love person to person, body to body, and so be drawn forth and trained to become human."[1]

Living outside the community of faith as a "lone-wolf Christian" can greatly inhibit the process of deep-level healing. Sharing our sin burden with others and letting them share theirs with us are powerful components of a complete healing process.

Within the process, we must have an overall attitude of transparency. The Enemy tries to keep us from opening up to ourselves, or to God, or to others in confession. This allows rooms of darkness within us to remain hidden from the penetrating light of Christ. The light of Jesus desires to flood every room in our "house" with cleansing light. And where the light shines, there, no darkness can overcome it! (Jn 1:5).

THE AUTHORITY TO FORGIVE

In working to bring deep-level healing, it is important to make use of all of the resources for ministry that God offers us. One of these is the authority to forgive people of their sins. Jesus said to his followers, "If you forgive people's sins, they are forgiven" (Jn 20:23a).

We deal with people who cannot seem to receive the mercy and forgiveness of God directly from him. They often are deeply mired in self-condemnation and feel their pleas for forgiveness are not heard. They feel distant and unable to relate personally with God. Though the verse seems to give us permission to forgive them directly, I am cautious in the way I use this authority. I ask the person if all known sin has been confessed. If they say "yes," I say something like, "In the name of Jesus Christ, on the authority given me by John 20:23, I speak forgiveness to you." The resulting release the person feels is sometimes dramatic.

CALLING SIN "SIN"

Though a fairly narrow range of behaviors come to most people's minds when the term "sin" is mentioned, the Scriptures define sin more simply and more broadly. Any disobedience to God is sin (Rom 14:23b). On the other, in addition to the "biggies" such as murder, sexual promiscuity, and open robbery that come to most people's minds, we need to list such things as holding grudges, refusing to forgive, keeping anger or bitterness (Eph

4:31-32), desiring revenge, not loving ourselves, jealousy, being materialistic, envying, being competitive, being individualistic, to name a few. The fact that many of these sins are approved by our society keeps many of us from even recognizing them as sins.

Neil Anderson gives a more scriptural definition of sin when he says, "You commit sin when you willfully allow yourself to act independent of God as the old self did as a matter of course. When you function in this manner you are violating your new nature and your new identity."[2]

It is usually "out-of-focus" sins that we have to deal with, those falling under this kind of independence from God, rather than those we ordinarily think of. This is why it is usually unloving to use the word *sin* as a rubric for labeling what the problem is. Though we may have studied the Scriptures and developed this broad understanding of what sin involves, most of our counselees will only think of the gravest of activities. Or, worse yet, they may develop a broader but inaccurate understanding of sin and condemn themselves for a multitude of things they should not feel guilty over. As pointed out above, then, *it is our practice to be very careful in the way we use the word sin, even when it is obvious to us that the root problem is a sin the person has committed.* Since Jesus almost never used the term, except when teaching his disciples, we choose to use it very sparingly.

We must, however, deal continually with sins and their effects, whether or not we use the word sin very much. When a person is involved repeatedly in some type of sinful behavior, there are a few things to consider.

1. The person must be willing to give up the sin and submit his or her will to Christ. Without such willingness, we (and God) are blocked in our attempts to deal with deep issues. The person's will must be engaged on God's side of the problem. One who continues in willful sin is taking Satan's side and blocking God's working in her or his life. To choose to give up a favorite sin may, however, be difficult and require constant recommitment on the part of the person and constant encouragement on the part of the counselor until victory is obtained in that area. Great patience and prayerfulness on the parts of both are also needed.

2. The roots of difficulty in choosing to abandon a sin often lie in emotional wounding. Pointing to this fact, the Sandfords say, "Love, being good, produces no bad fruit. Bad fruit has to come from bad roots in a bad tree.... What happened between your father and mother, or with your brothers and sisters? Somewhere there's a bad root. Let's find it."[3]

People's determination and ability to choose may be quite weak, stemming from events early in life. As issues are worked through in inner healing, however, they usually gain strength to exert their wills more effectively.

3. There may be demons giving strength to sinful habits. It is a part of a demon's job description to enhance sin while getting people to blame themselves for the problem. When people are having difficulty giving up a sin, it is a good idea to probe to discover if there is a demon present, piggybacking on their weaknesses. Deliverance from spirits that enhance such things as lust, pornography, drunkenness, stealing, lying, unforgiveness, hatred, and pride will allow the person much more strength of will to resist temptation in the future. See chapter twelve in this book and my book, *Defeating Dark Angels,* for more on dealing with demons.

THE GRAVITY OF SEXUAL SIN

In 1 Corinthians 6, the Apostle Paul indicates that sexual sin is in a separate category from all other sins: "Avoid immorality. Any other sin a man commits does not affect his body; but the man who is guilty of sexual immorality sins against his own body. Don't you know that your body is the temple of the Holy Spirit, who lives in you and who was given to you by God? You do not belong to yourselves but to God; he bought you for a price. So use your bodies for God's glory" (vv. 18-20).

Sexual intimacy bonds people to each other. And such bonding is more than a physical thing. It is spiritual. I believe that the Greek word *soma* ("body") in the above verses should be interpreted (in keeping with regular Greek usage) as referring to our whole *self*, not simply as referring to the physical part of us. As the Sandfords say, "It is impossible to touch body only, because it is the spirit living in every cell which gives life to the body (James 2:26)."[4]

The sexual part of us is of particular interest to the Enemy. He is, of course, against life. Thus, he mounts many of his strongest attacks on that part of us that creates life. He has also found that there is no better way to degrade us and to damage our self-image than to attack the sexual part of us. The invasiveness of sexual mistreatment of women is a particularly potent method in the Enemy's hands. He is especially hateful toward women because, as I have heard from many demons, "They give life."

We have found in ministry that sexual sins, especially adultery and fornication, need to be dealt with in a special way. When people have been bonded to each other, that bonding will interfere with the persons both internally and relationally. Marriage relationships are often damaged considerably when past sexual bonding has not been taken care of, whether or not the spouse knows of the previous affair(s). God is, however, willing to heal us from the effects of such bonding if we come to him.

To deal with adultery, incest, rape, homosexual encounters, or any other extra-marital sexual relations, we first make sure the person has confessed to God any sin involved and received his forgiveness. If it was adultery or homosexuality, the whole thing needs to be confessed as sin. Rape or incest, however, since they were not the fault of the victim, don't get confessed as sin. But there may be attitudes of anger, bitterness, unforgiveness, and the like that need to be confessed to God as sin before the person can be helped.

Once the sin has been dealt with, we ask the person to go back to the affair(s) under the guidance of the Holy Spirit, picturing the person and, if necessary, forgiving that person for his or her part in the relationship. The person then is guided to renounce, in the name of Jesus, all bonding to all persons he or she has had sex with, except the current marriage partner. It is my habit, then, as the person renounces the bonding, to take authority in Jesus' name and to break any satanic power that exists in the person's life as a result of the illicit sex. To do this, I say something like, "In the name of Jesus, I break all satanic power in this person's life and cancel all right to access the Enemy may have gained through these sexual relationships."

As we minister in this way, we find that frequently God gives the person a picture to signify the breaking of the bonding with the other person(s). In one case, where the woman I was helping had been repeatedly raped as a child in a satanic cult, God showed her all the men lined up one behind the other. As she renounced the bonding, then, the whole line of men fell down like dominoes and she was free.

Nonsexual bonding relationships can be dealt with in a similar way. Sometimes spiritual bonding happens when one person is dominated by another (including parents), when one strongly admires another, or when there is a very close friendship. Such relationships create what are often called "soul-ties." These are spirit-to-spirit ties to other people which need to be broken if the person is to be free. The steps are the same: deal with any sin through confession, renounce in Jesus' name any tie empowered by Satan, claim Jesus' blessing on any part of the tie empowered by God, and forbid the Enemy to continue to interfere in or make any further use of this relationship.

RESPONSIBILITY AND VICTIMIZATION

God has given his creatures a certain amount of freedom to make choices. It is clear that humans can choose to do right things or wrong things. And these choices have consequences in our lives for which we are responsible. It is also clear that when such choices are made, they often affect other people. Indeed, many people suffer greatly through no fault of their own because someone else chose to do something that hurt them. And in addition to the choices and activities of people are the things Satan and his dark angels choose to do that affect humans. These facts underlie at least three important areas relating to how people get into difficulty:

1. People often choose to run their lives outside of God's will. Whether they choose to sin or simply to ignore God, people are responsible for the choices they make and will be judged in accordance with how they have used their freedom.

Much illness, whether spiritual, emotional, or physical, is the result of the person's own poor choices. In spite of the fact that our Enemy, the Devil, is often involved in encouraging such choices, the Scriptures indicate clearly that it is our responsibility to deal with our sinfulness. In ministering at a deep level, we frequently find that problems caused by the person's own choices need to be dealt with first.

2. Not infrequently, though, a person's difficulties are the result of others' choices. Other people may have abused the person. An ancestor may have allowed demons into the family line. Those in authority over the person may have dedicated him or her to evil spiritual powers. As a result, such people have become victims because of someone else's choices.

Victims are those who are hurt, often badly hurt, through no fault of their own. As Rich Buhler tells us in his book *Pain and Pretending,* "A victim is a person who has experienced destruction at the foundation of who that person is and in a way that has caused significant hindrance in the living of life."[5] The majority of the people we minister to fall into the victim category.

When Jesus announced "good news to the poor" (Lk 4:18b), he was making a statement concerning his relationship to victims. The term "poor" in this context refers to those who are oppressed and, through no fault of their own, live in poverty.

Jesus never condemned those who were sick or demonized. He even refused to condemn at least certain people who had obvious sin in their lives, like the Samaritan woman (Jn 4), the woman caught in the act of adultery (Jn 8) and Peter (Jn 21), none of whom could rightly blame anyone but themselves for their difficulties. He treated them as if they had simply made mistakes, as if in learning to walk they had stumbled and fallen. Rather than condemning them as evil or as failures, he simply offered them his hand to lift them again to their feet.

Jesus seems to have divided up the human landscape into three groups: the victims (oppressed), the victimizers (oppressors), and the "righteous" (Mt 25:31-46, esp. vv. 33, 37). He saw the common people as victimized by those in power (namely, the Pharisees and rulers of the Jews) and set himself to rescue as many of them as possible.

If we are to follow Jesus' example, our eyes are to be focused on helping the needy, whether their problems result from their own bad choices or from victimization by others. We are to serve them automatically, because they have a need. And, when we help the needy, we minister to Jesus (Mt 25:37-39).

If Jesus' world produced victims, how much more does ours? Whether we look at worldwide poverty, or at political turmoil and warfare, or at widespread social dysfunction, ours is a world in which humans create an incredible number of victims.

3. There is an Enemy who is very active in messing up our lives. He instigates the temptations to sin and the inclinations of people to victimize others, and he is right there to take advantage of each negative event. He is the victimizer *par excellence*. While we are not allowed to duck our own responsibility by adopting Flip Wilson's "the Devil made me do it" theology, we need to recognize the nature and extent of his activities.

It is our job to deal intelligently with a fallen world in which people sin and victimize each other. We are expected to understand the Enemy's devices (2 Cor 2:11). But we are not to shoulder this responsibility alone. We are to help each other get free from the things that bind us.

Deep-level healing is a way of working in the power of the Holy Spirit to restore to health both victims and those who have made bad choices.

IDEAL RELATIONSHIPS WITH GOD, SELF, AND OTHERS

The Scriptures, either by specific statement or by implication, present us with certain ideals concerning our relationships with God, self, and others. Victimization disrupts these relationships.

The ideal relationship with God means that a person is a new and growing creature (2 Cor 5:17), united with the Lord, one with him in spirit (1 Cor 6:17), filled with the Holy Spirit (Acts 10:44-48) and living as close to the Father as Jesus did (Jn 5:19, 30).

The ideal relationship with oneself involves loving yourself as God does, accepting and forgiving oneself. Each person is to see him or herself as a full-fledged child of God (1 Jn 3:1; Gal 4:4-7; Rom 8:14-17) who can hold her or his head high as a prince or princess. Such a person is free to accept and forgive those who have hurt him or her.

The ideal relationship with others involves loving them as God loves them and as one (ideally) loves oneself (Mt 22:39). We are to follow Jesus' example and serve others (Mt 20:28), relating to them as members of the same family, the same body with Christ as the head. Humans have a basic need for mutual interdependence with others and cannot be emotionally healthy without such closeness. This means we need to fight our Western individualism to attain good, close relationships with others, especially within church contexts.

SPIRITUAL ROOTS OF DEEP-LEVEL PROBLEMS

The emotional and the spiritual areas of life seem to be so intertwined that illness in either tends to produce symptoms that are usually labeled emotional. I am not certain, therefore, that it is possible to distinguish between spiritual and emotional illness by looking at the surface symptoms. We may, however, attempt to distinguish spiritual from emotional roots for such problems.

We can identify at least seven spiritual roots to deep-level problems. And we can say that each of these causes spiritual illness, even though the obvious surface symptoms are emotional.

1. *Sin* is a primary cause of spiritual illness. We are told that our human nature ("flesh") is no good (Rom 7:18). It is full of all kinds of sin (Gal 5:19-21). When, therefore, we give in to the "works" of our human nature, either consciously or unconsciously, we become spiritually ill. Our relationship with God is disrupted until we confess our sins and receive his forgiveness (1 Jn 1:9).

2. *Neglect of one's relationship with God* also causes spiritual illness. We are made for closeness to God. Such closeness requires time spent with him. Jesus valued this intimacy so much that he frequently went off to solitary places to be with the Father (Mt 14:13). If Jesus needed to spend much time with the Father, so must we if we are to maintain our relationship with God.

3. Many people experience a kind of spiritual illness because they hold a *wrong view of God*. For many, God is too distant to concern himself with us. Others see him as so judgmental he refuses to help us, or even as so angry at us that his primary concern is to punish us. Still others see him as determining everything without reference to any freedom of choice on the part of humans. Each of these views participates in satanic deceit and flies in the face of Jesus' representation of God articulated in his words to Philip, "Whoever has seen me has seen the Father" (Jn 14:9b). These faulty perceptions also lead to serious misimpressions concerning the reasons for difficulties in the lives of Christians.

4. Akin to the above problem is *anger at God*. People often assume that God can do anything he wants to do (including overruling the free will of those who hurt others) without regard to the rules he has built into the universe. If this is true, he certainly could have prevented the abuse they have experienced. They are, therefore, angry at him for what they perceive as abandonment or neglect. Wallowing in such anger, bitterness, and unforgiveness creates spiritual illness.

Though God accomplishes his purposes ultimately, and though "in all things God works for good with those who love him" (Rom

8:28b), many things do not go the way God wants them to in the here and now. For example, God "does not want anyone to be destroyed, but wants all to turn away from their sins" (2 Pet 3:9b). But many will perish. That God seems to have limited himself in his relationships both with humans and with Satan is one of the most difficult things to explain to hurting people who feel God has let them down.

5. A fifth cause of spiritual illness is *satanic harassment allowed by the "garbage" inside a person.* If there are spiritual, emotional, mental problems, or disorders of a person's will, the Enemy can attack that person. He likes to harass by taking advantage of such things as fear, guilt, anger, and lust. Launching his attacks from such problems he often disrupts sleep and other normal functions as well as prayer, worship, and Bible study.

Curses and vows may be involved in such attacks. Proverbs 26:2 speaks of curses not being able to "land" or have an impact without a reason. The implication is that, if there is a reason, they can have an impact. I believe a lot of cursing goes on. Most of it is informal in the sense that it consists of angry words spoken against a person that are empowered by the forces of darkness. Some of the cursing, however, is initiated by more formal procedures, sometimes reinforced by ritual. It is, therefore, more powerful. One way or another, if the curses hit their mark, they will be experienced as satanic attack.

People who are angry at themselves often say things such as, "I hate myself (or my body or my name)," or "I wish this part of me wasn't so...," or "I vow not to be like my father and mother." When we say such things against ourselves, we often find that the Enemy sneaks in and empowers the words as curses or vows. He thus gains the right to harass. To break such curses or vows, a person usually only has to say something like, "In the name of Jesus Christ, I renounce any curses I have made against myself or any part of me and any vows I have made that are empowered by Satan." The person who makes a curse or vow has the authority to recall it.

6. In addition to such harassment from outside, there is *demonization,* the living of evil spirits within a person. As already mentioned, it is not uncommon for us to have to deal with demons living in those who come for deep-level healing. In *Defeating Dark Angels,* I have treated this problem in detail. Suffice it to say here that when a person who has demons living within becomes a Christian, the demons leave the person's spirit but still live within other parts of the person. As the Christian grows in the faith and, hopefully, deals with the emotional and spiritual garbage to which the demons are attached, they are weakened and suppressed and their ability to influence the person decreases. Even such growth often does not get rid of them, however. Though many Christians have been able to do it themselves, getting rid of demons living within usually requires the help of someone who knows how to cast them out.

7. The final spiritual problem I'll mention is *generational spirits or curses.* People can inherit satanic interference in their lives from parents and ancestors who have allowed demons into their lives. People who are parts of occult groups such as Freemasonry, Christian Science, Scientology, and Eastern mystical groups frequently, if not always, pass their demons on to the next generation. When these people take on themselves the curses involved in dedicating themselves to the spirits and gods behind their organization, the curses often attach to the following generations of their families. In this way the Enemy gains access to the lives of countless innocent children. They, then, experience interference in the spiritual part of their lives, especially if they turn to Christ.

EMOTIONAL ROOTS OF DEEP-LEVEL PROBLEMS

As pointed out above, many of our apparently emotional problems have spiritual roots. Now we will turn our attention to the following two major emotional roots: 1) reactions to life experiences; and 2) what the person has done and usually continues to do to him or herself.

1. Reactions to life experiences. During the course of our lives, *we react to what happens to us.* Life is difficult, even for those from good backgrounds. There often are factors to deal with such as childhood illnesses, parental neglect, the fact that a person was born out of wedlock, or born the "wrong" sex. Seamands writes in *Putting Away Childish Things,* "You cannot cut yourself off from your own history. You are a complex tapestry, woven with a million strands, some of which reach back to Adam and beyond him to God who created you in His image. But many of the most important strands were introduced in your childhood, especially in the parent-child relationships.[6]

Childhood or school experiences may have been difficult. Adolescence is a difficult time for most, sometimes involving sexual experimentation or occult involvement. Adult experiences, too, often leave scars. Even good parents, teachers, and other acquaintances make mistakes that hurt us.

In addition, many have experienced mild to severe abuse in emotional, physical, sexual, or spiritual areas of life. When hurt, people usually respond by suppressing the emotion and quickly "bandaging" the wound, so no one can see they have been wounded. The wound, then, not having been cleansed, festers. Later in life, the bandages begin to leak the infection. This allows the unhealed wounds, though the result of long-past experiences, to influence the person's present life.

Life experiences, especially the negative ones, affect a person's physical, emotional, and spiritual health. They usually affect relationships in a major way—relationships with God, self, and others. Typically, people blame themselves for their difficulties, even difficulties caused by others. Victims almost always blame themselves for their problems.

When hurt, people usually respond with anger, resentment, and the desire for revenge. These reactions enable them to survive at the time. Though the reactions are natural and legitimate, they become a major problem to the person who hangs onto them. These attitudes create the garbage we have been talking about. Thus, the hurtful event is not as much of a problem as is the reaction to the event and, often years later, the memory of it. Such negative attitudes can result in illness in any or all areas of a person's life. They can also provide opportunity for demonic harassment and invasion. Rich Buhler, in *Pain and Pretending* says, "God has given us the ability to blow fuses in the face of something overwhelming and that mechanism can enable people to survive, but that's the only thing it is good for, surviving, not living and relating to our families and friends. Even though I believe God gave us these safety valves, I don't believe he meant them to be a permanent way of life."[7]

For this reason, God has provided us with a spiritual and emotional excretory system. Note from the verse below that it is no sin to get angry. That's normal. But to not rid ourselves of our anger as soon as possible is risky. Hear the Apostle Paul on the subject: "If you become angry, do not let your anger lead you into sin, and do not stay angry all day. Don't give the Devil a chance.... Get rid of all bitterness, [rage], and anger. No more shouting or insults, no more hateful feelings of any sort. Instead, be kind and tenderhearted to one another, and forgive one another, as God has forgiven you through Christ" (Eph 4:26-27, 31-32).

With regard to anger, Buhler points out, "Sometimes the anger the victim feels is a righteous anger, a feeling that something very unjust has been done by one person to another, and that something needs to be done about it. This is a healthy anger and can lead to some wise decisions on the part of the victim, such as getting help for himself or herself and identifying the abuser and holding the abuser accountable for what he or she has done."[8]

So the problem is not with the angry reaction. It is with *keeping* the anger. God, knowing that keeping anger will damage us badly, has made it possible for us to give him our right to anger and revenge. So we are to give up our right to these emotions in order to be free. As God commands, "Never take revenge, my friends, but instead let God's anger do it. For the scripture says, 'I will take revenge, I will pay back, says the Lord'" (Rom 12:19).

2. What people have done and usually continue to do to themselves. This is a second source of emotional problems. Often, spinning off from the kinds of things we have just been discussing, people turn in on themselves and continue the victimization. Many people dislike or even hate themselves. This usually involves large amounts of negative "self-talk," the constant internal verbalizing of messages to oneself such as, "You stupid fool," or "You'll never get it right," or when something goes wrong, "What do you expect, things usually turn out wrong when you're involved." Or a person may repeat phrases often heard from parents such as, "Shame on you" or "Damn you."

The Enemy's fiercest attacks are in the area of self-image (see chapter eight). He doesn't want us to know who we are. So he attacks us constantly through other people. Unfortunately, humans have a propensity for internalizing and replaying "tapes" in their minds of the negative things heard from others. Seamands in *Healing Grace* underlines this fact saying, "People will remember a single hurtful criticism most vividly, while tending to forget a string of compliments. And they will feel a positive or a negative statement about what they are much more deeply than one concerning what they did. Thus it's easy to see why the put-downs of being can be so completely shattering to our self-esteem."[9]

We thus abuse ourselves, usually as a continuation of the abuse we received from our elders as children. This results in moderate to severe emotional illness that requires deep-level healing to correct.

CAUSES OF SICKNESS IN RELATIONSHIPS WITH OTHERS

All of the above problems can and frequently do result in relational illness. In addition, demons love to mess up relationships. They stimulate gossip, criticism, competitiveness, and fear that others will discover what we are really like.

If our self-image is poor, it will affect how we relate to one or more categories of people. Those who have had damaging childhood experiences with authority figures will probably have difficulty relating to those in authority. Likewise in relationships with the opposite sex and even relationships with peers. Here are three additional causes of relationship problems:

1. Individualism. One source of relational illness stems from our Western worldview. It is *our individualism.* God made humans so that *we function best when we live in genuine interdependence with others.* Whether in our families, in society at large, or in our churches, we relate to many other people and relate very closely to some. I believe we are not as healthy as God intended us to be when we are not in close relationships with others. The fact that American males usually do not have even one really close friend is a tragedy that makes for relational illness in most American males. I have no doubt that a major reason why American women live longer than men is the fact that more women establish and maintain close relationships with others.

People are often relationally ill because they are so individualistic. They keep to themselves, refusing to ask for help when they need it, for fear of admitting they are needy. In addition, there is often an extreme competitiveness. Such competitiveness and refusal to interdepend are particularly troublesome between marriage partners and between those working in an organization (for example, a church) that requires teamwork.

2. Broken relationships. This is a second source of relational illness. When people do get into a close relationship, such as in marriage or family, but it breaks down, a typical response is to shy away from further relationships. Often this is accompanied by self-blame, fear of getting close to anyone else, and anger.

3. Personal characteristics. A variety of *personal characteristics,* usually rooted in deeper-level problems, serve as a third source of relational sickness. Fear of intimacy ranks high among these. This is often rooted in fear of discovery of sin or other things in a person's background that the person is ashamed of. Other characteristics include the need to control or dominate, always blaming others for one's problems, arrogance, superiority or inferiority complexes, extreme shyness, overdependence, and inability to make decisions. All of these result in interpersonal illness.

The Enemy loves to make use of such relational "garbage," especially among Christians. The more he can stir up relational trouble in churches and other Christian organizations, the better he likes it. One of Satan's primary concerns is to mess up Christians. He will gladly attack any vulnerable relationship, especially of those in ministry. Notice how many clergymen and others in "full-time" ministry struggle and often fail in their marriages. Notice how many have difficulty with their children, not to mention problems relating to members of their churches or other constituencies. Both within families and Christian organizations, Satan especially likes to disrupt authority relationships.

EFFECTS OF SUCH DAMAGE

The effects of such damage are many and far reaching. Spiritually, there is often great damage to a person's relationship with God. If there was not already a wrong view of God, relationship problems can often produce it. For example, victimized people often develop a concept of God as far away and either unconcerned or powerless to help when they are being hurt. Frequently, they see God as one who abandoned them in their time of need.

These attitudes can lead to such reactions as fear of God's closeness, extreme feelings of guilt when thinking of God, an expectation of his condemnation, punishment, and even the belief that he is in the business of exploiting people. Not infrequently, people who feel this way give up any attempt to please God or other people and even gravitate toward rebellion against him and his standards. These responses can, in turn, lead to greater vulnerability to demonic influence.

As mentioned, such damage usually turns a person against him or herself, resulting in self-rejection, self-hate, perfectionism, a performance orientation, or a sense of unworthiness and inadequacy. Furthermore, the person often experiences an inability to forgive self, recurring guilt (even concerning things confessed), and an inability to accept forgiveness. This is often accompanied by self-cursing and other negative wishes toward the self or parts of self (including one's name, body, mind, emotions), along with a large amount of self-deceit.

People often experience unreasoning fear of facing any memories of the past. Psychologists tell us that the human brain records everything that happens to a person. But to survive, a person often suppresses the memories of past hurts without getting them healed first. Buhler points out that, "Victims who have experienced blocked memories will sometimes forget whole categories of childhood. Many, for example, can't remember childhood at all... It is important to point out that even if a person remembers abuse from childhood, it is common that what I call the 'branding experience,' the particular event that caused the most destruction, is blocked from memory."[10]

The possibility of those unhealed memories coming to the surface, then, frightens the person. Yet, in spite of attempts to suppress them, the memories affect the person's present life in some or all of the following ways: depression (often rooted in anger), upset sleep patterns (for example, disturbing dreams, restlessness, noisiness while asleep), or lack of control of one's emotional reactions to certain events or people. Sometimes the person loses control of the ability to suppress the memories and experiences flashbacks of the hurtful events. This usually results in even greater fear of the memories.

Spiritual, emotional, and interpersonal damage all tend to show up in emotional difficulties. Such emotional problems seem to cluster into groupings. Thus, people with one of the problems in a group tend to also have one or more of the other problems in that same group. (See lists on page 73.)

It is clear to medical doctors that emotional problems weaken the body. The vast majority of the physical problems I deal with have emotional roots, often even when the immediate problem was an accident. When the body is weak, sickness or accidents have a greater and longer lasting effect on it. Certain illnesses are notoriously psychosomatic, among them asthma, allergies, arthritis, and migraine headaches. In addition, any weak part of one's body may regularly manifest pain or other dysfunction under stress. Some people carry their stress in their backs, others in their stomachs, their heads or other parts of their bodies.

Typical Clusters of Emotional Problems

Unforgiveness:
anger at others,
bitterness,
resentment

Fear:
wide variety
of kinds
(e.g., of rejection,
dark, heights,
being alone,
being in crowds,
pain, disease,
death, intimacy)

Rebellion:
stubbornness

Self-rejection:
anger at self,
feelings of
inadequacy and
unworthiness,
performance
orientation,
critical spirit,
feelings of
rejection by others,
hypersensitivity

Critical spirit:
faultfinding,
judgmentalism,
intolerance,
condemnation

Confusion:
frustration,
forgetfulness

Discouragement:
disappointment,
anger at God
or fate or
life in general

Hatred:
desire for revenge
or even murder

Guilt:
shame,
embarrassment

Typical Compulsions and/or Addictions

Need to control:
possessiveness

**Performance
orientation:**
need to please
others

Masturbation
(obsessive)

**Need to
understand:**
intellectualism,
rationalization

Lust:
sexual fantasy,
pornography

Religiosity:
doctrinal obsession,
ritualism

Homosexuality
(gay or lesbian)

Addictions:
drugs, alcohol,
nicotine, etc.

We humans are complex creatures, to state the obvious. The previous pages have given us an outline of the various wounds that require deep-level healing. Such compulsions and addictions usually point to deeper problems. We also might note that physical problems can stem from any of the difficulties on the charts.

Now we will turn to advice for those who minister in deep-level healing.

For Further Reading

Neil Anderson, *Victory Over the Darkness,* 69-85; 193-207.

John and Paula Sandford, *The Transformation of the Inner Man,* 107-19; *Healing the Wounded Spirit,* 1-73; 369-91.

David A. Seamands, *Healing Grace,* 125-38.

4

An Orientation for the One Who Ministers

IT'S GONE!

I was standing before about two hundred people leading a seminar on deep-level healing. Having learned from past experience that the Enemy likes to distract people in such settings by causing headaches, stomach ailments, and other kinds of physical pain, I stopped to ask if anyone in the audience was experiencing such discomfort. As I expected, quite a number of people raised their hands.

Seeing this, I simply said, "I take authority over each of these headaches, stomach ailments, and other problems. I command them to go away, in the name of Jesus Christ."

I had hardly gotten the words out of my mouth when a man sitting midway back in the room began shouting, "It's gone! It's gone!" At my request, he explained that he'd had a fairly severe headache for most of the day, a headache that had disappeared as soon as I had commanded it to. And most of the others in the room who had had headaches or some other physical discomfort also indicated that they were now free.

A headache doesn't seem like a big thing, unless, of course, you're the one who has it. However, the fact that these disappeared on command indicates something about our authority.

Apparently, God has given us the authority to use Jesus' name to command things to happen that are according to his will (1 Jn 5:14-15).

I believe we are to do our best to ascertain what God's will is in any given situation and then to use the authority he has given us to bring about what he wants. This is what Jesus did. He lived in dependence on the Father (Jn 5:19) but ministered in powerful authority, an authority that he then passed on to his immediate followers (Lk 9:1) and through them to us (Mt 28:20).

I am convinced that God does not want people who are trying to concentrate on his instruction to be sidelined by headaches and other such ailments. I'm quite sure that it is often the Enemy who is behind such distractions. So I have no problem assuming that God wants us to use his authority to banish such interference. And God backs up the assertion of this authority by healing people as he healed those in the seminar.

OBEDIENCE AND GIFTING

The authority God gives us is truly impressive. And we will discuss that authority later in this chapter. But there is a prior consideration to deal with, the matter of *obedience*. When Jesus sent his followers out to minister to people, he *commanded* them to communicate the gospel and to heal (Lk 9:1-6; 10:8-9; Mt 10:7-8). He did not simply invite them to heal if they chose to. They were ordered by their Master to minister to the needy through the use of God's healing power. Later Jesus told his followers that whether or not they loved him was to be evaluated on the basis of whether or not they obeyed his commandments (Jn 14:21-24). *Refusing to minister healing, then, is disobedience to our Lord and a refusal to demonstrate our love for him.*

Some may feel this is putting it too strongly. But just as it was Jesus' highest desire to obey the Father by doing his will (Jn 4:34; 5:30; 6:38), so it is to be our highest desire to obey our Lord and Savior Jesus Christ by doing his will. If we call him Lord, we are to acknowledge his lordship in our lives by being obedient to him.

But "What about gifting?," I am often asked. "Not all of us have the gifts of healing." This is true. First Corinthians 12:29-30 says so. When someone raises this issue, my reply is usually to ask, "How do you know you don't have a gift of healing?" The usual response is, "No one has ever been healed through my prayers."

I once used these arguments myself in trying to excuse myself from the command to pray for healing. On one occasion, I told John Wimber, a good friend and a pioneer in the healing ministry among evangelicals, that I was quite convinced I had no gifts of healing. His reply was something like this: "They tell me you have the gift of teaching. How did you get that gift?" Then I recalled my early struggles with teaching and preaching. I remembered what a difficult time I had controlling my knees, my voice, and the color of my face whenever I stood in front of people to speak. I also remembered the great difficulty I had in preparing messages and lectures, the many hours it took me each time I had to prepare something for a public presentation.

But with determination and practice, I got better at it. And apparently the Holy Spirit was in it. I've seen confirmation that there is more than simply human ability in at least some of my teaching. As I recalled these facts for Wimber, he pointed out to me that the gift of healing is developed·in just the same way. We obey the Lord's command to heal. We practice and practice, determined to obey what Jesus has commanded us. And we discover that God is pleased to use us in bringing healing to those who hurt.

I needed to learn that *obedience many times precedes gifting*. God distributes his gifts liberally. Most people have several. Some are obvious. Simple observation of ourselves and others enables us to discover them. But other gifts are often there as well, waiting to be unlocked through experimentation in obedience to the commands of Christ.

As we obey Jesus and pray for people, we discover where we fit with respect to gifting. There are at least three possible levels: *role*, *ministry*, and *office*.

Role. When the Holy Spirit gives a gift in a particular situation, the person he uses performs whatever *role* that gift entails. People without gifting in areas such as teaching, preaching, hospitality, encouragement, and administration are occasionally called on to exercise such functions. And with the Holy Spirit's empowerment, they do well. They exercise the role of teacher, preacher, encourager, administrator, provider of hospitality, or healer, whether or not there is any evidence that they are gifted in these areas in an ongoing way.

Ministry. Those who see a pattern of effectiveness in their gift, however, may be said to have a *ministry* in that area. As we experiment in obedience to God with praying for healing, for example, we may discover that God chooses to use us often to bring freedom from certain types of problems. Such frequency suggests that God has given us a ministry. One who regularly teaches, preaches, exercises hospitality, encourages, or heals under the direction of the Holy Spirit can claim to have a ministry in the area of gifting.

Office. I believe that God wants some of those with demonstrated gifting in such ministries to be appointed to professional *offices.* An office is an official position, usually involving a salary. For example, ideally everyone who is a pastor would be appointed to that office on the basis of proven gifting. Unfortunately, there are many people in pastoral and other church offices who have little, if any, gifting in the areas required by those offices.

There are two points to remember: The first is that obedience in praying for healing is the primary consideration for all Christians. The second is that we need to experiment to discover our God-given gifts and at what level those gifts are to be exercised.

OUR AUTHORITY

Authority is not something someone simply assumes. It has to have a source, someone who grants it. It also involves someone who makes use of it, someone who has a right given by the source to exercise that authority. Our spiritual authority has at least three important components: it is rooted in God, authorized by Jesus, and maintained through our intimacy with our Lord.

1. Our authority is rooted in who God is. He is the Source of any authority we have to bring healing and freedom to others. Unless he gives it, we have none. We by ourselves can heal no one. We can only draw on the One who is both powerful and deeply concerned for those who are hurting.

Who is this God? First of all, he is the Creator of all things and all people. And people are his favorite part of creation. He made us like him, in his image (Gn 1:26). He breathed his own life into us (Gn 2:7). Even when we disobeyed and fell, he continued to seek contact with us (Gn 3:9).

Second, God is the sustainer of the universe, including humanity. It is he who continues to sustain and give life. He protects the creation, including humanity, against the destruction the Enemy would bring to it.

Third, our God is One who relates to his creatures. He is not far off and unconcerned. Even after the fall, he sought a relationship with Adam (Gn 3:9ff.) and with each of his descendants. He walks and talks with anyone who will spend time with him.

And he has shown himself to be concerned and compassionate toward us, even though we frequently stray from him and his path. His concern and compassion have taken him even to the point of paying the price to redeem us from the Enemy to whom we (in Adam) had given ourselves. In addition, he has forgiven us for our rebellions and wanderings.

Furthermore, God is all powerful. He has the power not only to create and sustain, but to fix whoever has been damaged and to free whoever has been imprisoned.

2. Our authority is authorized by Jesus, our Lord. Jesus said to his disciples, "I have been given all authority in heaven and earth," and then commanded them to go make disciples and teach them "to obey everything I have commanded you" (Mt 28:18b-20b).

Furthermore, he also said, "As the Father sent me, so I send you" (Jn 20:21b) and predicted that "whoever believes in me will do what I do—yes, he will do even greater things, because I am going to the Father" (Jn 14:12b).

In so doing, Jesus authorized his followers to continue working in the authority he had been given to bring freedom to those the Father loves. The Father had sent him "to bring good news to the poor... to proclaim liberty to the captives and recovery of sight to the blind, to set free the oppressed..." (Lk 4:18b-19). So he sends us into the world to do the same (Jn 17:18). We are authorized by the King of Kings to carry on his ministry in the world today.

3. Our authority is maintained through our intimacy with Jesus. Just as Jesus' authority was maintained through his intimacy with the Father, so is ours. Jesus did not depend on his sonship to maintain his relationship with the Father. He constantly fed that relationship by spending time with the Father and by obeying what the Father told him to do. Jesus maintained his relationship with the Father perfectly. He set an extremely high standard by doing only what the Father wanted (Jn 5:30) and what he saw him doing (Jn 5:19), saying only what the Father instructed him to say and always pleasing him (Jn 8:28-29). In spite of the fact that this level of intimacy is beyond us, we are to aim at it.

The Holy Spirit supplies the power for us as he did for Jesus. From our intimacy, then, comes the authority to use that power. Jesus found it necessary to spend considerable periods of time alone with the Father to be sure he had his directions straight. He depended on the Spirit for power and on the Father for guidance.

It is not because we are gifted that people are freed, it is because our wills are lined up with God's in such a way that what we claim is what he desires. This happens as we practice intimate discussion with and dependence upon God. It is probably what Paul has in mind when he tells us to "pray at all times" (1 Thes 5:17).

I once had a discussion with a friend who was discouraged in her prayer life. It seems that she had prayed for several things "in Jesus' name" but was not receiving what she prayed for. We discussed some of the possible reasons. Praying in Jesus' name, I told her, is not so much about how you pray or what words you use in prayer, but more about who you are in prayer.

Many Christians take Scriptures like praying "in Jesus name" and use them like magic incantations. They think that if they get the phrasing right, then the desired answer will follow. My friend needed to understand, though, that praying "in Jesus' name" meant living in Jesus' name so that the desires of her heart would be more closely associated with the desires of that "name." Her desires would be more in tune with God's desires. Powerful prayers are initiated by those who live and pray in Jesus' name.

Such intimacy doesn't have to be a mysterious thing for us, however. I don't think it was for Jesus. We need to spend time in the kind of give and take that cultivates a close relationship. When we talk with God, we usually call it "praying." This term, however, obscures the fact that talking and listening to God are to be natural and constant, not an occasional ritual. We are prepared for ministry if we try to practice intimacy with the Father in Jesus all day, every day.

MINISTRY GUIDELINES

Experience shows that there are guidelines and general principles to follow as we work.

1. *It is very important that the person's will be engaged* before we minister to him or her. People must come of their own free will or, in the case of children, with the parents' permission and willingness, under their parents' authority. Since healing can be quite a difficult process, the individual must be fully committed to it and willing to work as hard as necessary with God to attain it. The very act of the person coming for prayer is a step in the right direction, but many people have misconceptions about what deep-level healing entails. They may be looking for a "quick fix" and not expect to put much effort into it themselves.

People must often be reminded that we do not have any special gifting or power in ourselves to solve their problems. Rather, we are coming alongside as partners with them and the Holy Spirit in a team effort. Some do indeed receive quick healing. But most require a process, sometimes an extended process, during which the Holy Spirit brings to light layer after layer of experiences that need healing. Their commitment and willingness to work with the Holy Spirit and the ministry team is, therefore, crucial. God does not violate the human will (he has too great a respect for us), but he stands ready to take our hand and lead us when we hold it out to him.

2. We must *be careful to seek and work under the guidance of the Holy Spirit.* There is no step-by-step formula to be followed each time we minister because the Holy Spirit deals differently with each person. Indeed, as I mentioned earlier, we must avoid at all costs what I call "the Moses mistake"—our tendency to simply do what we did before instead of listening for God's direction in each particular situation (see Ex 17:1-6).

No formula is right for every person every time. It is clear from a study of the ways in which Jesus ministered, that even he dealt with each person differently. Though there are general principles to be followed to facilitate healing, none is nearly as important as the need to discover the leading and to work in the power of the Holy Spirit. *Learning to listen carefully to him and to obey him exactly, then, is the most important principle.*

Before anything else, commit the session to the Holy Spirit and listen for his voice throughout the session. Ask him to bring to light whatever needs to be addressed. Insight often comes in the form of words of knowledge when the Holy Spirit suddenly leads you to understand something about the person or the situation that you would have no way of knowing unless he revealed it. Such insights must be shared tentatively and with wisdom since we are not perfect receptors of such messages and can easily be wrong. Carefully ask questions to determine if you are on the right track before sharing the word and share it as a possibility rather than a definite "word of the Lord." Sometimes what God reveals is for our benefit, not for that of the one receiving the ministry.

Another means that the Holy Spirit uses to identify the issues is simply by bringing things to the person's mind when we ask. There may be long-forgotten incidents or attitudes that will prove to be important pieces of the puzzle. The Holy Spirit usually quickens common sense as well. People who come for ministry are often so wrapped up in the problems they are experiencing that they are unable to see the most obvious truths. Common sense, of both those receiving and those giving ministry, is a gift from God and must never be "shelved" during the course of ministry in favor of more "spiritual" resources. God uses every available means to speak to us.

3. We must *pray with authority*. There are at least six types of prayer, all of which are valid at certain times and all of which relate in major ways to praying with authority.

a. Petition. What most people think of when we speak of prayer is *asking God for things.* Jesus invites us to pray this way saying, "... ask and you will receive, so that your happiness may be complete" (Jn 16:24b). Jesus portrays God as a loving Father who delights to give his children good things and, therefore, encourages us to ask, seek and knock (Mt 7:7-11, Jas 1:17).

b. Gratitude. Paul recommends this kind of prayer when he says, "... be thankful in all circumstances" (1 Thes 5:18a; see also Eph 5:20). Throughout the New Testament we see an attitude of thankfulness and praise to God exemplified and recommended, even in difficulties (for example, Rom 1:8; 1 Cor 1:4; 15:57; 2 Cor 2:14; 9:15; Phil 4:6; Heb 13:15).

c. Confession. It is important that we who minister to others be clean ourselves. By acknowledging and confessing our deficiencies and disobediences, we are able to take advantage of God's gracious offer to forgive and cleanse us (1 Jn 1:9). In turn, an important part of the healing we seek to bring about depends on those to whom we minister confessing and ridding themselves of all their sin.

d. Intercession. In this form of prayer, we enter into battle against the forces of darkness, on behalf of those to whom we minister. In addition, we ourselves need intercessors to support and empower the ministry God has given us. Intercession is the concentrated beseeching of God for any given person or cause. In Scripture we see Abraham interceding for Sodom (Gn 18:23-32), Moses interceding for the Israelites (Ex 32:11-13, 31-32; 34:9; etc.), Jesus interceding for Peter (Lk 22:32) and for the disciples (Jn 17:9-19) and Paul interceding for many (Rom 1:9-10; Eph 1:16-19; 3:14-19; Col 1:9).

In each of these first four types of prayer, our posture is *toward* God. That is, we face him as we ask, thank, confess, or intercede. In these next two types, however, we stand *with* God, first in intimacy and then in taking authority.

e. Intimacy. Perhaps the most important basis for the authority we have in Christ is what I call *intimacy prayer.* This consists of spending time with God, as Jesus did when he went off into "lonely places" to pray (Lk 5:16; 6:12; 9:18, 28; 11:1; 22:41). In choosing his disciples, then, Jesus says, "I have chosen you *to be with me*" (Mk 3:14, emphasis mine), to experience with him the kind of intimacy he modelled with the Father. On this basis, Jesus would send them out "to preach and [to] have authority to drive out demons" (Mk 3:14b-15).

This intimacy that Jesus wants us to have with him is, I believe, what lies behind his promise of *rest* if we bring to him our heavy burdens (Mt 11:28). Unfortunately, when we spend time with God, we often fill the time with talking. Little of our time is spent listening and simply relaxing in his presence. I picture Jesus relaxing in the Father's presence and he and the disciples on many occasions simply relaxing with each other. *As Jesus' intimacy with the Father was the basis for his authority, so our intimacy with Jesus is the basis for our authority to bring freedom and healing to others.*

f. Taking authority. With this experience of intimacy as the foundation and buttressed by intercessory prayer, we are to engage in the same kind of *taking authority* that Jesus demonstrated. Though I call this "authority praying," it may be a misnomer, since we are simply exerting the authority Jesus delegated to us.

Like Jesus, we are privileged by God to speak authoritatively against demons and diseases (Lk 9:2), confident that it is God's will to free people from such problems. In exercising our authority, we posture ourselves *with God,* speaking on his behalf for or against whatever he leads us to deal with. Jesus used most of the above types of prayer (except confession) at various times, but when freeing people from bondage, he did not ask, he asserted his authority. He thus demonstrated God's love through exerting his power. And as the Father sent him, so he sends us to do the same (Jn 20:21).

With this authority, we are to work as Jesus did to bring freedom from disease (Lk 4:39), to bless, protect, bind or loose, forgive (Jn 20:23), and deliver from demons. Jesus is our model.

4. We must keeping ourselves spiritually strong. Ministering freedom to others puts us in direct opposition to Satan, who "prowls around like a roaring lion looking for someone to devour (1 Pt 5:8b, NIV). He has quite a number of devices to hinder us if we get to be too great a threat. The number one rule, then, is to keep close to God, as Jesus did. We should not neglect such disciplines as prayer, Bible reading and study, worship, fellowship with those who help us grow, and devotional reading.

COMPASSION TOWARD THE PERSON BEING MINISTERED TO

Over and over, we are told that Jesus had or was "moved with" compassion (Mt 9:36; 14:14; 15:32; 20:34; Mk 1:41, etc.). It is important that anyone attempting to minister deep-level healing be a person of compassion, deeply moved by the hurts of those he or she seek to minister to. Perhaps this is the gift of mercy.

There are those who seem to have little or no patience with

those who are hurting. Their attitude seems to be, "Why doesn't Joe get his act together and stop bothering people with his problems?" Such an attitude is very un-Christlike. Jesus was moved with pity when he saw people with physical, emotional, or spiritual problems. Having the power and authority to make a difference, he helped them. We are to do the same.

We need, however, to be very careful how we go about trying to help. One important rule is to treat others as we would like to be treated if we were in their place (Mt 7:12). It is not a pleasant thing for most people to have to admit they are needy. Our society does not make it easy for people to admit deep problems. People with broken legs will elicit sympathy and not be expected to walk normally. If, however, the problem is emotional, other people make them feel condemned because they are not functioning normally. We need to overcome our judgmental tendencies.

We must put concern for the person first, trying at all costs to avoid as much embarrassment as possible. We should ask for information patiently and sensitively, avoiding any unnecessary probing. Seamands advises us to "Watch and pray; wait and pray; listen and pray; probe and pray. But don't push and pry. It's supremely important [for people to] freely choose to share with us."[1]

As much as possible, let people bring sensitive things up at their own speed. Many people feel that they are being asked to strip naked in front of strangers when they are questioned about their inner life.

Often it helps for us to share some aspect of our own experience that relates to theirs. This usually enables them to feel more comfortable, knowing that they are not the only ones who have ever faced the problem in question. Be careful, though, not to get carried away with sharing your own experiences. I have observed some who took so much time sharing about themselves that there was too little time for ministering to the one who came for help. Sometimes, too, people will encourage you to elaborate on your experience, consciously or unconsciously using the focus on you as an opportunity to avoid dealing with their own problems. So, keep such sharing brief and keep the focus on the person you are trying to help.

Remember to keep your ears open to what the Holy Spirit is saying. "While carefully concentrating on what is being communicated to you, at a deeper level you must be using your spiritual radar to tune in to the discernment of the Holy Spirit."[2] See chapter five for more information on how we can hear God in this way.

Our motivation to minister is compassion for people who are hurting. Seamands, pondering the disturbing fact that many will not come to church leaders with their hurts states, "The reason is that all too often the atmosphere in our churches, the attitudes of other Christians, and the very way we proclaim the gospel do not create the trust conditions necessary for healing."[3]

BE CAREFUL ABOUT THE NATURE OF YOUR INVOLVEMENT

Genuine compassion is required if we are to do this kind of ministry in Jesus' way. There are, however, ways in which our compassion can become counterproductive. I will deal with three examples.

1. *Don't get overemotional.* Emotion tends to block ministry, whether it is the emotion of the one you are helping or your own. Often the story you hear will lead you to tears. Frequently, such an indication of your empathy will help the person to trust you. If, however, you lose control of your emotions, you probably will lose control of the ministry session. Likewise, much that you hear will make you angry, even angry at God. You must give that anger to God.

2. *Don't let a person become overdependent on you.* It is easy to make mistakes in this area. Some people are so troubled that we naturally want to take charge of them ourselves. I have heard of situations where counselors allowed clients to move in with their families or paid for their expenses. This level of involvement, though sometimes necessary, is usually not a good idea, since it teaches vulnerable people to be dependent on their counselor rather than on themselves and their relationship with God.

3. *Be careful not to internalize other people's problems.* We are to be empathetic and compassionate but are not to take on the problems of others as our own. If we do, we can become burdened and emotionally damaged ourselves. I once ministered to a pastor's wife who had suffered for thirty years with a severe back problem that disappeared when she learned to stop carrying other people's problems. *Worrying about others' problems is not compassion.* We need to learn to cast all our cares on Jesus (1 Pet 5:7), even the cares others have shared with us.

KEEP WHAT YOU LEARN ABOUT OTHERS CONFIDENTIAL

As we minister, we are trusted with a lot of private information. This is one of the things that makes this kind of ministry so scary to those who come for help. It is important that they be able to trust you with their secrets. Love demands that we treat their secrets just as we would like others to treat our private information.

Those of us who teach and write on deep-level healing are especially tempted to share publicly information about ministry situations. Such information is often very valuable in helping others in their ministries. When illustrations from ministry sessions are used, it is very important to disguise them carefully so no one can identify the person. I've even found it important to disguise illustrations if the person involved has given me permission to use the material.

It is best not to use illustrations from close to home unless you generalize or give the impression the ministry probably happened somewhere else. I've sometimes found that an illustration I wanted to use involved someone in the audience I was speaking to. On such occasions I have tried to disguise the subject of the illustrations.

Sometimes we may find that we have failed to protect a person's privacy, either through carelessly sharing with others something about a ministry session or by not properly disguising the details of a public illustration. On such occasions, it is important to apologize to the person involved. Always remember to treat others as you would like to be treated.

For Further Reading

Neil Anderson, *Victory Over the Darkness*, 227-45.

Charles H. Kraft, *Defeating Dark Angels*, 79-98.

Fred and Florence Littauer, *Freeing Your Mind From Memories That Bind*, 234-48.

John and Paula Sandford, *The Transformation of the Inner Man*, 401-12.

David A. Seamands, *Healing for Damaged Emotions*, 149-59.

5

How to Do Deep-Level Healing

JUST LEARNING

When I lead seminars on deep-level healing, I like to bring people to the point where they lead in ministry themselves. The following is a composite story of the first experience of a typical person leading a ministry session while I was an observer.

We'll call her Mary Jo. We were in the third day of a five-day seminar. She had attended every session, had listened intently, and observed as I and my colleagues did ministry. She was willing to give it a try herself, as long as one of us was nearby to help if something came up she couldn't handle. Mary Jo set things up as she had seen us do it—chairs in a circle with two chairs in the middle, one for herself and one for the client, a woman named June in her mid-thirties. Several other attendees at the seminar joined us to pray and pass on to Mary Jo whatever insights they received from God. Mary Jo told them, as she had heard me tell those who assisted me, to write anything that came to them on small slips of paper and hand them to her. No vocal interruptions would be allowed unless she requested them.

Mary Jo then led us in prayer, asking the Holy Spirit to take complete charge, to reveal whatever we needed to know and to do what he wanted to do. She spoke against any interference from emissaries of the Evil One. She then blessed June with God's peace to combat her evident uneasiness. At this, many noticed that June became more relaxed in posture and facial expression.

Mary Jo was loving and kind during the interview. She began by asking what it was that led June to volunteer to receive ministry. The main problem June described was an intense self-rejection that was affecting her relationships with God, her husband, children, and work associates. Until attending our seminar, June felt there was no hope of overcoming this problem. She had been to several counselors over the years and felt they had helped her a bit, but not enough to justify the cost.

June had been brought up the first child of four in a dysfunctional family headed by an angry, "macho" father. She had always felt ignored by him until her teenage years when he began paying attention to her. This resulted in sexual abuse that went on for several years until June's mother discovered it. Then when June was sixteen, her mother kicked her father out of the house. By that time, though, June had become sexually active with several of her schoolmates in order to get their attention, and at age seventeen she discovered that she was pregnant. Telling her mother was traumatic. So was the abortion.

June continued her sex-for-attention behavior through college, but much more carefully. She found that it helped a lot with school fees, studies, and eventually in landing a husband. Now, after twelve years of marriage and three children, she described herself as a "basket case," filled with fear that her husband, out of dissatisfaction with her sexually, would abuse their daughters as June had been abused by her father. Though she had given her life to Christ five years ago, she received little support from her husband for her church activities and feared that even these, though very meaningful to her, were widening the rift between her and her husband.

June blamed herself for everything that had happened to her. If only she had not let her father take advantage of her, her parents might still be together, she reasoned. If only she hadn't given herself so freely to men, she would have more self-respect. If only she could give herself more completely to her husband, maybe he wouldn't get interested in their daughters.

Mary Jo had learned well. She took June back to conception, using the "back-to-the-womb" exercise outlined in chapter six. In this way Mary Jo helped June to experience a bit who she really was in God's eyes—a child of the King, a princess, one planned and wanted by God himself from before her conception. June was able to picture Jesus holding her, to feel his love and care for her. She then was able to picture herself holding "the baby" (herself as a baby) and to feel more love toward herself than she could ever remember feeling.

Next Mary Jo asked the Holy Spirit to lead June in dealing with whatever events of her childhood, adolescence, and young adulthood he chose to and in such a way that she could experience Jesus' presence in the midst of them. We all experienced a special joy with June as she was able to feel and picture Jesus in event after event, including the sexual encounters with her father and the other men. Though many of the events, especially the latter, were not pleasant for June to recall, the release she felt in experiencing Jesus in them was tangible to all of us. Both June and all of us wept frequently as she described the gentleness of our Lord toward her and as she gave to him her right to hold anger, bitterness, and resentment toward those who had hurt her. Perhaps the most moving parts of the session were when she chose to give Jesus the anger and condemnation she had long felt toward herself.

Sensing the need for something more than she was doing when June got to the abortion, Mary Jo asked me if I would take over for awhile. My first concern was to break the spiritual bonding between June and each of her sexual partners, including her father. This we did, using the procedure outlined in chapter three. As June renounced these bondings, she remarked that she experienced a wave of release accompanied by a feeling of cleanness she had not felt since her first sexual experience with her father.

Dealing with the abortion was especially painful. I asked June to picture her baby in her arms, to decide which sex it was, and to give the baby a name. She felt the baby had been a girl and named her Elisa. She then held the baby, apologized to her, and, after further conversation, lovingly handed her to Jesus. Even after all this, June had great difficulty forgiving herself for taking Elisa's life.

After a bit of a struggle, however, she was able to accept an embrace from Jesus and to forgive herself. She then embraced herself as a sign of self-forgiveness.

June went away from the session truly renewed in her relationships with Jesus, others, and herself. She had to keep working against the well-entrenched habits of self-rejection, self-doubt, and fear in her relationships with others. But since the roots of these attitudes were now gone, she found that dealing with the habits was usually not difficult as long as she remained conscious of them. What we had observed was typical of the kind of release the Holy Spirit brings during deep-level healing sessions.

PREPARING FOR MINISTRY

Before we start a ministry session, it is important to have several things in place. Among them are supportive intercessors and our own prayer and fasting.

1. Prayer support. It is important to *have personal intercessors and prayer partners to support our ministry* in general and to support every specific ministry session. The real battle is a spiritual one and is, therefore, fought and won primarily in prayer. My colleague C. Peter Wagner has seen this clearly and has written several useful books on the subject (see bibliography). In them, he categorizes the types of intercessors needed to support ministry in terms of their commitment and gifting.

"I-1" intercessors are those most committed to supporting a given minister or ministry. These are the gifted ones who really know how to pray and are willing to commit sizeable amounts of time to interceding for us. There need to be several of them to sustain a ministry. We also need several "I-2" prayers who commit less time but pray regularly for our ministry. Beyond them, we need a larger number of "I-3" prayers—prayer partners who make a significant but lesser commitment to support our ministry.[1]

These groups of intercessors should be active at all times but especially during times of ministry. They need to be kept informed of ministry times and progress. Their part of the battle is crucial. Wagner states, "I have come to realize [that intercessors] are the elite in the Kingdom of God. They are the green berets, the Phi Beta Kappas, the Olympic teams of God's community."[2]

2. Giving ourselves to prayer. It is important for us to regularly submit ourselves to God's will and plan in personal prayer. We need to agree, among other things, that he can do whatever he wants with us, even to the point where we agree he can allow us to be embarrassed if he so chooses. In addition, prior to any given ministry event, we need to request a new infilling of the Holy Spirit to provide the right amount of power and authority to deal with whatever comes up. In ministry, then, we need to be constantly in prayer that he will guide our every plan, word, and action both during and after ministry.

3. Fasting. It is frequently advisable to fast before a ministry session, especially if it promises to be difficult. Fasting was practiced by people in biblical times to get close to God when faced with difficulty (Neh 9:1; Est 4:3; Dn 6:18; 9:3) or when seeking God's guidance (Mt 4:2). Though the Pharisees fasted out of wrong motives (Mt 6:16; Lk 18:12) and the frightened sailors taking Paul to Rome fasted superstitiously (Acts 27:33), we are not to neglect this form of seeking God's empowerment.

There seem to be spiritual rules in the universe that enable us to hear God more clearly and to work in increased authority and power when we fast reverently and from correct motives. Fasting is, however, a discipline that needs to be learned. People should not attempt to fast for several days unless they first have successfully fasted for a shorter time. Also while fasting, one should be sure to drink plenty of liquids.

A MINISTRY MODEL

When ministering to a person, it is helpful to follow a sequence of steps. Though it is sometimes advisable to follow a different ordering, the following sequence seems to be the most useful with frequent repetition of steps three though five. That is, any given ministry session should involve several interviews (step 3), each of which is followed by the development and implementation of another strategy (step 4) and more authoritative prayer (step 5) before the session is finally concluded.

Step 1: In prayer invite the Holy Spirit to come in a special way. The Holy Spirit is always with us and in us. Indeed, one important part of our pre-ministry praying should be to ask for a new infilling of the Holy Spirit. Ephesians 5:18 commands us to be continually filled with the Holy Spirit. But in addition to his constant presence, we see from Luke 5:17 that he comes in particular ways for special purposes. We need him to provide a number of specific things in each ministry event. Among them are:

    a. to lead and reveal his will during the ministry;
    b. to empower whatever happens;
    c. to give us the right thoughts, ideas, and words;
    d. To provide protection from the Enemy for everyone involved, plus all of our families, friends, and personal affairs, both during and after the ministry session.

This initial prayer time should be followed by continual silent prayer by all involved during the remainder of the session. It is good, however, for them to keep their eyes open while they pray, lest they miss the many clues that come from observing what is happening with the person being prayed for.

Step 2: Bless the person. Bless the person with such things as peace, freedom from fear or embarrassment, openness to whatever God wants to do, and whatever else the Holy Spirit leads you to say. Often, the person being ministered to is extremely ill at ease, sometimes nervous to the point of shaking, fearful—not knowing quite what to expect. Blessing the person with peace usually takes care of such things. If not, you may want to spend more time in prayer, or in sharing your own or another's experience, to bring trust and calmness. High emotion usually blocks the working of the Holy Spirit. Bringing in calmness and trust is, therefore, an important part of these first two steps.

Step 3: Interview the person. In the interview, we are looking for information that can aid us in the healing process. It is helpful to remember that God seems to prefer to lead us through ordinary means rather than through extraordinary means whenever possible. An ordinary interview, then, is usually quite important in the process of bringing a person to healing. While we ask questions, however, we need to be constantly listening for information from the Holy Spirit as well. *A major key to successful ministry, then, is to listen to God as we listen to the person.*

As we start the interview, we should expect God to answer our request that he lead. His leading will usually be through guided "hunches." Some people seem to think it important to distinguish which information comes from oneself and which comes directly from God. I think such attempts are both unnecessary and potentially distracting. If we ask God to lead and he does lead, what difference does it make where he pulls the information from? Information that God pulls from our experience is just as much from God as information that he gives us directly. He freely mixes both types as we minister.

There are several possible starting points as we seek to discover what to deal with first. The most obvious starting point is to check out the problem that brought the person to you. This will usually be some fairly surface-level difficulty, but it has roots at a deeper level in the person's life. As we ask questions concerning that issue, it is important to look for indications of a deeper problem.

Often there have been unpleasant, abusive, or at least misunderstood childhood experiences that provide the roots for the present problems. Seamands points out that "... children learn a language of relationships long before they can learn a language of words. And the painful memories of unhealthy relationships often cry out so loudly that they interfere with learning the new relationship with God."[3]

Family relationships are often involved. It is, therefore, often good to question the person concerning his or her relationship with father, mother, siblings, grandparents and others. Relationships with authority figures and peers often need to be explored as well. Much damage occurs in school experiences.

Another frequent source of emotional damage is illness. If the person has been separated from parents in a hospital situation, the result can be intense feelings of abandonment that produce considerable emotional and spiritual disruption in the individual's present life. We need to search out all such traumatic experiences in early childhood to discover whether they have produced emotional "garbage" affecting the person's present life.

Such a trauma occurred in the life of a woman I'll call Charlene. At the age of four, Charlene was left with a babysitter for two months while her parents went on a vacation. They did not tell Charlene they were leaving, perhaps because they felt she was too young even to notice their absence. At any rate, this event left a deep wound in Charlene, a feeling of abandonment that she carried with her into adulthood and for which she needed deep-level healing.

We are looking for events in the person's life that may possibly relate to present problems. We are also looking for attitudes that underlie his or her response to such events, attitudes that can be healed by the Holy Spirit. We look especially for damaged attitudes toward self, others, and God. They are frequently signaled by the presence of such emotions as unforgiveness, bitterness, anger, a critical spirit, self-rejection, fear, inadequacy, unworthiness, worry, anxiety, control, domination, depression, discouragement, rebellion, guilt, and shame.

It is usually not a good idea to spend more than five to ten minutes at a time in interviewing those we pray for. If we spend longer, we are likely to forget important things when we turn to prayer. It is ordinarily best to interview for a short time, then go on to the following steps, "looping back" later to get more information before going on to pray over another set of issues. A typical ministry session, then, consists of several interviews followed by several prayer times before the session is over.

It is of the utmost importance that we be loving and non-condemning as we interview. Responding to our questions can be a frightening experience for the person; we are entering his or her secret life. We also need to keep careful control over our motivation for probing. Curiosity has no place in a ministry session. We need to remember that our object is ministry, not uncovering fascinating data.

I often quote a West African proverb to my clients in this regard: "When it's time to bathe, don't try to hide your belly button." That is, if they sincerely desire healing, they must be willing to reveal even the most secret parts of their experience. However, I also tell them that I don't need to know all their garbage. If they want to hide certain details from me, that's okay. But they need to recognize that if God has brought something to mind, it should be dealt with, even if simply between the person and God, without me knowing the details.

Step 4: Develop a tentative strategy. Once we have enough information to enable us to begin the move into prayer, we need to seek the direction of the Holy Spirit. This is the step at which we decide what kind of prayer or other activity we will do next. We usually do this silently, so that the session flows from interview into ministry. The information received during the interview gives us clues as to where to start and what to do as we go along. All we need to decide at first is where to start. The Holy Spirit will then lead us on from there, even if we do not start with a clear idea as to what is to follow.

Often the first thing the Holy Spirit leads us to do is to invite the person to forgive everyone who has hurt her or him. Sometimes individuals will need to confess sin or renounce all opportunities they have given the Enemy to gain power over them. Often intergenerational curses or self-curses need to be broken. On occasion, demons need to be challenged, though it is usually best to do this later on in the session.

Though I present below a possible order of ministry, let me warn the reader against planning any set pattern; instead, follow the leading of the Holy Spirit. Galatians 5:25 tells us, "Since we live by the Spirit, let us keep in step with the Spirit" (NIV). Often the Spirit will lead us to do much of what is listed below, but in a different order. Often he will lead us to skip certain parts or to lump together several experiences of the same type, so we can deal with them all at once. Frequently, the Holy Spirit will guide the session by bringing suggestions to the person's mind, rather than to ours. In any event, be careful not to fall into the Moses mistake by following the same pattern in each session—unless the Spirit clearly guides you to do so.

Step 5: Engage in authoritative prayer. This step is the ministry proper. Having learned enough about the person's life to suspect which areas need to be dealt with and having worked out a tentative strategy, it is now time to pray through the issues and to bring God's healing to the person. Remember that we are working *with* God in authority over the situations, not begging God for something we're not sure he wants to do. As Jesus did, we speak healing, we don't beg for it.

A typical sequence might go something like this:

1. Intergenerational. Treat any suspected intergenerational problems such as spirits, emotions, or sins that may have been inherited. Though such problems often need to be dealt with specifically, sometimes a general prayer such as "I break the power of _____ in Jesus' name" will suffice.

2. Prenatal. Treat any suspected prenatal problems such as emotions and attitudes passed on by the mother before birth. If the person's mother had one or more miscarriages, deal with these early in the session. As a part of dealing with prenatal matters, it is often helpful to use the back-to-the-womb exercise, which will be discussed in chapter six.

3. Early life. Treat early life experiences such as birth, disease, accidents, and relationships with parents or siblings. Picturing Jesus in these events or putting the cross of Jesus over them usually brings healing.

4. Later life. Move through later childhood, adolescence, and adulthood, dealing with such things as school experiences, friendships, sexual development, sexual relationships, emotional relationships, work experiences, accidents, and deaths of family members and friends. In each part of the process, it is usually healing to invite Jesus to bring difficult experiences to mind and to invite the person to picture Jesus there when they occurred.

Step 6: Use post-prayer counseling. The person's will is at least as important after ministry as during ministry. Just as none of the healing could take place without the active participation of the person's will, so healing cannot continue without ongoing cooperation. Though the power of the Holy Spirit during ministry releases the person from the roots underlying dysfunctional habits, the habits themselves usually have to be dealt with on a continuing basis. The person needs, therefore, to work earnestly on the replacement of the old habits with new ones. And this takes willpower.

Often the people we minister to expect all their problems to end once they have been prayed for. This is seldom the case. Usually they will need to continue on their own to work on their habits. A good way to start the post-ministry counseling, then, is to bless individuals with the strengthening of their will. Here we should point out the need to resist Satan when he returns to bring back the same old problems or to deceive them into thinking nothing has changed.

People need to learn to claim the power of the Holy Spirit over their own problems in the same way we have claimed such power during the ministry session. All Christians have the same Holy Spirit and the same privilege and authority to claim his power at any time. They must learn to take this authority on their own in order to prevent further attacks from the Enemy.

I remember a woman who came to me with severe neck and back pain related to her relationship with her husband. When she dealt honestly with her problem before the Lord and experienced his freeing power, she was healed. I warned her, however, that the Enemy usually brings the pain back in an attempt to deceive one into believing that nothing has happened. So I told her that whenever the pain returned, she should simply assert her authority by telling it or the Enemy to go away.

A week later she reported that the pain had indeed come back several times. Each time, though, she commanded it to go away and it did. "Amazing!" she exclaimed.

In addition, we all need to engage regularly in spiritual disciplines that enable us to grow and be renewed in mind and spirit. We are commanded to be transformed through the renewing of our perspectives and attitudes (Rom 12:2). For those in the process of getting healed at deep levels, this usually involves replacing destructive mental "tapes" with messages that fill their minds with "things that are good and that deserve praise: things that are true, noble, right, pure, lovely, and honorable" (Phil 4:8b; see also Eph 4:22-32).

They should, furthermore, be spending time alone with God in prayer, meditating on God and the things of God, picturing themselves in Jesus' presence (for example, on his lap, in his arms, or walking together). Bible reading is crucial. It is, however, important to learn to read the Scriptures more to hear God's voice than just to get new information. In addition, those seeking wholeness need to give much attention to participating often in praise and worship, both alone and in groups. Satan doesn't like praise and worship music and has great difficulty doing his work when praise and worship is going on. We can play praise music in our homes and automobiles as a means of waging war against Satan. The more we fill our minds with praise and worship, the less he will be able to tempt and otherwise harass us.

Another important part of growth is to learn to express love and blessing toward ourselves. As John Wesley once said, "Self-love is not a sin, it is an indisputable duty."[4] As children of the King, we are princes and princesses in the kingdom, chosen by him and given an inheritance with Jesus (Rom 8:14-17; Gal 4:6-7; 1 Jn 3:1-3). It is good to advise people to learn to thank God for themselves and to bless themselves, especially any parts of themselves they don't particularly like.

Neil Anderson in his book *Victory Over the Darkness*, is particularly helpful in this area. Neil contends that "No person can consistently behave in a way that's inconsistent with the way he perceives himself."[5] If this is true, we all need to align our self-perception with God's perception of us. For "self-worth is not an issue of giftedness, talent, intelligence, or beauty. Self-worth is an identity issue. Your sense of personal worth comes from knowing who you are: a child of God."[6] See chapter eight for more on building a healthy self-image.

The support of others is important in the healing process. Ministry sessions provide "spurts" of healing. Individual and small-group support is, however, crucial to undergird the slower continuing process of healing and growth. Close relationships with people who have served on the ministry team are often very helpful. It is, furthermore, important that ministry team members be part of a caring church.

Finally, it is usually a very healing thing for counselees to begin ministering to others. We are healed for our own sake. But we are also healed to help others, especially those who suffer in the same areas in which we have been helped (2 Cor 1:4). Freely we have received, freely we are to give to others (Mt 10:8).

For further information on the steps of ministry, let me recommend both John Wimber's excellent presentation in *Power Healing*, and my own in *Christianity With Power*.[7]

GENERAL MINISTRY GUIDELINES

In ministry, it is good to remember certain guidelines. The following were first suggested to me by George Eckart, a colleague in ministry:

1. *Treat the whole person.* As we have pointed out, people are tightly integrated and need to be treated as whole entities; not simply as bodies, emotions, or spirits. Look for and deal with any problem in any area, but always in relation to all other areas of the person's being. And be *loving*.

2. *Never ask a person to "claim" anything that hasn't happened yet.* There are schools of thought that encourage people to simply name whatever they want and to claim it on the assumption that God wants to give us almost anything we desire. I believe this approach is in error. God stands for honesty. If he has healed, it will be evident and we can claim it. If he has not healed, it is not honoring to him to claim what has not yet happened.

Wonderful things happen when God chooses to work. But we are to serve him; he does not serve us. Praying is our obedience. Healing is his choice. And we should not try to coerce him into doing our will by claiming something has happened when it has not.

3. *Share "words from the Lord" tentatively.* God is generous in revealing things to those who minister. But we must be careful how we deal with such insights. We should never "lay something on" another person in an unloving way. I have heard people who received what they thought was a word from the Lord say bluntly, "The Lord says, you are to…" Much better an approach that asks a question such as, "Does… mean anything to you?" or that says something like, "I have an impression that perhaps…. Does that correspond with anything in your experience?" The rule is to always be loving, as you would want others to be loving toward you.

4. *Shouting is unnecessary.* Neither God, nor Satan, nor most of us are hard of hearing. And contrary to what some people seem to assume, turning up the volume does not increase the amount of God's available power.

5. *It is good to minister in teams.* With more people, there is more gifting, insight, and power. Furthermore, more people are able to express more love. I've found that a team of three or four works best. When working in a team, it is important that one person be in charge, with the rest speaking out only if invited to by the leader. If team members simply speak out whenever they hear something from the Lord, or worse yet, try to take charge of the ministry, it can get very confusing.

It is my practice when I lead in ministry to have the others write what they hear from the Lord on small pieces of paper and to slip them onto my lap. I can then read them and follow the suggestions if I feel led. Sometimes, I will stop and ask if others on the team are getting anything they think I should know. At such times they can contribute vocally.

My co-worker, Mark White, tells how he was in the middle of a ministry session with a team when suddenly his mind went blank. He felt blocked as they tried to work through an event in the person's past.

After trying to "plow through" the block for a few seconds, he felt that someone else in the group had a word of knowledge for the person being ministered to. So Mark stopped to ask the team members if any of them was getting something specific from the Lord. Just at that time, one of the team members received a vision that took the ministry session to the next step. When we minister in teams, God uses the whole team, not just the leader.

6. We must always *be clear as to who is responsible for what in a healing ministry.* It is our responsibility to *minister*, not to heal. It is God's responsibility to *heal* and our privilege to help. We are to be faithful in praying for people whether or not God does what we think he should. It is discouraging when nothing seems to happen. But we are to continue being faithful and obedient to what he has called us to do anyway. Don't let the Enemy work on your discouragement to get you to stop.

WORDS OF KNOWLEDGE

There are several typical ways in which God reveals information directly. Frequently, 1) we'll simply get an *impression.* God often leads through what feel like hunches, intuitions, or guesses. Often 2) he also puts in our minds a *word or combination of words.* We may think them, audibly hear them, or visibly see them written in our mind or in some other place. 3) Further, God can lead through *pictures*. Frequently, he puts a picture into our minds to show us what he wants us to know. Sometimes this will be a picture of the person in a difficult situation, such as an abusive event. Sometimes it will be a picture of some event or situation in the future—for example, the person walking in newfound freedom. Sometimes it will be a picture with symbolic meaning.

4) God may reveal information through a *feeling of pain or an emotion*. Though some people never receive information from God in this way, with others, this seems to be God's preferred method. A pain in some part of our body or a stirring of our emotions is quite effective as a means of identifying someone else's physical or emotional problem.

In a recent meeting, during the worship time, a colleague of mine got a burning sensation in both of his ears. He felt he should share it with the group afterward to see if it meant anything to anyone in the group. A woman in the back of the room spoke up, saying that she had experienced the same burning sensation in her ears earlier in the week when she was in a situation of intense emotional and spiritual distress. During subsequent ministry, it became clear that this was God's way of seeing to it that she got help for some deep-level problems in her life.

Lastly, 5) in ministry we often find ourselves *speaking words we hadn't planned to say*. This method is sometimes called "automatic mouth." Without warning, we hear ourselves saying things that seem to be coming directly from the Lord through our mouth.

During ministry, it is important for both leader and ministry team members to let the others know whatever thoughts come to them. Often we get thoughts that do not seem relevant or even intelligible. When leading ministry, I have learned to share even the strangest thoughts, knowing that God often leads us into major insights in this way. On many occasions, I have had team members who received such information and have not shared it, only to discover later that what came to them could have aided the ministry considerably. On other occasions, people have shared what seemed to be strange or irrelevant words or pictures and discovered that these provided important keys to the ministry.

A man we will call Dan came to my colleague Mark White for prayer. Dan was having trouble breaking free from the authority of his parents. Though grown up, he still did what they told him to do, even though sometimes he knew better and wanted to do differently. He became angry at his parents and sought to be free of this oppressive part of his relationship with them.

In questioning Dan about his childhood, it was discovered that Dan's parents had always told him who he was to be and what he was to do. During one of the early sessions, the Holy Spirit gave Dan a strange mind-picture. He saw a "football coming out of a womb."

This seemed to be a strange vision, so Mark questioned him about it: "Have you ever played football?," Mark asked.

"No," Dan answered.

"Have you ever wanted to play football?"

"Yes," he said, "when I was in high school."

"What happened?"

"Well, my parents strongly suggested that I join the marching band and play the trumpet! I didn't even like the trumpet!"

At this time, the Lord showed Mark that the football coming out of the womb meant that he had created Dan and gifted him, in part, to play football. Unfortunately, his parents failed to recognize this as they forced him into music instead. No wonder he had hated the band and resented his parents' decisions to control him!

After Dan forgave his parents, he was free to seek the things now in his life that are like that football coming out of the womb —those things he was born, gifted, and empowered to do by God from the beginning.

One of the worst things we could do would be to add hurt to someone who is already suffering. The love we felt for the person when we agreed to minister to her or him needs to be expressed in a variety of ways during the ministry sessions. The hurting person needs to experience love during every part of the ministry process if true healing is to occur.

Now we turn to helpful techniques in ministering.

For Further Reading

Rich Buhler, *Pain and Pretending,* 223-69.

John and Mark Sandford, *A Comprehensive Guide to Deliverance and Inner Healing,* 127-58.

David Seamands, *Healing of Memories,* 123-62.

6

Helpful Techniques in Ministering

MEETING JESUS IN JENNA'S PAST

We were in our sixth inner healing session with Jenna and she was making remarkable progress. I had just asked the Holy Spirit to direct us to the agenda for this meeting when Jenna interrupted me and said, "Wait a minute, I think the Holy Spirit is bringing a memory to me." I allowed her some time for the memory to become clear to her, then asked Jenna to describe it for me.

"I see myself standing on the porch of my grandfather's house," she said. "I'm in ragged clothes and my face is dirty. My hair is unkempt and I am experiencing some sort of deep emotion."

"What is the emotion," I asked.

"It's pain, deep emotional pain. I think my parents have left me," Jenna said. She then went on to describe a deep sadness almost beyond her ability to handle. Along with the sadness came great fear of her pain, plus great insecurity. "I don't know what to do," she complained. It makes me feel like putting the whole experience in a sealed box, so it won't hurt so much, and then quitting. In fact, I think that's what I did at the time."

"Keep watching," I told her. "I want to ask Jesus to come and minister to you there. Do you think Jesus was there with you at that time of deep pain?" She wasn't sure. I then explained to her that based on Scriptures like Hebrews 13:8, John 1:1-3, Revelation 4:8, and Colossians 1:15-23, we can know that Jesus was indeed there when these things happened to her. He's everywhere, not only in the present, but also in the past and future. He's intimately involved in every detail of our lives whether we recognize and respond to him or not. I then asked her if she could see Jesus there with her on the porch.

She watched for a couple of minutes with her eyes closed and then a smile came over her face. I asked her what she saw, and she said that a great big Jesus (in comparison to her) in flowing robe and sandals had walked up the sidewalk in front of her grandfather's house. He ascended the steps of the porch and stood in front of her. She was so small compared to him that all she could see were his feet and shins. Jesus stooped down and picked her up, holding her in his strong arms. He then declared to all who were there that day, "This one is mine!"

Jenna allowed herself to be held by Jesus for a long time, just enjoying his loving presence. As she did, she committed to him her feelings of abandonment and worthlessness and found that her pain ebbed away, replaced by a sense of Jesus' closeness in the past as well as in the present.

Jenna still has work to do, adjusting to her new freedom on the one hand and mopping up areas that still need healing on the other hand. But the process is well underway and she can do much of what remains on her own. She has experienced the healing hand of the Lord applied to the roots of her problems and knows that "God, who began this good work in [her], will carry it on until it is finished" (Phil 1:6b).

WHY DEAL WITH TECHNIQUE IF THE HOLY SPIRIT IS LEADING?

In the course of learning to minister deep-level healing, we have found certain methods very effective. But discussion of technique in a ministry committed to doing what the Holy Spirit indicates can seem contradictory, almost as though we were trying to manipulate the Spirit instead of following him. This is far from what is intended. Indeed, none of these techniques are failproof. Nor do the techniques contain any special power in and of themselves.

We all need suggestions for good methods to enable us to bring long-buried emotions and attitudes to the surface. Simply advising people to "pray about it" or to "forget it" has proven very unsatisfactory.

We do have a scriptural precedent for seeking specific techniques in spiritual matters. The disciples were asking for just such a thing when they asked the Master to teach them to pray. What many of us call the "Lord's Prayer" or the "Our Father" was the technique Jesus showed his followers in answer to their request. He did not, of course, want them to use those words like the "meaningless words" of the pagans (Mt 6:7b). Rather, he was providing them with a pattern they could follow. In presenting that pattern, he was showing them the vital elements in a healthy prayer life: honoring the Father, seeking and submitting to his will, and asking him to meet our daily needs for food, forgiveness, and protection.

At the same time, we need to recognize that Jesus' major "technique" was listening to the Father. This he modeled constantly, with the expectation that his followers, and that includes us, would make it the basis for whatever they seek to do in his name. Thus, listening to the Holy Spirit becomes our primary technique.

THE NEED TO GET BACK TO ROOTS

Before we begin to deal with specific techniques, it is important that we understand our reasons for needing them. In deep-level healing, we seek to get at deep-level problems. We aim to get back to any hurtful events that have resulted in attitudes that make life difficult today. Since the roots of most such attitudes are buried in a person's subconscious memory, this quest requires methods that go beyond what might come to light in ordinary conversation or even in an interview.

What we need are methods for revealing both memories and any satanic incursions into the person's life.

1. Memories. Those who study the human brain tell us that everything that happens to us is committed to memory. The memories are all there, encoded in our brains, including memories recorded before we were born. "Think for a moment about what a massive storehouse of information you are. Everything you have ever experienced or felt, thought or learned has been filed away in your brain somewhere. The brain, much like a computer, accepts enormous amounts of data and does amazing things with it."[1]

The memories are all there. However, we cannot retrieve a lot of them, either because what happened didn't impress us enough for us to keep it in our consciousness or because it was so painful that we repressed it. Most of us have had many painful experiences. If we lived every day conscious of these, we would not be able to function. Knowing this, God has built into us the ability to repress unpleasant memories.

Each time we are wounded emotionally we feel the need to hide our reaction in order to save face with those around us. It's like slapping a bandage on each wound as it occurs. If we pictured our bodies with one bandage for every time we have been emotionally hurt, we'd probably all look like mummies! But it's as if the emotional wounds under the bandages are still raw, bleeding, and often infected. The memory of these events may be repressed, but the infection under the "bandages" produces harmful material that "leaks" and affects our present life.

Repressing these memories requires an incredible amount of energy. It is as if the memories are pushing against the walls of the enclosure they are stored in, seeking to get out. "No one completely understands the mental, emotional, and neurological process. But we do know that it requires a great deal of continuous emotional and spiritual energy to keep the memory in its hidden place. It could be compared to a person trying to hold a bunch of balloons under water."[2]

We repress memories because they are unpleasant. But if, with God's help, we let our memories out and face them honestly, we can be healed from the deep wounds. If the experience is sinful, we are to admit it (1 Jn 1:9). If the experience resulted in anger, we can be angry without sinning if we give our anger to God (Eph 4:26). We are to get rid of all anger, bitterness, and hate by admitting such feelings and forgiving (Eph 4:31-32).

I have a scar on my hand that has been there for fifty-eight years. The wound the scar represents once hurt very much. But it hasn't hurt for a long time now because it was dealt with at the time it occurred and soon healed. The truth of the fact that I was injured was not changed when the wound was healed. But it doesn't hurt anymore. It's similar with emotional wounds. Healing does not change the history. Those wounds remain a part of the person's life story. There is, however, an enormous difference between wounds that are still open and festering and those that have healed and turned into scars. God is willing and able to turn festering emotional wounds into painless scars.

2. Satanic influence. We need to be aware of the possibility of Enemy infiltration in a person's life and to know what to do about it.

If there is a family history of occult involvement (for example, divination, witchcraft, palmistry, ouija board, tarot cards) or of membership in a cult (including Freemasonry, Christian Science, Scientology, or Mormonism), the power of God needs to be brought to bear on whatever part of that inheritance has been passed on. Frequently, the person will be demonized. (See chapter twelve, and my book, *Defeating Dark Angels*, for more on dealing with demons.) Whether or not there is demonization, the person needs to renounce any allegiance to or relationship with such activities or organizations. All such bondage needs to be broken through an authoritative word, speaking specifically to the family line through which such influence has come.

When dealing with prenatal experience, it is my practice to assert God's authority and power over both father's and mother's family lines to break all ungodly influences and to cancel the

Enemy's right to the person. When this is done in such a general way, however, it is not always enough. It is often necessary to go back to the specific generation in which the satanic influence entered the family line, claiming God's power to break the influence and cancel the Enemy's right to the family at that point.

Seeking the roots, whether in memory or in satanic influence, is what deep-level healing is all about.

MEMORY RETRIEVAL

The need to be able to retrieve memories is crucial to deep-level healing. As we commit the ministry session to the Holy Spirit, we ask him to bring to mind whatever will be helpful in bringing freedom to the hurting person. Often, among the most helpful things are the memories of past events (before or after birth) long hidden from the person's consciousness.

Fred and Florence Littauer have helped us a lot with this area of memory retrieval in their two books, *Freeing Your Mind From Memories That Bind* and *The Promise of Restoration*. Though there is too much of value in these books to present here, it will be useful to summarize the chapter in the latter book entitled, "Guidelines for Memory Retrieval." As we do, keep in mind that the Littauers' emphasis, like ours, is that the beginning, middle, and end of the process of memory retrieval are to be bathed in prayer and continual attention to the guidance of the Holy Spirit.

Fred Littauer defines memory retrieval as "the rediscovering of experiences we endured in childhood which were too painful to accept as reality at the time. They were then either consciously or unconsciously suppressed deep within our memory bank. There is obviously no need to find every childhood memory that has lapsed into obscurity. Our minds would be cluttered with useless trivia. It is only when there are adult issues which are troubling us that we need to dig up certain specific roots."[3]

When we ask the Holy Spirit to bring things back, he does. While dreaming, praying, reading, or during ministry sessions, fragmentary memories of scenes from the past often begin to come to mind. These flashbacks are like the pieces of a jigsaw puzzle. When they come, it is helpful to keep them in focus long enough to see if any other parts of the picture will come to mind. It is also helpful to write them down.

Flashbacks frequently contain material that upset the persons who see them. I have spent parts of many sessions helping people to deal with disagreeable and often disgusting revelations concerning their parents. One of the biggest problems was allowing themselves to believe their parents would have done the things the flashbacks were revealing.

Littauer presents three steps toward memory retrieval. The first step is to *desire the truth*. Such a desire needs to be so strong that the person as an adult can face the hurt he or she suppressed as a child. *Those who would be healed need to be determined both to seek the truth and to accept it.* And for many, especially those who have been badly hurt, neither seeking nor accepting are easy tasks. Praying against blockage by asking God to make one willing to face whatever comes may be an important step toward healing.

The second step is to *believe that God is leading* and that he will not push a person beyond what he or she is able to handle. Third, we *ask the Lord to reveal whatever he chooses*. If healing is to take place, we need to ask, seek, and knock (Mt 7:7) to discover what is hidden. It is a good practice to have the individual pray aloud, asking the Lord to reveal.

Littauer gives an example of how they go about seeking memories:

> After the seeker of truth has prayed, we usually suggest that he (or she) sit back in the chair and relax. We ask him to shut his eyes, explaining this is only to blank out any distractions that might occur in the room. This enables him to keep his attention focused on wherever the Lord may take him, on whatever the Lord may reveal. Then we will ask, "I want you to try to find yourself as a little child, perhaps at four or five years old, somewhere in your childhood. When you find yourself anywhere, I

want you to tell me where you are...."

We remind him that we are not asking him to remember anything or any place, but simply to find himself as a child.

Once a location is set, we ask the person to look around: "Tell me what you see," always asking for more details, helping to make the scene clearer.[4]

Star Cole, one of the Littauers' associates, suggests in an insert in Fred Littauer's *Promise of Restoration Workshop Manual*, that there are four ways in which memory retrieval is experienced:

1. Graphic recall. Some people find their memories coming back *graphically*, "in crystal-clear vision like a photojournal or video recording." This is, however, the exception. Most people retrieve memories in one of the following ways.

2. Hazy impressions. The most frequent way of memory retrieval seems to be through *faint but plainly discernable images*. These impressions usually are hazy but definable and tend to become clearer when focused on. For many, focusing on the impressions results in fairly clear pictures of people, places, and things. Even sounds and smells sometimes become clear.

3. Strong impressions. These can be "body sensations such as changes in breathing or sensations of tightness, tension, pressure or pain in the head, throat, chest, stomach, genitals, arms, legs or elsewhere; dizziness or sensations of movement; emotional responses such as anxiety, fear, panic, crying, anger, etc.; smelling fragrances or odors, hearing sounds or voices, etc. These impressions can be so strong that it is *as though* you 'see' what you are experiencing without an actual *visual* image. Many people experience memory this way."

4. Medley. This consists of any combination of the first three types of recall in various ways and proportions.[5]

5. Nonvisual, nonsensory impression. This is a final way not mentioned by Cole. Not infrequently, the person simply knows what happened, even without pictures or feeling. Such recall is sometimes adequate. Sometimes, however, when there is a lack of feeling it is because the person is repressing the memory or, at least, is not as fully involved in it as he or she needs to be to work toward healing.

FAITH PICTURING

Since so much memory retrieval involves picturing the events in focus, the above discussion leads naturally into dealing with the place of visualization or what I prefer to call "faith picturing" in deep-level healing. This is simply the practice of having people go back in their minds to picture events, people, or places, to enable them to feel again the emotions associated with those memories. Faith picturing is for many of us who work in deep-level healing our most useful technique.

Throughout the Bible, God has revealed himself and his messages in pictures, whether through visions and dreams or in word pictures and analogies. He spoke through visions and dreams to just about all of the heroes of the Bible, including Jacob (Gn 28:10-17), Joseph (Gn 37:5-11), Samuel (1 Sm 3:1-15), Isaiah (Is 6), Peter (Acts 10:10-16), Paul (Acts 16:9), and John (Rv 1:10-22:5). In addition, as Gary Smalley and John Trent point out, "Jesus' primary method to teach, challenge, and motivate others was word pictures. When discussing love, He launched into a word picture about a good Samaritan. Or to describe the forgiving heart of a father, He shared a story about a prodigal son. Interestingly enough, word pictures are also the most frequent means of describing who Jesus is."[6]

It is picturing that brings the Scriptures to life as we contemplate the great events of salvation history. We picture creation, the murder of Abel, the flood, Abram leaving his home, Joseph in the pit, Moses and the burning bush, Joshua taking the land, the con-

flict between Saul and David, Job on the ash heap, the events surrounding Jesus' birth, life, death, and resurrection, the travels of
Paul, and all the other events to which our faith is tied. In addition,
we can picture the Lord as our Shepherd (Ps 23), the person who
trusts the Lord mounting on wings like an eagle (Is 40:31), the
righteous person as a tree planted by good water (Ps 1:3), the run-
ner pressing on to win the prize (Phil 3:12-14), and countless
other word pictures, as we receive God's messages to us.

We should not think it strange, then, that when God seeks to
free people, he uses pictures to reveal the memories that bind
them. Just as he speaks through and empowers words, so he speaks
through and empowers pictures to lead people to truth. *Faith picturing, then, is the use of our God-given ability to picture under the
leading and power of God.* This takes place under the direction and
empowerment of God and, I believe, is a function of our spirits,
not just a product of our imagination.

We rationalistic Western Christians are often suspicious of this
technique because we are captured by our "left-brain" orientation.
Unlike Jesus and the Hebrew world of which he was a part, we
often fear anything emotional or picture-oriented. Dave Hunt, in
his book, *The Seduction of Christianity,* points out that visualization is heavily used by psychologists (whom he considers anti-
Christian), those in the New Age, and other occult groups. He
judges that, since the technique is used by such groups, any use of
it by Christians will necessarily draw us into their errors. His conclusion is that the method itself is evil.

This viewpoint neglects to take into account the fact that no
technique, activity, or created thing is completely sacred or profane
in and of itself. Satan can use even the most sacred things, including prayer, the Bible (see Lk 4:1-13), worship, spiritual gifts, and
the church to serve his purposes. Are these things therefore evil
because Satan uses them? Nothing should be labeled "evil" simply
because the Enemy finds a way to make use of it.

In fact, a focus on whether the forms are good or evil obscures
the real issues. The crucial aspect of the argument should be, not
the nature of the techniques, but the way they are used and the

source of the power behind them. Within New Age and other occult organizations, the power source behind such techniques is not Jesus, but Satan. Whether knowingly or not, practitioners of such faiths are receiving their power from demonic sources and, as such, any benefits they receive or bestow will ultimately do more harm than good.

Hunt rightly warns us to be careful when we see people using visualization techniques. But he warns us against the technique, rather than pointing to the real problem, the source of the power. Our power source is Jesus. When we begin each ministry session we ask the Holy Spirit to be in charge of what takes place and we believe that he honors that request. Thus, our use of faith picturing is submitted to the Lord's control along with every other practice we employ, like prayer, anointing with oil, and blessing.

However, even when we use faith picturing under God's power, I would raise one more caution. When we are dealing with memories, we are dealing with things that actually happened, not things as we wish they had happened. Some who minister are in the habit of guiding the imagery in such a way as to change what actually happened. Such "re-creation" of the history is, I believe, ultimately harmful since it is a kind of deceit. Lying and distortion are never condoned by God. In the long run, such an approach will not help the person. We cannot deny or rewrite the past to suit our desires. Our aim is to heal the damage to emotions that resulted from actual events.

The way we use faith picturing is to ask people to close their eyes and go back in their minds to an event in which emotional damage was done. We ask people to let themselves feel the emotion. We point out that *Jesus was there when the event happened.* This is fact. Seamands puts it helpfully, "Remember that Christ is alive. He is here now. And because He transcends time, He is also back at that painful experience. Confess to Him, turn over to Him each experience, each emotion, each attitude."[7]

We try not to suggest what people ought to see but ask the Holy Spirit to lead. When they have been able to go back into the memory, we ask them to allow themselves to experience the feelings. This is often difficult, since avoiding these feelings has been their method of coping and is the reason they are now in need of help. At this time, preferably without having them leave the memory, it is often necessary to give lots of encouragement or even to ask questions concerning how they felt about the situation, the other person(s) involved, themselves, and God.

The process of feeling the emotions again, plus the realization (usually pictured) that Jesus was there protecting them from greater harm, usually results in turning the painful wound into a painless scar. The true emotions have been felt and the truth of the Lord's presence made clear, paving the way for healing.

With a little experience, we can often predict at least part of what will happen as the person sees Jesus in the painful events. Sometimes, too, God reveals part or all of what is going on through words of knowledge. Often, however, the results are surprising and the healing spectacular. Usually at least some of the things that happen are new to even the most experienced ministry leader.

We need to be on our guard as we lead people through faith picturing since Satan often tries to interfere with this process. He has a lot to lose if the person becomes aware of the Lord's presence in the painful events and gains healing. Demons will sometimes pose as Jesus in the picture. At times this is evident, as when one of my clients saw "Jesus" holding a knife behind his back. Another time a woman reported being kissed by "Jesus" in an unwholesome fashion. These uncharacteristic behaviors tipped us off to the fact that we were dealing with an impersonator, not the real Jesus.

At other times, it is not so clear that an imposter has appeared. Frequently, though, when this has happened, the Holy Spirit has alerted me and I have challenged the being the person is seeing. My challenge is simply to command any false Jesus to disappear or to turn black. If the being is an imposter, it will usually disappear or turn black immediately. Precautions can be taken against this type of interference by forbidding it at the beginning of the session, though occasionally it still occurs.

Sin in the person's life or an unforgiving attitude can block faith picturing, especially the picturing of Jesus in the event. Likewise with feelings of shame, guilt, unworthiness, rejection, fear, anger, or other negative emotions. Not infrequently, a person will feel shame over the thought of Jesus seeing her or him in the situation. Feeling that people have always rejected him or her, the person believes that Jesus is no more accepting than the others were. Often such attitudes need to be dealt with before the faith picturing can be effective.

Donald had such an attitude. He felt totally ineligible for help from anyone, especially one as righteous as Jesus. "I must be bad in God's eyes or all this horrible stuff would not have happened to me," was his feeling. So, he was angry, hurting, hopeless, and wishing he could die. He refused to believe what we said about Jesus' willingness to take on himself Donald's heavy burdens.

When I strongly affirmed Donald's right to be angry, bitter, and resentful, though, he began listening in a new way. Did I mean that Jesus wouldn't reject him because he hated those who had hurt him? Donald admitted he didn't enjoy being so angry. I suggested he take a chance on Jesus. If it didn't work, he could back out later. The words came haltingly, "I want to forgive those who hurt me. Please help me, Jesus."

We didn't ask for a picture of Jesus. Without any suggestion on our part, though, God gave Donald a beautiful picture of Jesus in a shining robe with his arms spread wide to receive Donald. I asked if Donald would move into those arms. He said, "I'm running toward them!" The embrace was long and sweet. And Donald is a completely different person now.

Survivors of abuse like Donald often cannot even look at Jesus due to the shame and anger they feel. It is important for them to know that Jesus never blamed people for their condition. Nor does he blame them for what happened to them. Indeed, he was hurt by it too. For reasons I don't understand, Jesus often appears behind the person in the faith picture. When people tell me they cannot see Jesus in the picture, I frequently suggest that they picture themselves turning around and there he is!

One woman in her fifties, dealing with a painful childhood memory, found it impossible to face Jesus, though she could picture him in the event. Her shame and guilt were too great. When at last she was able to turn, however, she experienced immediate release from those feelings that had kept her bound.

Once people have seen Jesus in the event, they need to give all the painful feelings to Jesus. At this point, they may find it difficult to approach Jesus. Or they may find it difficult to give up the anger, bitterness, or desire for revenge that the event arouses. Experiencing the emotion, seeing Jesus there and giving him the feelings requires that people be willing to forgive all others for their part in the painful scene. Then they usually need to forgive themselves as well. Often they will also need to "forgive" (really, release all anger toward) God for allowing the hurtful events to happen.

Forgiveness does not mean saying it was all right for the event to have happened or that it no longer hurts. Indeed, forgiving is often extremely difficult. Since unforgiveness binds us to the past and does not permit healing to flow freely, though, we must forgive. Sometimes the best a person can initially do is to "be willing to be made willing" to forgive. But that's usually enough to bring a considerable amount of healing. The person usually feels a great sense of relief. Given the depth of the hurt, we cannot expect everything to be taken care of quickly. Many years have gone into the making of the problem and the healing is likely to be a process. God accepts whatever steps we take toward obedience, and he will give the strength and grace to further the forgiveness process.

After working all the way through an event, it is good to ask the person to revisit it to see if anything has changed. This request is often met with a good deal of surprise and unwillingness. The person doesn't want to have to go through the pain again. This step is important, though, to demonstrate the difference in the feel of the memory now that it has been "defused." Going back, the person will most often find a significant decrease in pain. For what was once like an open wound is now healing into a scar that will no longer hurt.

John and Mark Sandford point out, "Inner healing does not erase a memory or change our personal history. Rather, it enables us to cherish even the worst moments in our lives, for through them God has inscribed eternal lessons onto our hearts and prepared us to minister to all who have suffered in the same way (Heb 2:18). We know we are healed and transformed when we can look back on everything with gratitude."[8]

There are quite a number of possible variations in faith picturing. Often, when we are focusing on one memory, the Lord will bring a quick succession of memories to the person. In this way, God may bring healing to several memories at the same time. God led one young woman to see several very traumatic events as pictures hanging on the wall of a room. As she and Jesus walked past each one, he healed it and removed that picture. On another occasion, when the emotions aroused by the memory were so intense that the woman pleaded with me not to make her relive it, God enabled her to see the event as a still picture on which Jesus poured his blood, turning the picture white as he healed her emotional hurt. Once people have experienced this type of ministry, they can often work through other memories on their own with the Lord.

Some people are unable to visualize. Or they may object to doing so for personal reasons. Some have been exposed extensively to visualization and guided imagery as members of occult groups. It may be unwise to use visualization with them. With such people, recalling the event and feeling it again as best they can may be just as effective. Techniques such as covering the event with the cross, planting the cross between the person and the event, or claiming the blood of Christ over the event can be used (see below). The healing that takes place through these methods can be just as great as through faith picturing.

THE BACK-TO-THE-WOMB EXERCISE

A tool we have found very helpful is what we call the "back-to-the-womb" or "back-to-conception" exercise. This procedure enables us to take people back under the power of the Holy Spirit to conception and to deal with prebirth experiences that provide roots for present problems. As noted above and detailed in chapter seven, human beings are capable of recording memories even within the womb. These can be powerful forces in their lives. Such prebirth experiences as physical traumas, hearing parents fight, and experiencing the mother's negative feelings shape our responses and actions throughout life. Praying through this period can bring great healing to those damaged before birth.

This exercise can be done either with individuals or with groups. When done with a group, it is good to warn people that, though most will probably have a positive experience, some may have a neutral or negative reaction. Those for whom this process turns up negative or difficult emotions will need to go to someone for individual ministry.

We start by inviting people to close their eyes while we lead them through the following steps:

1. We were planned by God. At the start, we focus attention on the fact that God planned us before we were conceived and that our parents did his will by coming together to bring about our conception. Whatever our parents' desires, whether we were planned by them or not, we were planned by God. It is God who brought about our conception and gave us life. Nothing about us, then, is a mistake from his point of view—not the timing of our birth, not our sex, not our genetic inheritance, not even our parents. As with Jeremiah, he says to us, "Before I formed you in the womb I knew you, before you were born I set you apart" (Jer 1:5 NIV). As David said, "You created every part of me; you put me together in my mother's womb.... When my bones were being formed, carefully put together in my mother's womb, when I was growing there in secret, you knew that I was there—you saw me before I was born" (Ps 139:13, 15-16a). He planned each of us from eternity and carefully put us together in that secret place inside our mothers.

2. Jesus was present at our conception, signifying it was all right we were conceived. We then like to ask each person to try to picture Jesus' hands outstretched toward them, with a sperm in one hand and an egg in the other. I ask then that each person put his or her hands outside of Jesus' hands and press them carefully together to fertilize the egg with the sperm. This signifies agreement that it was all right for the person to be conceived.

This part of the exercise may be very difficult or emotion-laden for those with very low self-esteem and especially for those who hate themselves. People may have to pause here to forgive their parents for not wanting them or for wanting a child of the opposite sex and agree with God that they are what he wanted.

3. We take authority over any satanic power in the family line. As this takes place, I take authority in prayer over the father's line and then over the mother's to break any satanic power that may have come to them through inheritance. I usually say something like,

> In Jesus' name I take authority over your inheritance through your father (mother), to break any satanic influence that may have come down to you by inheritance. I break the power of any dedications, curses, or entrance by deceit that gave the Enemy any right to influence you. I break this power at the point of your conception, or at any other point at which it may have entered you.

Some feel the breaking of such power over them as these words are said. Others, unfortunately, do not seem to experience the breaking of power during a general procedure like this. They need specific attention to such influences. Others, of course, don't have such interference in their family lines and, therefore, aren't affected by this part of the process.

4. We work our way through the gestation period. Once this is accomplished, we journey through the gestation period month by month. We bless the child during each month of development. We take authority over all negative influences the child may have experienced. We speak against any anger, fear, negative self-image, discouragement, and the like, as the Spirit leads, that may have come from the mother. We then break any additional curses, dedications, or vows that may have allowed satanic power to enter.

Quite often, people will experience intense emotion or even blockage at certain points during this process. They can often feel the very emotions their mother was experiencing at certain times during the pregnancy. Such happenings usually signal the surfacing of some critical issue or event that occurred at that time. This may be known or unknown to the person. As I was working with one woman, she felt a poking sensation as we dealt with the second month. This reminded her that her mother had once told her she had tried to abort her, though she had not told her the month. On checking with her mother, the woman discovered that the attempt was indeed during the second month.

When there are such feelings or intense emotion or blockage, they signal the need to work with the person individually to discover what the event involved and to bring healing into it. Whenever such signals point to abuse on the part of parents or others, the person will need to forgive them to gain release from the reaction. If the feelings relate to some traumatic event over which the parents had no control, the person may have to release all anger toward God for letting it happen.

5. We picture our birth and see Jesus holding us. When it is time for the birth, we invite people to picture their birth. As soon as they are born, they allow Jesus to pick them up and hold them. Most people are able to do this and find it a positive experience as they feel the love, safety, and protection of being held in Jesus' arms. Persons with feelings of unworthiness, though, sometimes find this difficult. They may see the baby and Jesus but not be able to get into Jesus' arms. Such people need to be worked with individually.

We suggest that people spend as long as they would like in Jesus' arms, letting themselves feel wanted, noting the pleased expression on his face, and soaking up his love and care for them. We also ask them to look to see if the umbilical cord is still attached. If it is, it is to be taken care of in the next step.

6. We hold the baby and cut the umbilical cord if it is still there. We then ask people to see themselves entering the picture as adults and holding themselves as a baby. If the umbilical cord is still there, they are to tie and cut it. This often signifies the severing of some unnatural bond with or overdependence on their parents. As they hold the baby, they should help him or her to feel wanted and secure, blessing the child with whatever the Lord leads them to say and committing themselves to love and care for the child (since that baby still lives inside them).

Again, those with feelings of inadequacy or self-hate will have difficulty holding their inner child in this way. Once they have worked through such feelings, it is useful to return to this part of the exercise to allow them to experience the change.

On occasion, demons will show up during this or any other part of the procedure. If this happens, the ministry leader may choose to deal with them at the time or may shut them down and deal with them later.

DEALING WITH CHILDHOOD AND LATER LIFE EXPERIENCES

The process of dealing with childhood and later experiences is relatively simple. We start by asking the Holy Spirit to bring to mind the events he chooses to deal with. If we have just gone through the back-to-the-womb exercise, it is often useful to continue with early life experiences, either moving along year by year or jumping around as the Spirit leads.

When the Holy Spirit brings an event to mind, we invite the person to get back into it, either visually or nonvisually, with the aim of feeling the hurt and inviting Jesus to take it on himself as he promised in Isaiah 61:1b-3a (see also Lk 4:18-19): "He has chosen me and sent me to bring good news to the poor, to heal the brokenhearted, to announce release to captives and freedom to those in prison.... He has sent me to comfort all who mourn, to give [them] joy and gladness instead of grief, a song of praise instead of sorrow."

As people experience again the hurtful event, I have found it helpful to affirm the validity of their negative feelings toward those who hurt them. I will often say something like this:

> You have a right to be angry, hate, and even seek revenge for what these people have done to you. But if you exert that right, there's a law in the universe that says you will be enslaved to those feelings. And furthermore, you will probably never be able to get back at the perpetrators anyway. So Jesus says forgive them and get free.

> So we invite them to forgive everyone they need to forgive—usually others, self, and God. They can then usually see Jesus in the situation and turn their feelings over to him. At this point, they often find that Jesus embraces them or shows them his love and acceptance in some other way. And they go free!

We repeat this kind of process for each event the Holy Spirit brings directly to their attention or, through words of knowledge, to ours. Often, though, when one of a certain kind of event gets healed, others of that kind are also taken care of.

PUTTING THE CROSS OF CHRIST OVER THE EVENTS

A technique that is often very useful, either in place of faith picturing or in addition to it, is to "put the cross of Christ over" the event or "between" that event and the person being prayed for. In the experience cited above in which the woman pictured the event as a still picture on a wall, we used the blood of Christ rather than the cross to cover the event.

Though the power that heals is in Christ himself, not in symbols such as the cross or his blood, it is often helpful to use such symbols to apply that power in a meaningful way. For example, when working with a person who has difficulty seeing Jesus in the hurtful events, sealing the ministry time by placing the cross of Christ over the experience is often a good approach. After the person has experienced the hurt, forgiven whoever he or she needs to forgive, and given Jesus the pain, the ministry leader can say something like,

"In the name of Jesus, we place his cross over this event (or put his cross between this person and the event), and claim freedom from all emotional or spiritual damage stemming from it."

We can also use this method in dealing with inherited satanic interference. For example, when it appears that an ancestor has allowed the Enemy to enter the family line, we can, if possible, identify the ancestor (for example, a grandfather on the mother's side) and place the cross of Jesus between that ancestor and the person we are praying for. In working with a child, the Sandfords describe their use of this technique as follows: "... we place the cross of Christ (the stopping place for all sin) between the child and his parents and his parents' parents all the way back through his generations, declaring that all of his inheritance be filtered through that cross. This is not magic. It is simply a way of putting the Lord in charge, and of claiming His blessing and protection."[9]

I often use this symbolism when obtaining a client's freedom from a place where terrible things have happened. Sometimes in faith picturing, people will be able to see themselves in a room or a house but find it impossible to picture their escape from that place. Even inviting Jesus in to rescue them doesn't seem to work. I have, therefore, had them picture me entering that place and leading them to safety. Once we are outside the door, I describe myself as closing and locking the door, then placing the cross of Christ over the door to seal it so that whoever is in that room or house cannot get out. Nor can anyone take the person back into that place.

I also use this symbolism when casting out demons. Once they are gone, I place the cross of Christ and his empty tomb between the client and the demons and forbid them to ever return or to send any others. (See *Defeating Dark Angels* for more on this subject.)

SEPARATING THE GOOD FROM THE BAD PARTS OF THE PERSON

Persons who have been abused by someone close to them experience a great deal of confusion in their attitude toward that person, especially if the person is a parent who was supposed to nurture and protect them. Both love and hate are there, a desire to be close to that person, but an intense fear of him or her as well. When such a "love-hate" relationship exists, the process of healing is often helped by guiding people to distinguish between the parts of the other person they like and those they don't like.

First, as always, we invite the Holy Spirit to direct the whole process. We then instruct the person, with or without the use of picturing, to divide the abuser into two people, the good, loving person and the bad, hurtful person. We invite the person to picture the abuser and to ask Jesus to come and escort the good part of the person out of the room, while the bad part remains. The person is then free to tell the bad part of that individual exactly how she or he feels about the abuse, without the risk of hurting the part of that person he or she likes. During such a discussion the counselee needs both to hold the person responsible for such actions and to forgive him or her.

Later, the good part of the person is brought back and the bad part taken elsewhere. The client can then talk to the good part of the abuser, again without the confusion of having to deal with the other part of the person at the same time. This discussion frequently centers around how much the client loves the other person and desires that he or she prosper.

This technique allows the counselee to express real feelings concerning the abuse, while at the same time acknowledging the special place the abuser may have in the client's life. Interestingly, when the good part of the abuser is brought in and spoken to, the counselee often sees him or her as a child. To see one's parent or another adult abuser as a child is often startling, and it can be remarkably healing for the client. Perhaps this is God's way of helping the hurting one to recognize that there is a wounded child within the abuser, a child that needs love and forgiveness.

CHANGING CHAIRS

Not infrequently, especially with people who have been severely abused, memories come back with great intensity. Seamands points out, "... the harder we try to keep bad memories out of conscious recall, the more powerful they become. Since they are not allowed to enter through the door of our minds directly, they come into our personalities (body, mind, and spirit) in disguised and destructive ways."[10]

Perhaps the most intense form of memory is what is often called a "body memory." In a body memory, the person experiences the event as a present experience, believing and feeling that she or he is actually in the abusive situation at the present time.

Such memories frequently involve feelings of pain and terror which overcome the person and are not easily stopped through simple reasoning. When such body memories occur, they disrupt the ministry session until they are over. Indeed, they sometimes so exhaust the counselee that little can be accomplished even after the episode is finished.

When such episodes occur, we have learned to invite the client to change chairs as a means of obtaining release from the experience. I often explain that the chair the client is sitting in is "the past" and invite the person to move from that chair to my own chair, which I have labeled "the present." The change of chairs usually results in the person coming out of the body memory into the present. Then, by claiming the cross of Jesus over the memory, much of the pain of the memory may be healed. Even when healing of the memory doesn't happen, however, this technique has worked dramatically in extricating the person from the body memory and returning him or her to the present.

PRAYING FOR YOUNG CHILDREN

Very young children can be ministered to as they sleep or as they are being held. Parents and others authorized by the parents can take authority over any satanic interference in a child's life while the child is asleep, talking aloud to any emissaries from the Enemy and claiming the child for Jesus. It is very important to assert our authority over the child in this way so that no one in the universe is in any doubt as to who's in charge. At the same time, we should dedicate and commit the child to Jesus.

Sometimes the results of this kind of ministry are surprising. I joined the parents of an eighteen-month-old boy once in praying with authority over him while he slept, and the release was so great it woke him up. Not only that, but he felt so good that he stayed up and kept his parents from sleeping the rest of the night!

It is good to do this on a regular basis, dealing both with satanic interference and with early (including prebirth) emotional influences and biological inheritance. Often, parents need to apologize to young children in this way for not wanting them initially—say, when an unexpected pregnancy occurred to which their first reaction was, "Oh, no!"

In conclusion, in using all of these techniques, we must always remember to let the Holy Spirit lead us. That means we must be prepared to lay them aside at any time. After all, they are only tools. What we are after is deep-level healing, and the Holy Spirit is our guide.

For Further Reading

Neil Anderson, *Victory Over the Darkness,* 193-207.

Francis and Judith MacNutt, *Praying for Your Unborn Child,* 143-52.

John and Paula Sandford, *The Transformation of the Inner Man,* 191-266.

David A. Seamands, *Healing of Memories,* 33-42.

Part Two

Issues and Problems in Deep-Level Healing

7

Our Reactions Are Usually the Main Problem

A LOAD OFF HER CHEST

"Wow! That was incredible! I feel ten pounds lighter! Now I won't have to go on a diet!" Amy had come with a fairly typical set of problems. Her early experiences with her family had left her with a poor self-concept. She had struggled to survive, dragged down continually by the feeling that somehow she was responsible for most, if not all, of the things that went wrong around her. Intense guilt was her constant companion. And now her marriage had fallen apart and her husband was placing all the blame on her. As is typical of a person with such a life history, she was internalizing all the blame and feeling that life was not worth living.

Could God help her? she wondered. Nothing she had done so far seemed to bring much hope. We went back over her early life to see where Jesus was when she was being verbally abused. The Lord appeared to her, embraced her and showed her that he was indeed present in each of the events he brought to her mind. This helped enormously and she experienced a good bit of release from the grip that regrettable past had had on her.

But not everything was right yet. Amy was still blaming herself for causing these events and feeling shame and guilt over them. This did not surprise me, given the fact that she had become a "magnet" for guilt, willing to take full blame for anything around her that went wrong. So we reasoned a bit about her part in the things that had happened to her. "Amy, do you honestly believe you are totally to blame for your divorce?" I asked. "Or for the things that went wrong while you were growing up?" She admitted it was unreasonable to blame herself for everything.

At that point, I asked Amy if she had confessed all known sin. She said she had. So I claimed the authority Jesus gave us in John 20:23a ("If you forgive people's sins, they are forgiven") and said, "In the name of Jesus, I speak forgiveness to you, Amy." And the load lifted.

As we will discuss in this chapter, the Enemy works hard to get us to feel shame and guilt over anything we are involved in that works out badly. It is a fact that victims tend to blame themselves for the crimes perpetrated against them. They reason, "If these things happened to me, I must somehow have deserved or allowed them. Therefore, I am to blame for them happening. This must be because I'm bad."

Furthermore, many have a hard time believing what God says about sin, that if we confess it to him, it is forgiven. The Enemy takes full advantage of this and regularly raises doubts in our minds about whether or not we are actually forgiven. He likes to say things like, "After what you've done, do you think you can get off that easy? No, you've got to pay for it!" So there are many Christians who have confessed their sins but still carry heavy loads of guilt.

Some of those in both these categories are like Amy. They seem to gladly accept all guilt attached to actual sins and mistakes but also to reach out for guilt that doesn't belong to them. It is as if they are in the habit of claiming whatever guilt there is in the atmosphere! They are ready to blame themselves for anything, no matter whose fault it might be.

IT'S REACTIONS, NOT EVENTS, THAT REQUIRE HEALING

As pointed out in chapter three, sin is a major issue in deep-level healing. We are sinners, therefore, we sin. When we sin, then, we react to what we have done. And these reactions are often unhealthy. Our tendency is to hide what we've done, both from others and often from ourselves. Though this is a time-honored tendency, going back to the Garden of Eden, it is just as damaging today as it was then. For there is a law in the universe, put there by God, that says if we confess our sins to him, we receive his forgiveness and go free (1 Jn 1:9). If, however, we hide our faults, we become captive to them and to our Enemy, the Devil.

Being sinned against is also a major issue in deep-level healing. When we are victimized by others, we react automatically. Anger is a normal reaction to such mistreatment. So are other natural but troublesome emotions such as fear, resentment, bitterness and the like. Though the immediate emotion, if dealt with and released right away, is not much of a problem, we tend to hang onto such reactions as anger, resentment, and bitterness.

In addition, we may, like Amy, turn in on ourselves and feel guilty. As we have mentioned, when we are victimized we tend to blame ourselves for what others have done to us. The perpetrator's action is treated as if it were in response to our behavior and is thus our responsibility rather than his or hers. Our anger over the mistreatment, then, is usually complicated by the feeling that we deserved what we got because of some defect or badness in ourselves.

So there may be more than one level of reaction to deal with when we seek to bring deep healing to people. Forgiving the persons who hurt us may be easier than forgiving ourselves for supposed defects that we believe brought about the victimization.

It is, however, the reactions, not the events themselves, that have to be dealt with in deep-level healing. The events cannot be changed. The events cannot be healed. Our response and the abiding attitude toward others, self, and God that sprang from the events can, however, be redeemed. Guilt and shame over sins committed can be replaced by self-forgiveness based on claiming and accepting God's forgiveness. Anger, resentment, and bitterness over being wounded can be replaced by freedom. And this in spite of the fact that we seldom understand why the hurtful events happened to us. We have little ability to figure such things out and God doesn't explain. He simply says to us, as he said to his disciples concerning the man born blind, "He is blind so that God's power might be seen at work in him" (Jn 9:3b). He then reminds us that "in all things God works for good with those who love him" (Rom 8:28b).

PREBIRTH REACTIONS

Though when we talk of memories our thoughts usually go to things that have happened since birth, frequently the experiences people are reacting to happened while they were in the womb. In working with people to bring healing from deep inner wounds, we frequently find that much damage was done before birth. Praying through prebirth experiences is especially helpful to those conceived out of wedlock, those conceived at an inconvenient time in their parents' lives, those whose parents wanted a child of the other sex, and those whose parents were experiencing marital discord or other difficulties, during the pregnancy.

Those who study preborn children have a number of very interesting things to say about their activities and level of consciousness. A University of California professor, John T. Noonan, states that by the tenth week of gestation a baby's "adrenal and thyroid glands are functioning. He sucks his thumb and responds to pain. He can kick, curl his toes, and turn his feet. His brain is formed much as it will be in adulthood. And his fingerprints already bear the pattern that is uniquely his. His heart has now been beating for seven weeks—pumping blood that he has made himself."[1]

So at least by the time the gestation process has reached two and a half months (and probably much sooner), babies are experiencing life and recording those experiences in their brains. Though the outside world remains somewhat of a mystery, it has been shown that they will recognize certain voices and other frequent sounds (e.g., music) and know a good bit about the attitudes of parents and others toward their presence. I have heard of one study that showed that virtually the only way to quiet a crying child after his birth was by playing a particular song his mother had played repeatedly during his time in the womb. A study by Thomas Verny, M.D. entitled *The Secret Life of the Unborn Child* contains reports of clinical studies from all over the world concerning in-the-womb experiences. Dr. Verny says, "The womb is the child's first world. How he experiences it—as free or hostile—does create personality and character predispositions. The womb, in a very real sense, establishes the child's expectations. If it has been a warm loving environment, the child is likely to expect the outside world to be the same."[2]

While in the womb, babies are probably aware of any discord among those closest to the mother. They are likely aware of their parents' marital situation and other facts about the family they are entering, including their father's attitude toward them. If the mother experiences any violence, especially sexual violence, the baby will be aware of it.

Unborn children are especially sensitive to the mother's emotions and attitudes. Seamands in *Healing of Memories* tells us that, "The mother's attitude toward her baby has the greatest single effect on how an infant turns out... and the quality of a woman's relationship with her husband rates second and has a decisive effect on the unborn child."[3]

Unborn children are, therefore, likely to pick up any rejection, anger, fear, dissatisfaction, and resentment that the mother is carrying. They will, however, interpret those emotions as directed toward themselves, whether or not this is the mother's intent. Thus, even though a mother may be angry at her husband rather than at the child, the child interprets the anger as directed toward her or him. Likewise, even if the mother's rejection was toward the pregnancy, not the child, the latter is likely to feel it is he or she that was not wanted.

There are several types of situations in which parents signal rejection to their unborn child. Rejection is felt in the womb by a child whose parents wanted a baby of the other sex or by one who was conceived out of wedlock. Or the pregnancy may not have been wanted even though the parents were married. It may have come by surprise or at an inconvenient time. In addition, a child whose mother feels rejected will likely feel rejected also.

As we minister to people who feel they may have experienced emotional damage while in the womb, it soon becomes apparent that praying through such experiences brings great freedom. One thirty-five-year-old man to whom I ministered came to freedom from a lifelong guilty feeling over the fact that he was a male. The issue was that his mother had one boy, then lost a girl. His mother's desire for a girl to replace the one she had lost seems to have been communicated to him in the womb, leaving him with an intense feeling that he disappointed his parents by being male.

In their valuable book, *Healing the Wounded Spirit,* John and Paula Sandford have recorded a helpful listing of certain roots and their fruits that stem from prebirth experiences. These come from their own and Dr. Verny's observations. I list here a few of the more important of these:

Roots and Fruits of Prebirth Conditions

The Root Condition	Fruit of Condition after Birth
1. Child not wanted	Performance orientation, inordinate desire to please or rejecting before rejected, apologizing, wishing death, frequent illness, refusing affection, or insatiable desire for affection
2. Conceived out of wedlock, or before parents were ready	Deep sense of shame, lack of belonging, believing "I'm a burden or an intrusion"
3. Wrong sex	Trying to be other sex, striving to please, defeatist attitude ("I was wrong from the beginning"), sometimes contributes to homosexuality
4. Next child after miscarriage/abortion	Trying to make up for the loss, over-serious, striving, anger at

	being a "replacement," not getting to be "me"
5. Mother's fear of childbirth	Fear, insecurity, fear of childbearing
6. Mother loses loved one during pregnancy	Deep sadness, depression, death wish, fear of death, loneliness, fear of loss of loved one, feeling he/she has no one to depend on except self
7. Mother heavy smoker, drinker of alcohol or coffee	Predisposition to severe anxiety, chemical damage, baby absorbs negative attitudes that caused mother to drink, low activity level
8. Fighting in home	Nervousness, uptightness, fear, jumpiness, keeping people from quarreling, feeling guilty when in conflict, taking emotional responsibility for parents
9. Father dies or leaves	Guilt, self-blame, anger, expectation of abandonment, inordinate hunger to find substitute, death wish, depression
10. Violent and/or unwholesome sex during pregnancy, more than one sex partner	Aversion to sex, fear of male organ, unhealthy sexual attitudes
11. Induced labor or C-section	Bonding problems, intense craving for physical contact, sexual perversion
12. Unusually painful delivery	Unacceptably expressed anger, depression
13. Cord around neck	Throat-related problems, problems with swallowing, speech impediments, anti-social behavior[4]

To illustrate a selection of these conditions from real life, the Sandfords share some of the connections between prebirth experiences and present problems in their own and their children's lives. Paula discusses her own defensiveness by pointing out that her mother had had an operation just before her pregnancy and had to have her abdomen bound up for support. She feared that the pregnancy would burst her incision or that she would lose the baby. In the womb, therefore, Paula felt guilty for being there. This resulted, she says, in my "trying to perform to earn a right to be, and taking responsibility emotionally for endangering my mother. Consequently, I developed an overgrown sense of need to control, to keep situations in manageable order. The sort of shyness with which I had struggled all of my life was identified by the one who prayed with me as being rooted in feelings deep inside me that if I grew, I would take up space that would threaten another. And so I would hang back in fear and with hidden (to me) anger."[5]

Their son Loren lived with a disturbing fear of death. He had from birth resisted going to sleep, no matter how exhausted he became. When he was born, Paula had had a difficult labor and no one was allowed in the labor room with her. She says,

> I remember fighting fear and loneliness and praying, "God, don't let me die!"... The doctor, without consulting me or my family, gave me a strong dose of ether, unaware that warnings had been given years before that I should never be given it. When I first saw Loren, he was pale blue, and extremely sleepy, and he remained that way long enough to cause everyone some concern. We had to work hard to keep him awake sufficiently to eat. Research has now revealed that alcohol, drugs, and anesthetics given to mothers are immediately experienced by the fetus. No wonder his little spirit was afraid to sleep. He had received the message, "I have to stay awake because if I go to sleep I might die."[6]

Their daughter Ami suffered from lethargy. According to some medical researchers:

ambivalence in the parents can result in lethargy in their child. Ami began life as a tubal pregnancy. I spent ten days in [the hospital] with my feet elevated. Prayer, a small miracle of moving by the Lord, and good medical care worked together to save that precious life. But Ami was so sleepy she would hardly eat. Throughout her early youth she seemed to be sleepily dreaming through life, unable to take hold. Further prayer for healing of the wounded spirit called her forth to blossom and take hold of her life dynamically. Prayer also set her free from fear of tight places.[7]

Their son Mark, suffered from a feeling of being unwanted. Paula says,

Mark was the next to be conceived while we were still in seminary, and we had to fight to prevent the repeated threat of miscarriage. He also had to be called forth by prayer to take hold of his life. And the Lord showed us that the dyslexia he struggled with in his early years was a physical manifestation of his spiritual fleeing from life. Feeling unwanted—a third child when two were a financial strain—he did not want to be born. His feelings of expecting to be rejected caused subsequent scramblings of other parts of his being.[8]

People who have been adopted often experience major self-image problems. The roots of these problems almost always lie in the person's reaction to the circumstances surrounding his or her conception, gestation, and birth. This is predictable, since the conception usually has happened out of wedlock, with a very young mother left to deal with the pregnancy virtually alone. She experiences tremendous shame and, not infrequently, fear, with or without violence, stemming either from the sexual relationship itself or from the girl's relationship with her parents. Such emotions as rejection, shame, fear, abandonment, and the feeling that the person was not meant to be, all get passed on to the child before birth, creating deep wounds that many live with all their lives.

In one of my seminars a young man we'll call Larry raised his hand after we had done the back-to-the-womb exercise complaining that everything had gone black for him as soon as we started it. So, as is our custom when that exercise done in public results in such blockage, we arranged to meet with him privately for prayer ministry. Larry had been adopted at a very young age by a childless couple whom he and everyone else I talked to contended were model parents. Yet he had lived all his life with intense anger toward them and himself. As we ministered to Larry, we discovered that the roots of his anger lay in his feeling that he had been abandoned by his birth parents and frustrated in his attempts to find out who they were and why they had abandoned him.

As we prayed and tried to imagine (and hear from God) the circumstances under which he had been conceived, we decided it was likely his birth parents were not married. One very important issue, then, was whether or not he could forgive them both. He needed to see their giving him up for adoption as an act of love and concern rather than of irresponsibility. Though it was difficult, empowered by the Holy Spirit, he was able to forgive his birth parents and to thank them and God for caring enough to provide him with a good family. There were a few demons to deal with as well, but they were easily cast out once the main problems—his anger, unforgiveness, and self-rejection—were dealt with.

REACTIONS TO CHILDHOOD EXPERIENCES

Children can perceive that they are not wanted after birth as well. Whether it is true or not, children can feel rejected because they feel they are a financial burden, a bother, the cause of family problems, are not good looking, lack ability, have a behavior problem (for example, crying too much or being too pushy), are the wrong sex, or are less favored by their parents than a sibling.

Julie had such an impression. She was born the second child, after a boy. This should have assured her of acceptance on her own merits, since a boy followed by a girl is what parents usually want.

Her brother was, however, unusually skilled in many ways, and Julie was constantly compared with him and found wanting. For example, from her earliest days, she was a complacent child, seldom crying or demanding attention and content wherever she was put. By her parents' own admission, she often got ignored. As she grew up, then, it was frequently noted in her presence that she learned to use a spoon, to walk, to talk and stopped wetting the bed later than her brother. The fact that she learned to use the potty earlier than he did was scarcely mentioned.

Things got worse when, shortly after her second birthday, her younger sister was born. This baby demanded attention and got it. Again, Julie got ignored. This pattern continued in her school experiences. She was the quiet one, too shy to raise her hand even when she knew the answer, who went largely unnoticed by teachers and peers alike. She had one good friend in first and second grades. But her family moved away before Julie started third grade, and she never made another friend like her first-grade buddy. And the rest of her story doesn't get any better, even though she turned to Christ as a teenager.

By the time Julie came for ministry, she suffered from incredibly low self-esteem. In ministry, she received a good amount of freedom as she was able to see and feel Jesus' presence in a number of these events. She is, however, still working on her habitual way of relating to herself. She has to work to keep from neglecting herself as her parents did, looking for disadvantageous comparisons between herself and others, using negative self-talk and the like.

The patterns we were dealing with in Julie's life were deeply ingrained, stemming from her childhood. Though the wounds themselves weren't her fault, she is responsible for dealing with her reactions. Julie doesn't seem to have been an unwanted child, but she interpreted the lack of attention she received as indicating that she was not worth much.

Reactions to perceptions of school experiences are another important source of emotional damage. Even if one has escaped such damage at home, schoolmates are often cruel. Furthermore, teachers often misjudge what we need even when they attempt to treat us well. And some of them, weighed down with their own problems, are not able to treat us the way we need to be treated. For whatever reason, Jill, though a very good student, was ridiculed by her teacher after doing poorly on a paper in fifth grade. This had never happened to her before and she was mortified, never again able to be comfortable in the classroom. In prayer ministry, however, Jill experienced Jesus standing by her side during the embarrassing event saying, "It's all right, I'm with you."

REACTIONS IN PUBERTY AND ADULTHOOD

Whether we experience any of this type of emotional damage in childhood, many are hurt badly during adolescence and later. Puberty can be especially hard on our self-image. The timing of our development is often out of sync with that of others. We probably were self-conscious because we seemed to be either ahead of them or behind them, bigger than the others or smaller, and laughed at by the rest of the group.

Barbara Rainey speaks of the emotional damage she experienced when, during adolescence, she was asked, "Are you sure you're a girl?" She was late in developing—by other people's standards— and treated cruelly by the other youngsters. Boys can be at least as cruel, as a visit to any junior high boys' locker room will prove. The boy whose penis is small and who has little or no pubic hair gets no pity from those who are farther ahead in their development. And many are scarred for life by such experiences.

Further down the road of life, rejections and betrayals are also likely to have a traumatic impact. These may come from people we perceive to be loyal friends or partners in romance, especially from our marriage partner. Career experiences such as uncertainty over or disappointment in one's present position, being fired, or even failing in business can also figure in—often in a big way—as emotion damagers. The man we call John in chapter eight was pressured to leave his first job and change careers. The deep sense of failure and shame in the presence of family and friends, combined with his own habit of blaming and condemning himself for whatever went wrong in his life, produced wounds he carried with him for some time.

We may imagine ourselves moving through life as tourists on a sightseeing trip. At each stop along the way, we buy more things. The things we purchase, however, mean heavier and heavier luggage to carry and greater difficulty getting into and out of cars, buses, trains and planes. So too in life, as we plod along our personal journey, our rejection-baggage gets heavier and heavier, more and more bulky and difficult to manage. As we move from place to place, we are off balance and always in danger of falling. We strive to look calm, cool and collected. But there is a very large struggle going on inside to conceal the load we carry. Such baggage makes us prime candidates for deep-level healing.

As with Larry above, the internal damage can allow demons to enter and remain. As stated earlier on, demons are like rats and rats go for garbage. Though it is the "garbage" on which they feed that is the biggest problem, the demons also need to be kicked out if the person is to be free.

EVEN CONVERSION MAY NOT SOLVE THE PROBLEM

How disappointing conversion is for many who carry such loads. They have been promised that all things will become new (2 Cor 5:17) when they accept Jesus as Lord and Savior. But often what they expect to happen doesn't seem to. Rather, the same old problems, both those outside and inside, seem to continue. I clearly remember my own personal struggle with habits and thoughts I had hoped would go away once I gave my life to Christ. Paul's struggle recorded in Romans 7, verses 15 and 19 was a very real one for me—I could neither do what I wanted to do nor understand what was wrong with me. This struggle led me frequently to the point of questioning the validity of my conversion.

I do not fully understand even now how Paul could so glibly promise the newness of life in 2 Corinthians 5:17 when he knew it would be so much work! What I know now, though, is that through prayer ministry, the power of God can be brought to bear on the reactions we struggle with in such a way as to free us. We can then not only be released from enormous burdens, we can also forgive those who misled us into thinking things would be easy.

TAKING RESPONSIBILITY FOR OUR REACTIONS

Though as humans we seem to be playing on what some might call "an uneven playing field," we cannot blame other people or demons for the problems raised by our reactions. True, we have a sin nature that tips us in the direction of sinning. And many of us have a life history, extending back to conception, that has left us with plenty of festering emotional wounds. On top of this we have to contend with the pressure put on us by the ever-active dark angels whose job it is to harass us. Yet *the Scriptures give us no right to blame others for our reactions, no matter how much pressure we may be under.*

The key to taking responsibility for our reactions comes from discovering the roots and dealing with them. This is why we spend so much time on early life experiences. For, as Seamands points out, "If we stop honestly to look at our behavior, we may discover that we really haven't reacted to the present situation as it is. Rather, that hidden child of the past has surfaced to respond to some childhood event or relationship. We have not acted with maturity; rather, we have responded to circumstances entirely different from those immediately apparent."[9]

We can discover the roots to our reactions with help from God and other people, but we alone can take responsibility for them. If we want to be healed we must be determined to face and work through the events and our attitudes toward them. Attitudes such as anger, bitterness, fear, and resentment, whether initially identified as sins or not, need to be admitted and handed over to God.

Satan tries to keep us from taking this responsibility by tempting us to blame others for our problems. Even though many of the things we struggle with are caused by others' actions, we still have no right to blame others for our resulting attitudes. Perhaps we can apply here Jesus' words concerning the fact that it is not what goes into a person that defiles him or her, but what comes out (Mt 15:11). *We cannot blame others, we cannot blame "the system," we cannot even blame Satan for our attitudes.*

Though God will judge those who hurt us for what they have done (Rom 12:19), he holds us accountable for our reactions. This is true even when what the perpetrators have done to us will result in great punishment for them. They are responsible before God for their actions, we for ours. Regardless of the source of the wounds in our lives, if we desire deep inner healing we will have to take responsibility for the attitudes and actions we have now internalized. Refusal to do this will only delay, if not completely impede, the healing process.

When we have been victimized, God's rules require us to give up all right to revenge against those who have hurt us. This is a hard rule but one we must obey if we are to gain freedom ourselves and minister freedom to others.

THE PROBLEM OF FEELING GUILTY

One of the major strategies of the Enemy is to get us to feel guilt or to keep us feeling guilty. He especially focuses on three areas: 1) if he can keep us from confessing a sin, he will; 2) if he can keep us feeling guilty for sins already confessed and forgiven, he'll do that; and 3) if he can get us to feel guilty over what others have done to us, he will. If allowed in and fed, guilt gives Satan a spiritual and emotional stronghold in us that can result in our viewing reality in a completely skewed way.

Seamands underlines the destructiveness of guilt in human life: "If it is true that forgiveness is the most therapeutic fact in all of life, then guilt must be the most destructive. We are simply not built for it, so we automatically try to atone for it, to get rid of it somehow. Often we carry it around in our bodies and minds and it affects our entire personality. Or we pour it into a bag and dump it on someone else."[10]

1. Unconfessed sin as the cause of guilt. The Enemy can often get us to leave sins unconfessed, especially if we have become discouraged and feel we can never do anything right. When we sin and fail to confess it, we give the Enemy an opportunity to burden us unnecessarily with guilt. What God intends is that when we sin we experience *conviction,* a response in our spirit generated by the Holy Spirit on the basis of which we confess the sin and receive forgiveness.

In contrast, the Enemy attempts to make us captive through hiding sin and developing guilt. Deep-level healing is often necessary to bring people to the point of distinguishing the difference between the Holy Spirit's gentle chiding (conviction) and guilt (the emotional reaction to unconfessed sin).

In the spiritual realm, guilt and conviction are poles apart. Paul points this out in 2 Corinthians 7:10 by contrasting the sadness or sorrow that comes from God (conviction) with what is human in origin: "For the sadness that is used by God brings a change of heart that leads to salvation—and there is no regret in that! But sadness that is merely human causes death."

2. Feeling guilty for sin that has already been confessed. If the Enemy is unable to keep us from confessing our sin, his strategy is to keep us from feeling the forgiveness God grants us. Though we have confessed our sin and have been "cleansed from all unrighteousness" (1 Jn 1:9), it is often easy for Satan to convince us that our sin is just too big to be so easily taken care of. We are indeed free from the sin, but we don't feel forgiven.

"The most helpful word I have ever heard on this [subject]," says Seamands, "was from a young man who said every time he started to pray, he would remind God of a certain failure in his past. One day when he started to do this it was as though God whispered to him, 'My son, enough of that. Stop reminding Me of that sin. I distinctly remember forgetting it a long time ago!'"[11]

Either the lack of confession or the retaining of guilt after confession often results in an inability of people to forgive themselves. With David, we may feel "I am always conscious of my sins" (Ps

51:3b). Guilt is one of the major roots of a lack of self-forgiveness. This inability to forgive ourselves also needs to be confessed, since we are to forgive everyone God has forgiven.

3. Feeling guilty because we blame ourselves as the victims. *Victims usually blame themselves for what has been done to them.* They blame themselves for the fact that someone else hurt them. They assume that these others knew what they were doing and hurt them because they deserved it. I have often heard from victims a statement such as, "If I wasn't bad, they wouldn't have done these things to me." It is frequently difficult to convince them that their treatment was the result of the badness in someone else rather than in themselves. They insist on feeling guilty, even if rationally they cannot find anything they have done to deserve such treatment.

Rich Buhler in his very helpful book, *Pain and Pretending*, calls this habit of blaming ourselves for what others have done to us the "doctrine of eligibility." He writes,

> Why do children blame themselves? I believe it is because of what I call the "doctrine of eligibility," which exists in a fascinating way in the heart of even the youngest child. We carry this doctrine with us into adulthood, and it affects many of us in ways we may not fully realize. This doctrine prompts a child to conclude, "I am the reason for the pain."
>
> What is the doctrine of eligibility? Quite simply, it is the belief that good things happen to good people and bad things happen to bad people. As we grow and develop, we learn there are "good" people and "bad" people in the world. We conclude that good people are associated with success and victory and bad people are associated with failure and defeat. In simple ways, we learn to have something good happen in our lives, we have to be eligible for it. We also learn that if we are bad, then bad things might happen to us.[12]

Hounded by guilt, a man I'll call Terry was experiencing intense physical pain in several of his joints. Though he wasn't aware of it until well into our ministry time, the pain and the guilt were closely connected. Terry was well aware of the feelings of guilt. They plagued him wherever he went. He described himself as feeling guilty over just about everything he himself did or anything that others did in relation to him.

We found the roots of Terry's guilty feelings in the fact that, from his parents' point of view, he wasn't supposed to be born. So he felt guilty about even existing. The slightest mistreatment by parents, playmates, teachers and others, was interpreted by him as his fault. Likewise, he felt guilty for whatever went wrong around him, even if he had nothing to do with causing it. Terry's whole view of reality was distorted by his guilt feelings.

In commenting on a view of reality like Terry's, Seamands says, "Some of us wouldn't know how to live if we didn't feel guilty; we'd go to pieces from spiritual anxiety. That guilty self becomes the basis of a "good conscience," while a good conscience somehow creates a feeling of guilt."[13]

Terry actually was experiencing all three of the Enemy's ploys mentioned above. Though guilt over the sins he himself had committed was not his major problem, he had left several of his sins unconfessed due to discouragement. In addition to the guilt he carried over those sins, the Enemy was able to get him to carry a much greater amount stemming from confessed sins he could not seem to forget and self-blame for wounds inflicted on him by others.

With people like Terry, the last thing they need is to hear their guilt related problems referred to as "sin." With these people it is almost inevitable that this will make them feel even more guilty. I choose, therefore, to refer to these problems as "holding onto guilt," an "inability to forgive oneself," and "blaming oneself for other's crimes." People dealing with these issues don't need to acquire any more guilt because we have labeled them as sinful.

THE IMPORTANCE OF DEALING WITH UNFORGIVENESS

The greatest block to receiving healing at the deepest level is unforgiveness. It seems to be a rule: wallowing in unforgiveness creates such disruption in our physical and emotional being that the consequences can be quite serious.

When people are hurt, it is normal to react in anger. But when people retain their anger, it easily turns into such attitudes as resentment, bitterness, and unforgiveness. These attitudes provide fertile ground for Enemy activity.

I can't count the number of people whom I have prayed with who have received emotional, physical, or spiritual healing almost immediately when unforgiveness was dealt with. On at least two occasions, women have come to me with extreme tightness and pain across the shoulders. When they forgave someone they were angry at, the symptoms left immediately. Another woman's whole personality and outlook on life changed dramatically when she gave up her unforgiveness toward scores of people against whom she had held bitterness.

Forgiveness is so basic, we are well advised to deal with it early on in ministry. The "rule of thumb" in deep-level healing is, *look for unforgiveness.* When we forgive, we release the one we have been holding something against from our anger, bitterness, resentment, and desire for revenge. We do not declare that person "not guilty." Rather, we recognize his or her guilt and give to God our right to pay the person back.

In other words, when we withhold forgiveness, both we and the person we are angry with remain captives. When we forgive by giving up to God our right of revenge, both that person and we ourselves get to go free.

When we look for unforgiveness, we should leave no stone unturned. We do well to start at the very beginning, at conception, to look for anger, bitterness, and resentment. As we see from the chart earlier in this chapter, many prebirth experiences need to be cleansed of such reactions if the person is to be freed. Likewise, childhood and adolescent experiences need to be taken seriously and cleansed through the change of attitude that occurs when we forgive.

Scripture shows that forgiveness was a major theme in Jesus' teaching. Our Lord taught his disciples and us that there is to be no end to the amount of forgiveness we give (Mt 18:21-35). He then set the example himself by forgiving those who crucified him (Lk 23:34). Following up on this, Paul tells us to "forgive one another just as the Lord has forgiven you" (Col 3:13b). It is part of the Lord's Prayer to ask God to "Forgive us the wrongs we have done, as we forgive the wrongs that others have done to us" (Mt 6:12). Jesus elaborates on this statement by telling us that only if we forgive others will God forgive us (Mt 6:14-15).

"For many victims," says Buhler, "the thought of forgiving those who caused their pain seems absurd and even impossible. Certainly forgiveness is contrary to the "get even" attitude of our society. It is a more important step toward a more complete healing, however, which is one reason forgiveness was so paramount in the teachings of Jesus Christ."[14]

Forgiveness is a kind of spiritual excretory system (please excuse the analogy). There is a law inherent in our biological makeup that sees to it that if we refuse to go to the toilet, we pay a price. If we refuse to go long enough, or if for some reason our excretory passages get blocked, biological law sees to it that we get poisoned from inside. So it is spiritually with unforgiveness. If we refuse to get rid of it, there is a law in the universe—a law just as firm and unbending as the law of gravity—that sees to it that we get poisoned from inside. The consequences of ignoring this principle are serious problems in emotions, body, and spirit. In fact, unforgiveness is like emotional and spiritual cancer. As it spreads, it blocks emotional and spiritual healing and can lead to a kind of spiritual death. It can even be one of the root causes of numerous serious physical illnesses.

During ministry be sure to affirm people's right to be angry and even unforgiving. Most of those struggling with unforgiveness have been badly wounded by others. They need to realize that they have this right. Affirming the fact that their feelings are normal and that they have a right to keep them can be very freeing.

They have many times been led to feel that the anger itself is sinful. This is not the case, as we learn from Ephesians 4:26. Seamands writes, "It's high time some of us get over our childish ideas on this subject. Anger is not a sinful emotion. In fact, there are no sinful emotions. There are only sinful uses of emotions...."

Anger is a divinely planted emotion. Closely allied to our instinct for right, it is designed—as are all our emotions—to be used for constructive spiritual purposes."[15]

God doesn't deny our right to choose even a reaction that he knows will be damaging. He simply invites us, saying, "Give me your burden. Keeping such burdens as anger, bitterness, and unforgiveness will enslave and destroy you." When he says, come to me with your heavy burdens so I can give you rest (Mt 11:28; 1 Pt 5:7), he has burdens like this in mind. When he says we should give up our right to revenge (Rom 12:19), he knows it is for our own good. He knows the laws of the universe and what is best for us as he uproots the spiritual cancer of anger, unforgiveness, and bitterness from our lives.

Giving our anger, bitterness, resentment, and unforgiveness to God is not a form of spiritual denial. It requires honest facing of our feelings and admitting that they are there. God requires complete truthfulness. God only heals those who face the facts and give the heavy burden of such feelings to him.

Often, though, releasing such intense feelings to God is a process rather than a single, once-for-all act. We who minister need to recognize this and not be impatient if people cannot shed all their anger and unforgiveness immediately. God understands this and often grants great freedom to those who have simply taken the first step of their journey toward completely forgiving those who have hurt them.

It is important for those struggling with forgiveness to recognize that they are not forgiving innocent persons. *They are forgiving the guilty.* Honesty requires that we recognize that there has been real hurt and those who have brought it about are responsible before God for their behavior. God will repay them. He simply tells us not to try to do his job for him. He will avenge our wounds in his time and in his way (Rom 12:19). When Jesus forgave from the cross, it was those who nailed him to that cross that he forgave. They were guilty and had to pay for it. But Jesus was not going to allow himself to become captive to anger, bitterness, and resentment, no matter what they had done.

When ministering to those struggling with how to forgive those who have hurt them, it is often helpful to lead them to look at the perpetrator's past life. Since victims create victims, those who hurt others have usually been badly treated themselves. Often a simple question such as, "What was your father or mother's early life like?" is sufficient to change the attitude of a wounded son or daughter toward his or her parent. When we see our parents or others who have hurt us as themselves victims in their earlier life, it is usually easier to forgive them. Sometimes the "good parent, bad parent" exercise described in chapter six is a help in this process. Often I point out to people that these who hurt them never had the advantage they have of receiving ministry to get their problems healed. Having such troubles is no excuse for the abusers to do what they have done. But understanding their pain makes it easier to forgive them.

Beyond forgiveness, then, lies what for many is an even greater challenge, the challenge to learn to love the persons they have just forgiven. Scripturally, love is a choice, not an emotion. *We are to choose to love people whether or not we like them.* We are to choose to love even our enemies (Mt 5:44; Lk 6:27, 35) and to bless those who have cursed us (Mt 5:44; Lk 6:28; Rom 12:14). The ability to love those who have harmed us is an undeniable demonstration of the freedom Christ bestows on us when we forgive.

FORGIVING SELF AND GOD

The need to forgive others should by now be obvious. Not so obvious, however, is the fact that wounded people usually also need to forgive themselves and God.

As mentioned earlier, victims tend to blame themselves for their problems, especially when they have been mistreated early in life. In ministry we frequently find such people unforgiving and angry toward themselves, as if they had been the perpetrators. In the wake of such attitudes often come self-condemnation, self-rejection, and self-hate, in many cases reinforced by demons.

Sally held all of these attitudes toward herself. She felt badly neglected by her mother and the series of husbands her mother had had while she was growing up. Sally responded to these feelings of neglect and worthlessness by doing things that got her into trouble with school officials and later with the police. Though recognizing the part her mother's neglect played in her woundedness, Sally steadfastly contended that her reactions proved she was bad to the core and didn't deserve to be forgiven.

In ministry, it was comparatively easy to get Sally to forgive her mother. It was obvious to her that her mother had been victimized in her early life and had never gained control over her reactions to that mistreatment. Sally could also accept with her mind that her reactions were forgivable. She could not, however, seem to give up the feeling that there was something defective and bad about her. "Otherwise," she said, "why would I react in such unacceptable ways?" It took some time for her to give her self-hate and unwillingness to forgive herself to Jesus.

One important step in the process was when she moved from knowing that Jesus forgave her to recognizing that he expected her to forgive everyone he forgives. Another important step was for her to exercise toward herself her own gift of compassion, a gift that God marvelously uses through her in working with disadvantaged people. Finally, she was able to forgive herself.

All of us have, of course, responded in anger toward ourselves for certain things we have done. It is easy, then, to hang onto such feelings, allowing them to fester and turn into bitterness and unforgiveness toward ourselves. Self has then become the enemy we need to learn to love (Mt 5:43-45). Those with a low self-esteem (see the next chapter) are especially vulnerable to allowing such feelings to escalate and to damage them emotionally. Like Sally, we need to call off our war against ourselves and forgive this self that Jesus has forgiven, accepted, and chosen to be his child (1 Jn 3:1-3). We need to accept ourselves as Jesus accepted Peter after his crushing failure. Though guilty of an enormous sin, he was as forgivable as a child who had simply made a mistake.

For many, a bigger problem is anger at God. Counselees ask, "If God loves me so much, why did he let these horrible things happen to me? Where was he when I was being abused? Why didn't he stop it?" It is painful to have to deal both with the unanswerable questions and with the immutable requirement that we must forgive. I don't know why God allows horrible things to happen to people.

But I do know what the Enemy had in mind. He wanted to destroy them. And the fact that he wasn't able to destroy them means that God prevented him from doing his worst (1 Cor 10:13). I can say with certainty that God was there. Satan did all he was allowed to do, but not all he wanted to. In the process the person was hurt but not destroyed.

Though we may never understand why in this life, we need to recognize that God often does not get his way in the universe. So we must accept what God allowed, and thank him that he kept it from getting worse. Beyond this, we know that he is willing and powerful enough to bring healing to even the most damaged of people.

Furthermore, God allows us to be angry at him. He knows we don't understand. With our human limitations, we probably would not understand even if he explained things to us. And he doesn't. He didn't even explain things to Job. But he allowed Job to get very angry with him without penalty. And when Job repented (Job 42:2-6), he released God from his anger, bitterness, and resentment. This is what I mean by "forgiving God." Though we don't understand, we can give up our right to be angry at him, in effect agreeing, as Job did (40:3-5; 42:2-6) that God can run things, even our lives, his way. This is hard to agree to, but it is the only way to freedom.

For many, though, it is difficult to admit that they are angry with God. This is not considered proper, even though we know Job, David, and undoubtedly many others have expressed their anger at God. Many, however, fear that God will disown us or punish us for our anger. So they, like Adam, try to hide their secret even from God himself. But, again, freedom lies in admitting our anger and frustration and giving it to God. Hiding such anger gives the Enemy an advantage. Facing it and dealing with it by giving it up brings freedom.

SETTING BOUNDARIES

One of the most difficult aspects of dealing with our reactions to those who hurt us comes when we are still in constant contact with the perpetrators. It is one thing to lead people to forgive those who have hurt them in the past. It is quite another to help them to forgive someone who is still hurting them. I frequently have to deal with wives who are being mistreated by their husbands and have to go right back to them when our sessions are over. This type of situation is among the most difficult we have to handle.

Many people think that forgiving a person means giving up all rights to protect oneself. This is not true. *To forgive means to release the other person and oneself from captivity to anger, bitterness, and resentment. It does not mean we give up common sense, reason, and those resources available to us for our protection.* These resources include: 1) setting boundaries, 2) taking authority over spirits, and 3) contacting civil authorities or other professional services.

1. Setting boundaries. This is often not easy. It requires carefully thinking through one's own rights and those of the abuser. It is frequently advisable for a person to work with a professional counselor or someone else who has had experience with abusive situations to strategize a course of action. Such a course of action usually requires setting clear and firm conditions of the "this-far-but-no-farther" type. These conditions, then, need to be communicated (often by another person) to the abuser, accompanied by a threat that if the person oversteps that boundary one more time, the victim packs up and leaves, either for good or until certain further conditions are met. One thing that is very important is that the victim be prepared to do whatever is threatened and carry it out if the abuse continues.

A woman I'll call Emily was blessed with a husband who wanted to see their marriage work. They had returned from overseas Christian service, however, largely because his abusive rages made life intolerable for Emily. She threatened to leave him several times and finally did by admitting herself into a facility for battered women. She also made arrangements with a friend to live with her if she needed to. During her stay in the facility, her husband sought help. He had sought help before, but only short-term change had resulted. This time, though, he went to someone who ministers in deep-level healing and the change in him seems to be permanent. As a result, there are now healthy boundaries of mutual respect and love in Emily and her husband's relationship.

2. Taking authority over spirits. Often those who abuse physically do so under the influence of evil spirits. Whether these spirits are working from inside of the person or outside, they frequently provide the push that results in a physical attack.

When an attack takes place, it is a good practice to speak directly to the spirit behind the attack rather than to the human perpetrator. The words we use can be something like, "If this is a spirit, in Jesus' name I forbid you to harm me," or "Stop it, foul spirit, in Jesus' name," or "I command this spirit to release this person in Jesus' name." I have heard the stories of several women who were able to successfully ward off attacks in this way. One told me she was attacked by a man with a gun. When she forbade the spirit to do that, the man's gun hand dropped to his side and he turned and walked sheepishly away.

When the abuse is verbal, rather than physical, one can assume that a spirit is probably involved. "If this is the Enemy, stop it!" may be said out loud or silently. If it is a spirit, the command will be heard and usually obeyed. I have seen quite a number of situations changed radically when this command is uttered.

3. Contacting civil authorities and other professional services. In some communities, women are able to go to a home for battered women for a time to escape a husband's abuse. Some have had to call the police for help. Though such measures are usually short-term, they often make the point that has to be made with perpetrators, that the victim is serious about setting boundaries. Sometimes this motivates the perpetrator to do something about his or her problem.

Now we move on to the emotionally charged issue of healing our wounded self image.

For Further Reading

Rich Buhler, *Pain and Pretending*, 65-84.

John and Paula Sandford, *The Transformation of the Inner Man*, 95-106.

David A. Seamands, *Healing for Damaged Emotions*, 25-38; *Putting Away Childish Things*, 112-19; *Healing Grace*, 125-66.

8

Healing Our Wounded Self-Image

MARGE AND JOHN

"How can I help you?" I asked.

"I hate myself," Marge answered.

The story she told was typical of many. Marge was the firstborn in her family and wasn't sure her parents wanted a child at that time in their marriage. And she was certain that if they had wanted a child, they would have wanted a boy. As she looked back, she added, she had tried hard to be a boy in what felt like a vain attempt to win her father's approval. When she reached puberty, however, she had to give up the pretense and tried to content herself with being a girl. But that, too, was disappointing.

Marge's hair never seemed to look right. Her hips grew too big and her breasts developed late, and were small. Menstruation came as a surprise and was treated by her mother as something to be hushed up. Marge's mother seemed to be both angry and ashamed about this part of womanhood, and about sex in general. Marge worked hard at her studies and made good grades. This was approved by her parents. But good grades added to her feeling that she was unattractive physically, sabotaging any hopes she had of becoming popular with the boys.

As she grew into young adulthood, Marge had a couple of brief relationships with men, both of which involved sexual encounters that left her feeling exploited, unwanted, and worthless. Though she had made a commitment to Christ early in life, her relationship with him did not grow enough to provide much of an antidote to her general depression and low self-esteem. So here she was, in her mid-thirties, unmarried, feeling very unattractive, lonely, and hating herself.

John, a man in his mid-fifties, had a similar story. He was conceived before his parents were married. Happily for him, they did get married and provided for him a fairly typical American home for his generation, with a largely absent father but a mother who spent most of her time as a homemaker. As he grew up, he, too, did well at school but could never quite make it in athletics in spite of a sizable drive to prove himself athletically to gain his father's approval. He was small of stature until late in high school. This set him up for a lot of teasing from other boys. In addition, he made few friends. Though this stemmed to some extent from his lack of self-confidence, it also contributed to it.

John, too, felt unwanted. He resented his father's absence and apparent unwillingness to spend time with him. He resented the fact that he hadn't grown faster, and wasn't more mature. He didn't like himself and assumed that others, including his parents, didn't either. Though he continued to do well in school, this fact didn't seem to attract his father's attention as he hoped it would.

I believe the roots of the self-rejection of both Marge and John lay in the knowledge they had before birth that their parents did not want them. As pointed out in the previous chapter, when feelings of rejection come to babies in the womb, they cannot understand that it is the pregnancy, not themselves, that is being rejected. The message of rejection gets personalized and they are born feeling unwanted. Since they trust their parents' judgments, they assume their parents reject them for good reason. So they agree with what they perceive to be their parents' opinion, feeling that that opinion was arrived at rationally and on the basis of good evidence. They, therefore, reject themselves.

Both Marge and John turned to Christ in their early years. This exposed them to the promise of 2 Corinthians 5:17, that if they were properly "in Christ" they would be "new beings." Their experiences did not, however, show the kind of newness they expected, leading them to wonder if they were indeed "in Christ" or simply faking. Furthermore, the frequent sermons they heard concerning human sinfulness were taken personally, reinforcing their negative attitudes toward themselves.

John, especially, kept feeling a deep sense of failure in the sexual area. He had been taught that masturbation is sin, so he felt guilty every time he succumbed to the temptation. Though he prayed sincerely and often and tried as hard as he could to overcome this habit, nothing seemed to work for more than a couple of days. This sense of failure in his Christian life compounded the effects of his negative self-image to such an extent that, even when he did succeed in athletics and in several other areas of life, he found it impossible to change his attitude toward himself. He still considered himself a loser, in spite of quite a bit of evidence that he really was a winner.

SATAN'S STRATEGY

Though we cannot blame Satan for our weaknesses and failures, we have to recognize that he lurks in the background, ready and waiting to take advantage of whatever is there to harass and, if possible, to destroy us. He hates God and anything God has done. He is sterile and cannot create anything himself. He can only disturb and destroy what already exists. He especially hates the creatures God has created most like himself—us.

This hate drives him to attack us where we are the weakest—in our sense of identity as the prized creation of God. "Satan's greatest psychological weapon is a gut-level feeling of inferiority, inadequacy, and low self-worth."[1]

He is envious of the position God has given us, just a bit lower than himself. As Psalm 8:5b says, "You made [man] inferior only to yourself; you crowned him with glory and honor."

Only we are created in the image of God. Only we have been given the privilege by God to procreate others in his image. When God created us, he positioned us above the angels. We are, therefore, number two in the universe. This makes Satan jealous and angry. Some have even suggested that God's plan to make a creature superior to the angels is what led to Satan's rebellion and fall.

Out of jealousy, then, the Enemy attacks us in whatever ways he can. He particularly attacks those things he cannot have, such as our creativity and our ability to procreate. He also zeros in on our ability to relate to God, to others, and to self. Furthermore, he and his followers envy the fact that we have bodies and seek to do as much damage as possible to them.

Not only is Satan jealous about the things God gave us at creation, he is also upset over our redemption. Only we, not the angels, have been redeemed. *Only humanity was adequate for the incarnation—the uniting of God with his highest creature.* Through Jesus, God worked out a way to redeem humans.

Out of envy, then, Satan assaults humans in at least four ways: 1) He tempts people to obey him and does his best to keep them from responding to God's plan of salvation by blinding them (2 Cor 4:4). Failing this, he 2) continues to tempt even believers to sin. 3) Even when we confess our sin, he tries to keep us from feeling forgiven. 4) In addition, Satan continually plants lies in our minds and emotions, especially lies concerning our identity before God. As mentioned earlier, Satan is the author of what some call "worm theology"—a theology that continually focuses on our sinfulness and inadequacy. Unfortunately, that is reinforced by the liturgies of many churches in which God is begged for a forgiveness he freely gives to all who confess their sins (1 Jn 1:9).

Satan is especially active in attempting to disable us emotionally and spiritually. No matter how strong we may be in mind and body, the Enemy knows that without emotional and spiritual health, we will be crippled in our effectiveness for the kingdom of God.

Satan's attacks on our self-image come in the form of accusations. They are in stark contrast to the picture God draws for us:

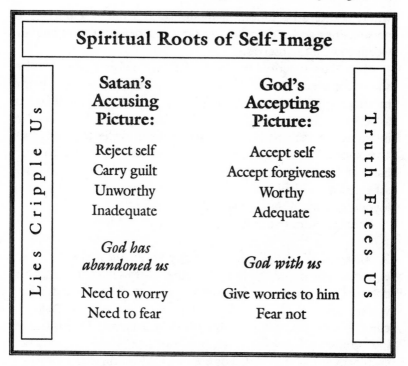

Spiritual Roots of Self-Image

Lies Cripple Us	Satan's Accusing Picture:	God's Accepting Picture:	Truth Frees Us
	Reject self	Accept self	
	Carry guilt	Accept forgiveness	
	Unworthy	Worthy	
	Inadequate	Adequate	
	God has abandoned us	*God with us*	
	Need to worry	Give worries to him	
	Need to fear	Fear not	

SYMPTOMS OF THE PROBLEM

For those whose self-perception is out of sync with God's view, here are at least nine symptoms that need to be dealt with. They seldom occur separately. It is not uncommon for a person to show all nine at the same time.

1. *Many dislike themselves or some parts of themselves.* Many, such as Marge and John, grew up with negative feelings toward their bodies, or parts of them. Since the cultural standards for the size and shape of our bodies are rarely attained, many of us, especially women, live with a continual guilty conscience. Many intensely dislike their faces, hips, stomachs, breasts, height, hair, or their whole bodies. In addition, many dislike their minds, emotions, or personalities and are constantly directing negative thoughts and words toward themselves.

Many have inherited or developed from before birth a sense of shame for even existing. In the case of a person conceived before marriage, this shame may have come from a mother who was ashamed to be pregnant. John Bradshaw speaks of the need to integrate the "shame-bound" parts of us in order to achieve self acceptance. "As a formerly shame-based person, I have to work hard at total self-acceptance.... Most shame-based people feel ashamed when they need help; when they feel angry, sad, fearful or joyous; and when they are sexual or assertive."[2]

These are sure symptoms of a self-image problem.

2. *Many people dislike the name they have been given.* John, for example, was called "Johnny" during his growing up years and detested it. Some see their name as a kind of curse. Indeed, I have worked with people from other societies whose name actually is a curse. For example, in Spanish, girls may be named *Dolores* (meaning "pains") or *Soledad* (meaning "isolation"). People who bear such names may feel cursed or even actually be cursed.

3. *Many wish they were someone else.* Sometimes, rather than facing the pain in our life, we find it easier to imagine being someone else. Though in some, this desire gets to be an obsession, there are many who keep it well inside. Wanting to be someone else can, however, powerfully erode our self-esteem if we don't come to grips with it.

4. *Christians with self-image problems are frequently obsessed with their own sinfulness.* We are indeed sinners. There is no denying that. But when we confess our sins, God forgives us and they are gone (1 Jn 1:9). Furthermore, since it is no longer our nature to sin (1 Jn 3:9), we do not have to continually focus on our sinfulness. It is enough to commit to God anything we may have done, knowingly or unknowingly, and to recognize that he forgives it as soon as we mention it.

5. *Many resort to mood-altering techniques to escape feelings of worthlessness.* Such techniques include, but are not limited to, substance abuse. Many of us mask our pain through such addictions as athletics, exercise, eating, TV viewing, and even religion. As Bradshaw says, "Toxic shame has been suggested as the core and fuel of all addiction. Religious addiction is rooted in toxic shame, which can be readily mood-altered through various religious behaviors. One can get feelings of righteousness through any form of worship. One can fast, pray, meditate, serve others, go through sacramental rituals, speak-in-tongues, be slain by the Holy Spirit, quote the Bible, read Bible passages, say the name of Jahweh or Jesus. Any of these can be a mood-altering experience."[3]

6. *Many people curse part or all of themselves.* A woman once asked me to pray for healing for lumps on her breasts. As it turned out, she had been sexually abused as a teenager with her breasts as the focal point of the abuse. This led her to curse that part of her. When she renounced the curse she had put on that part of herself, the lumps disappeared. Many people say hateful things to themselves or part of themselves. Frequently, these are empowered by the Enemy and become curses. Curses need to be broken by saying something like, "In the name of Jesus Christ, I renounce any curse I have put on myself (or some part of me)."

7. *Many are approval-addicted or accomplishment-oriented.* If we can't accept ourselves, we believe others can't accept us either, unless we do something to win their approval. In many cases, approval addicts are driven people, always striving to attain and never satisfied no matter how great their accomplishments. Indeed, many of those who seem to have accomplished the most during their lifetimes have done so out of deep feelings of unworthiness and inadequacy.

Such people often grow up feeling that their parents will never care about them unless they do something significant. They feel that they never experienced parental love for who they were, only for what they accomplished. They may have been praised, sometimes lavishly, by their parents, but only for what they accomplished, never for who they were. This results in a driving performance orientation in which the yardstick of "what others think" is used to measure everything they do.

A woman we'll call Jean recounts how her mother regarded her children's report cards as her performance report, indicating whether or not she was doing a good job at mothering. This made Jean and her siblings very fearful at report card time, lest they disappoint and discourage their mother. So they worked hard to gain and keep her approval by getting good grades. Now Jean is married and has lived away from her mother for two decades. Her mother's letters, however, still reveal her need for proof of her mothering abilities.

Sandra Wilson in her book, *Released From Shame*, relates a story of a man she calls Walt who was brought up in an upper middle-class family and who excelled both in athletics and academics. In recognition of his accomplishments, he received lavish praise from his parents. As he looks back, though, he cannot remember ever being affirmed for his own sake, only for his accomplishments. As an adult, driven, insecure, critical, and alcoholic, Walt exclaimed: "It just doesn't make sense to me. My folks were wonderful compared to some of the parents I hear about. So why do I feel so connected to all the stuff I'm hearing about self-hatred and codependent relationships? I'm really confused."[4] In discussing this case, Wilson continues,

> Praise without affirmation focuses on performance, not personhood. If you were subtly abused by this technique, you might feel hollow because all of your parents' emphasis was on outward performance to the neglect of inner development. You might be a person who experiences yourself not as a human *being* but as a human *doing*. In praise-without-affirmation families you hear phrases like: "Mommy loves Susie when she cleans up all her toys like that." Or, "I was never so proud of you, Dan, as the day you made the all-state team." You might also hear variations on the family motto: "second place is no place."[5]

Many of us as we grew up can't even imagine our parents saying to us things like, "I love you just because you're you," or "I'm so glad God gave you to us because you're such a neat kid." The only way we knew to receive approval was to work for it. Such a background leaves us with deep wounds that God is anxious to heal.

These wounds relate both to our attitude toward self and our attitude toward God. For it is at home that "we get our earliest 'feltness' of God through relating with our parents. A great many of their characteristics are woven into our idea of His character, from what is caught as well as taught."[6]

Such home influences, then, often propel us to develop what some have called a "Messiah complex," an approach to serving God that pushes us to incredible amounts of activity in service of him. Such activity, far from being the proper expression of total dedication, however, often springs from the same root that generates the "I must perform well to gain my parents' acceptance" syndrome.

"When you waste time and energy trying to be Super Self, you rob yourself of growth and the friendship of God. And you never let God accept and love the Real You for whom Christ died. This is the only you that God really knows and sees."[7]

Approval-addiction and accomplishment orientation are not from God. God wants to heal us from these defects.

8. *Many even seem to seek disapproval in a desperate attempt to get attention.* There are those who seem to have developed a habit of being bad. They have a way of doing things that provoke people to anger. The attention they get thereby seems in some perverse way to be an acceptable recompense for their need to be noticed by somebody, at whatever the cost. Since their low self-esteem keeps them from seeking positive attention, they settle for negative attention.

9. *Many simply give up on themselves.* Some people are so convinced they aren't worth anything that they simply give up. They often envy others, but can't bring themselves to imitate anyone who has succeeded. Indeed, they are often quite negative and critical of everyone who has achieved something, perhaps thinking that by tearing successful people down they win the right not to succeed themselves.

"THE BEST DEFENSE IS A GOOD OFFENSE"

In dealing with self-image problems, as with all of the other problems we struggle with, we need to recognize that we are at war. There is an Enemy who has his own plans for our lives and who works fulltime to implement them. Ours is not a smooth road to Christian maturity, it is a battle against "the wicked spiritual forces in the heavenly world" (Eph 6:12b). Though we are expected to know the Enemy's schemes and strategies (2 Cor 2:11), we in the Western world tend to be blind to them.

So learning Satan's strategy is the first step. It is important to know that he is there and how he does his work. Whether in warfare or in athletics, a good bit of time and energy is put into studying the Enemy and assessing his strengths and weaknesses. No good general or coach goes into the next battle or game without having studied the opponent thoroughly and having drilled his army or team concerning how to fight. We should do likewise so that we can mount both a good defense and a good offense.

On the defensive, we need to constantly claim the protection that is ours in Christ. We can daily put on the armor pictured for us in Ephesians 6:13-18. We can stop going to places where our self-image is wounded and stop associating more than necessary with people who wound us. We can stop allowing negative self-talk within our heads. We can constantly play praise and worship music. One of our best defenses is getting to know God better. The closer we get to him, the better able we are to recognize and combat the Enemy's voice.

We can also take the offensive, attacking the Enemy in prayer and in self-talk. In prayer, as pointed out earlier, our first concern is to be intimate with our God. We are accepted and loved by him. We should, therefore, act like it and spend as much time as possible with him. With this as our foundation, we can exert our authority to command the Enemy to stop telling us lies about ourselves.

Beyond this, we need to tell ourselves the truth constantly. Our self-talk should, "fill [our] minds with those things that are good and that deserve praise: things that are true, noble, right, pure, lovely, and honorable" (Phil 4:8b).

Our self-talk should embody a scriptural perspective on our identity. "No person can consistently behave in a way that's inconsistent with the way he perceives himself. If you think you're a no-good bum, you'll probably live like a no-good bum. But if you see yourself as a child of God who is spiritually alive in Christ, you'll begin to live in victory and freedom as He lived. Next to a knowledge of God, a knowledge of who you are is by far the most important truth you can possess."[8]

We now turn to a more detailed look at that scriptural perspective.

A SCRIPTURAL PERSPECTIVE

We need a solid dose of instruction about God's attitude toward us as we reach toward a healthy self-image. When we study what God thinks of us, we come up with a lot of ammunition to counter the Enemy's lies and our negative self-talk. We find, for example, that God planned and chose us before the foundation of the world (Eph 1:4; Jer 1:5). He created us in his image and likeness (Gn 1:26). He formed and cared for us while we were in our mother's womb (Ps 139:13, 15). Then, after we had sinned and turned our backs on him, he redeemed us while we were still in our sinful condition (Rom 5:8). Beyond this, he chose us and calls us his friends (Jn 15:15-16). He even calls us his children (1 Jn 3:1-2; Jn 1:12), chosen and rescued from slavery (Gal 4:4-7) to inherit the kingdom with Jesus as the eldest son did in Jewish society (Rom 8:14-17). In addition, we are continually referred to in the New Testament as saints (Rom 1:7 NIV; 1 Cor 1:2 NIV; Eph 1:1 NIV; etc.) and even as a "kingdom of priests" (Rv 1:6b; 5:10). As children of the King, *we are princes and princesses*, just the opposite of what many of us have felt about ourselves. This is our status, not because we have achieved it but because God has given it to us.

It is obvious that the Enemy has been quite effective in his strategy to mess people up in the self-image department. But we can count on the fact that our Lord both wants to and can reverse what Satan has done to people's self-concept. Jesus' intense commitment to the downtrodden of his day was an important part of his campaign to destroy what the Enemy had done. As he said when he announced the reason for his coming, God "has chosen me to bring good news to the poor" (Lk 4:18b).

Though the term "poor," as Jesus used it, does refer to material poverty, it usually has a wider reference, one more akin to that of the predominant Old Testament usage. In the Old Testament, the reference is usually to people who are oppressed: "Where there is no specific mention of an oppressor, the word becomes generally synonymous with the socially poor, with those without land. *That such poverty had been caused by disinheritance or unlawful injury and not by the person's own fault is shown by its being contrasted with violence, not riches.... The poor man is the one who suffers injustice; he is poor because others have despised God's law.*" [9] When we read "poor" in the New Testament, therefore, the meaning is close to our term "victim." This is why Jesus never condemned those he helped.

Jesus certainly knows the difference between mistakes and rebellion. He also knows our weaknesses and the pressure Satan puts on us to fail. Take the instances of the woman caught in adultery (Jn 8:1-11) and of Peter on the beach (Jn 21:15-19). Though both of these cases looked like rebellion, he treated them as if they were mistakes. Jesus came into the world not to condemn but to rescue (Jn 3:17). He extended a helping hand, lifted them up, and sent them off with his backing and trust. *There is incredible healing in such acceptance and trust.*

I think it is significant that it was Peter who later instructs us, "Leave all your worries with him, because he cares for you" (1 Pt 5:7). He learned that day on the beach something of the freeing acceptance of his friend whom he had treated treacherously. It was an undeserved acceptance and trust, and it transformed his life. Afterward, he could say of himself and us, "... you are chosen race, the King's priests, the holy nation, God's own people, chosen to proclaim the wonderful acts of God, who called you out of darkness into his own marvelous light" (1 Pet 2:9b).

He learned that a child of God is *special*. My colleague Barbara Sturgis has put together a helpful chart based on the word *special*. A child of God is:

A Child of God Is:

S   **Saint:**
     1 Cor 1:2; Eph 1:1; Phil 1:1; Col 1:2

P   **Priest, Prince/Princess:**
     Gal 4:6,7; 1 Pt 2:9-10

E   **Enemy of Satan:**
     1 Pt 5:8

C   **Child of God, Citizen of Heaven:**
     Jn 1:12; Gal 3:26, 28; Eph 2:6; Phil 3:20

I   **In Christ, In God:**
     Col 3:3

A   **Adopted Son/Daughter, Alien to this World:**
     Eph 1:5, 1 Pt 2:11

L   **Light of the World:**
     Mt 5:14

MINISTERING TO THOSE WHO REJECT THEMSELVES

It is this scriptural perspective that needs to pervade our ministry to those with self-image problems. Neil Anderson has written *Victory Over the Darkness* to help us communicate this perspective. I highly recommend this book to all Christians who struggle with their attitude toward themselves. Neil's position is, "Self-worth is not an issue of giftedness, talent, intelligence or beauty. Self-worth is an identity issue. Your sense of personal worth comes from knowing who you are: a child of God."[10]

Whatever our parents may have wanted, we were planned and brought into being by God. Conception is not simply a physical, human act. Only God can give the life that courses through our physical bodies. And he was not surprised at our conception. Rather, he affirmed it by granting us life. From his perspective, we were not an accident. So, as someone has said, "Don't let anyone tell you you're a mistake."

In ministry, it usually helps those struggling with their self-concept to do the back-to-the-womb exercise, dwelling on the above facts concerning God's place in our conception. It is good to focus on Jesus' pride in them after they were born. It usually helps, then, to work right through childhood experiences with Jesus.

Conceptually, it is often helpful to get them to see themselves as kids, as Jesus recommended (Mk 10:15; Lk 18:17). Kids are open and vulnerable, able to relax with Jesus and receive his love, just as they accept their parents' love. Guide the person to picture him or herself in Jesus' arms, first as an infant, then growing up in his arms. Note that as parents serve their children, so Jesus served his disciples and seeks to serve us (Mt 20:28), even to wash our feet (Jn 13:1-20). Try to help people let Jesus express his servant love to them.

Healthy, undamaged little children feel no shame. They find no need to feel ashamed of who they are or how demanding they may be on their parents. They just turn their problems over to their parents unashamedly. But they are very vulnerable to being hurt, especially at the emotional level. When this happened to us as children, we learned to repress our emotional hurts. That's how we got our emotional wounds. We bandaged them, but they kept festering and the bandages have been leaking. In addition, Satan kicks hurting people.

Jesus wants us to go back to the point of being like a little child, in order to simply acknowledge our problems as we do our sins (1 Jn 1:9), then to give them unashamedly to him (Mt 11:28; 1 Pt 5:7). Being God's kids means freedom, healing, self-acceptance, self-love and self-forgiveness. It also means the right to come boldly to God without shame (Heb 4:16) and the ability to receive God's love and forgiveness. He chose us and he invited us. We should not refuse the rights he has given us.

To work on this, it is often helpful to invite clients to close their eyes and picture the throne room of Isaiah 6:1-4 in which the prophet saw God sitting on his throne, high and exalted with his robe filling the whole temple and a multitude of heavenly creatures worshiping and praising God. Help clients to try to *feel* the awe, the worshipful atmosphere (not just to think about it). Then, once people are really into it, have them imagine a thump on the door to the room and a whole bunch of kids running into the throne room. Have them imagine the kids running right past the angels, the cherubim and seraphim bowing low with their foreheads to the floor, disrupting the whole worshipful scene, running noisily right up to the King and climbing into his lap. Have them notice that the King loves it, because they are his kids and always have a right to barge into the throne room. Kids have different rules. And we are God's kids, invited to come any time "boldly" into his presence (Heb 4:16).

Have people see themselves as children welcomed onto Jesus' lap, with the Lord's arm around each child's shoulder. See Jesus putting a crown on each child's head. Then, as this picture sinks in, have people picture themselves growing up on Jesus' lap. This part may be more difficult for those with poor self-concepts. They may be able to easily see themselves as children on Jesus' lap, but have difficulty seeing themselves in such a favored position as adults. Nevertheless, it is important to work through this part of the exercise until they can experience Jesus' present acceptance of them.

Other forms of ministry mentioned in these pages are likewise helpful. Especially useful is picturing and feeling every hurtful event the Holy Spirit brings to mind and experiencing Jesus' presence in the event.

BLESSING AND ADVICE

A good way to conclude any counseling session would be in prayer and blessing. We can speak freedom to people from such things as root problems, habits, and curses. Further, we can speak God's strength to them in order to help them accept and forgive themselves as God does. We can ask the Lord to work with them to break old habits of self-rejection and any patterns of envy, bitterness, anger, and unforgiveness that they project to others. We can bless them with the ability to love self and others in a way that has never before been possible.

It is important, furthermore, to advise people to take charge of their self-talk. They need to practice speaking the truth of God's acceptance. They should practice blessing themselves, even looking at themselves in the mirror and speaking their love to themselves, especially to any part of themselves against which they have a particular grudge.

We end this chapter with a quote from John Bradshaw's helpful book, *Healing the Shame that Binds You*. He lists seven things we can do to make positive self-talk work for us:

1. Work with the same affirmation every day. The best times are just before sleeping, before starting the day and especially whenever you feel "bummed out."

2. Write each affirmation 10 to 20 times.

3. Say and write each affirmation to yourself in the first, second and third persons, as follows:

   "The more I, _____, love myself, the more others love me."
   "The more you, _____, love yourself, the more others love you." "The more she/he _____, loves her/himself, the more others love her/him."

   Always remember to put your own name in the affirmation. Writing in the second and third person is very important since your conditioning from others came to you in this manner.

4. Continue working with the affirmations daily until they become totally integrated in your consciousness....

5. Record your affirmations on cassette tape and play them back when you can. I very often play them while driving the car on the freeway or when I go to bed.

6. It is effective to look into the mirror and say the affirmations to yourself out loud. Keep saying them until you are able to

see yourself with a relaxed, happy expression. Keep saying them until you eliminate all facial tension and grimaces.

7. Use visualizations with your affirmations.[11]

For Further Reading

Neil Anderson, *Victory Over the Darkness,* 17-67.

Charles H. Kraft, *Defeating Dark Angels,* 79-98.

John and Paula Sandford, *Healing the Wounded Spirit,* 53-73.

David A. Seamands, *Healing for Damaged Emotions,* 63-84; *Putting Away Childish Things,* 112-19; *Healing Grace,* 151-65.

9

Healing from Infected Wounds in Our Past

NEGLECTED

We'll call her Lila. At the time she was in her mid-thirties, married, and the mother of four. Outwardly, she seemed fairly well in control of her life. When she shared with those closest to her concerning her inner life, however, it was a very different story. She could hardly remember a day when it was easy to get up. Depression was her constant companion. But she was told that a young mother with small children had to expect to feel like that.

During a social evening with Lila and her family, she shared with me her suspicions that what she was experiencing was not normal. After the children were in bed, we began to check out her early life to see if there might be any roots there that would explain her present depression. Knowing that depression is often rooted in anger, I was especially concerned to ferret out any anger-producing events in Lila's life.

After prayer, I felt led to do the back-to-the-womb exercise with her as a means of uncovering any roots that might be there from prebirth experiences. Lila was soon in tears, feeling deeply that her parents didn't want her. We stopped the process, explored her parents' situation at the time of her conception, and invited her to release them from her anger by forgiving them.

When we got to Lila's childhood, the Holy Spirit brought back to her memory that she had been quite ill as a small child and had had to be hospitalized for a lengthy period of time. This meant that Lila had very little contact with her parents for more than a month. Intense feelings of abandonment accompanied this memory. As we prayed through this time, she experienced the presence of Jesus with her in the hospital, filling in for her absent parents. This wound, too, was healed through understanding and forgiving her parents.

As we went through Lila's growing-up years, the Holy Spirit brought to mind one experience after another when her father and sometimes both parents were absent just when she felt she needed them most. She thought that some of these experiences would have been pleasant if her parents had been present for her. Some of them, though, would have been unpleasant anyway but were made doubly so by the fact that she had had to go through them alone. Her feelings of anger, abandonment, and worthlessness were so intense that they didn't all disappear during our time together, but she was able to make a start toward forgiving her parents, especially her father.

At a later session, some colleagues of mine were able to help Lila through the memory of her wedding. This was an especially hurtful event, since she felt she had been given very little say in arranging it. This had left a gaping wound in her psyche, even though she believed a good marriage had come out of it. In releasing Lila from the pain of that memory, Jesus came to her in a faith picture, inviting her to plan and carry out just the kind of wedding she had always wanted. This she did and it brought newfound happiness and freedom.

Though Lila's healing was still in process the last time I talked to her, she's in a very different place now than when we started the ministry. Her present had been badly infected by her past. She had a storehouse full of hurt in which festered deep anger, resentment, unforgiveness, and bitterness, especially toward her father. And this was covered by a thick layer of guilt and shame over the fact that she was angry at him. She also felt very unworthy and alone, devalued and abandoned by those who should have valued, encouraged, and "been there" for her. She had a right to these feelings, but they were doing her in, robbing her of other rights such as those to peace, joy, and freedom. As Lila gave up her right to anger and unforgiveness, her depression lifted and she began to taste the freedom and rest that Jesus promised to those who give him such heavy loads (Mt 11:28).

INFECTED WOUNDS: THEIR SYMPTOMS AND SOURCES

Lila had been badly wounded by people close to her. Some of the wounding was not her parents' fault. They had no control over some of the circumstances. Unfortunately, though, much of her hurt was directly attributable to her father's behavior.

The healing she needed was not, however, simply a matter of getting at the pain of the wounds themselves. Wounds dealt with quickly are not nearly as difficult to heal as those that are allowed to get infected. Lila's wounds had not been dealt with and had become badly infected, producing a much larger problem than that caused by the original experience.

What had happened was similar to an experience I had in my final year of college. I awoke one night with excruciating pain in my abdomen. I was taken to a hospital and examined. The doctors decided that I had a ruptured peptic ulcer in my stomach, and operated. To their surprise, however, they found that there was no problem with my stomach, except for irritation that was coming from somewhere else. Examining me further, they discovered a sac that my body had produced around my appendix. Inside it my appendix was gangrenous and was producing a poisonous fluid that was leaking out of the protective sac and irritating my stomach.

Emotional hurts are like my appendix. If they are not taken care of, they fester and become gangrenous. Our natural reaction is to produce a sac in which to isolate the infection. But such sacs leak and affect our present life. *Then, in the present, we find ourselves overreacting to what are often minor irritants.* As David Seamands has said, "Whenever you experience a response on your part that is way out of proportion to the stimulus, then look out. You have probably tapped into some deeply hidden emotional hurt."[1]

The wounds we are concerned about are those that happen when people relate to each other in hurtful ways. Usually such wounds happen without the one who wounds intending to hurt anybody. Often they happen simply because the wounded one is too sensitive or misunderstands. For most people, a majority of such wounds seem to happen in prebirth, infancy, childhood, and adolescence, when our understanding of life and its twists and turns is not yet well developed. The important thing to remember is that these past wounds become infected. Here are some typical types of wounds and how they often come into being.

Abandonment. We saw with Lila that she had a deep sense that her parents, especially her father, were never there when she needed help. As a child she often felt alone, uncared for, unappreciated, unwanted, and generally had nowhere to turn, even when she wanted to share something good. Many children develop such feelings, feelings that they have been abandoned, when forced to stay in a hospital or continually turned over to a babysitter. An early divorce will often produce such feelings as well, with children blaming themselves for the fact that their parents did not get along.

Rejection. There seem to be many paths to feelings of rejection. Those experiencing what they interpret as abandonment often feel rejected. Neglected children usually feel rejected. Furthermore, they usually assume that their parents have a good reason for neglecting and rejecting them. "There must be something wrong with me," they reason, "or else my parents would pay more attention to me." Children often develop feelings of rejection if they are always being corrected by their parents or are constantly given the impression that what they do is not up to their parents' standards. Many times the rejection by others is internalized as *self-rejection*.

Feelings of worthlessness, inadequacy, and the like often stem from these same roots. Or they may come from the signals that came that the child was unwanted while still in the womb. Often such an impression will leave children with the feeling they were a mistake and have no right to exist. Later in life, the child may hear such things as, "You're useless," or "You're good for nothing." Such statements either cause or reinforce feelings of worthlessness and inadequacy.

Many develop a *performance orientation* in response to feelings of inadequacy and unworthiness. They feel they must earn their right to attention and respect, even self-respect. Many have the feeling from their earliest days that they are not acceptable to their parents or other significant people in their lives unless they achieve enough to prove themselves. Such attitudes as *perfectionism and hypercriticalness* are also manifestations of such feelings. These are especially likely in response to parents, teachers, and others who never seem to be pleased with the child's performance.

Shame and guilt. These feelings often accompany the impression that one is not living up to the expectations of the adults in one's life. Expressions such as, "Shame on you," or "You should be ashamed of yourself," are often leveled at children if they make a mistake. Such expressions reinforce the feeling that they should feel shame or guilt about nearly everything they do and even for who they are.

Anger, resentment, and bitterness. Such emotions often develop before or after birth in response to mistreatment of oneself or of one parent by the other. The anger of many women toward men is traceable to their awareness while in the womb of the abusiveness of their fathers against their mothers. If that abuse is sexual, the child in the womb experiences it firsthand. Children who experience abuse from their fathers (whether in or out of the womb) and who feel they were not protected from their fathers by their mothers often feel anger toward both parents. Anger and resentment can, of course, develop at any time, over any issue. Anger at others often involves self-blame as well, especially if the root events occur early in life, since young children tend to blame themselves for anything that goes wrong around them.

Fear. This is a frequent result of childhood and prebirth experiences that are not understood by the child. Children often develop intense fear of persons who react angrily, especially if their reactions are unpredictable. Drunk family members are a case in point. Various life experiences can result in such fears as fear of abandonment, fear of the dark, fear of death, fear of pain, and fear of failure.

Rebellion. This is a frequent reaction to a number of kinds of mistreatment that produce fear. One kind of person seems to react to such mistreatment by wilting, another by rebelling. A variety of difficulties in relating to authority figures often lie behind a rebellious attitude. Among such difficulties are verbal, physical, or sexual abusiveness, neglect, favoritism toward a sibling, and legalistic pressure to conform.

Confusion and indecisiveness. People who are greatly confused or can't seem to make up their minds have often experienced inconsistency in their upbringing on the part of their parents and others. This results in self-talk in which one "voice" regularly contradicts or out-reasons the other, leading to an inability to decide on even fairly minor issues. If, as often happens, perfectionism is also present, the person finds it virtually impossible to make major decisions.

Insecurity. Stemming from any number of sources, insecurity often manifests itself in the *need to control*. Children who had to take charge too early, as with the oldest daughter in the home of one or both alcoholic parents, often suffer from this problem. So do those who have experienced continual embarrassment and confusion concerning what was expected of them as children. They seem to reason that if they can control the circumstances, including conversations and relationships, they will be able to reduce the possibility that they will be embarrassed.

Desire to escape. The feeling that life is so bad or unpredictable that it would be better to escape often leads to *addictions*. Common addictions are to *food, alcohol, tobacco, shopping, TV, movies,* *sports, a hobby, sex, pornography, drugs, gambling, even studying,* or just about anything else. There is usually a sense of drivenness and inability to control the addiction. Often the roots lie in abusive relationships during childhood. Sometimes the feeling that they can never measure up to the expectations of parents and other adults leads people to give up trying to get ahead. "Why even try," they reason fatalistically, "nothing will work. So I may as well just give in to whatever comes along."

These are far from the only symptoms that could be mentioned. Please note the following caution, however: *since any given set of symptoms may indicate a range of causes, we need to be very careful not to diagnose a particular case too quickly.* Not everyone who manifests the above symptoms has experienced the problems we have suggested. In at least some cases, the characteristic may relate more to the person's personality than to any abuse he or she may have experienced. For example, some people may have had fairly normal upbringings but be extra sensitive in their reactions to certain stimuli. We mustn't assume that every reaction conceals an abnormality.

WILLINGNESS TO WORK AT GETTING WELL

It is highly unlikely, probably impossible, that people who are not willing to work at their healing will receive much benefit from prayer ministry. Though there may be exceptions, *as a general rule we can assume that not even God will work against people's will.* They have to choose at the start and continue to choose throughout the process to work with God toward healing. Such a commitment is often a considerable challenge to their strength and determination.

There have been times when the Holy Spirit has showed me that people who have come to me are not fully committed to working with him for healing. When this happens, my first task is to help them to become committed. Failing this, I have to tell them I cannot continue to work with them until they are willing to work hard at the process. For the process may be very difficult indeed.

To get healed, people need to be determined to do whatever is necessary to work along with God. With that determination, however, they can claim Romans 8:28: "We know that in all things God works for good with those who love him, those whom he has called according to his purpose."

Christians are often not highly motivated to work with God toward further growth and freedom because they have been misled concerning the relationship of salvation to the Christian life. They have assumed that a verse such as 2 Corinthians 5:17 promises almost instant total freedom. John and Mark Sandford helpfully trace such an assumption to the way salvation was presented during and after the second Great Awakening, roughly 1814-1914. Whereas the earlier Wesleyan renewal had recognized that "every born-again believer requires disciplined reshaping into Christian values, virtues, and moral strengths,"[2] this movement

> began to elevate the conversion experience above what the Bible proclaims for it. They began to preach that whoever came to the altar would be changed totally, instantly. Positionally that is true: We are all made perfect in Jesus. But salvation is to be worked out experientially as well, "with fear and trembling" (Phil 2:12b)....
>
> The false doctrine of instant, painless sanctification came to be preached throughout much of the church. If conversion made you a totally changed creature, there was no need to face sin and die to self daily on the cross (Lk 9:23).
>
> That teaching made an idol of the conversion experience, and Satan saw his opportunity. If he could build that heresy into a stronghold of deception, he could disillusion countless numbers of Christians and non-Christians alike.[3]

Those of us who persevere in the Christian life discover that our conversion experience is but a small part of it, providing only the essentials from which we are to become new creations in Christ. In fact, the creation of the new being is hindered when a person has been badly damaged before coming to Christ. Then the transformation process will require a great deal of work. But it is gratifying to see how faithful God is to those who pay whatever price is demanded in time, energy, and determination. For those who work with God find that God works with them and supplies the power they lack. Perhaps this is what Paul was advocating when he said in Philippians 2:12b-13: "Keep on working with fear and trembling to complete your salvation, because God is always at work in you to make you willing and able to obey his own purpose."

Since the biblical use of the word "salvation" covers much more than the saving of one's soul, it is not unlikely that these verses legitimately include the process of getting free from such hindrances to growth as sin and deep-level emotional problems. In both, God is willing to work with us if we work with him. In Ephesians 4:22-32, Paul elaborates on several aspects of what is involved, including what we have to do to carry our share of the load:

So get rid of your old self, which made you live as you used to—the old self that was being destroyed by its deceitful desires. Your hearts and minds must be made completely new, and you must put on the new self, which is created in God's likeness and reveals itself in the true life that is upright and holy.

No more lying, then! Everyone must tell the truth to his fellow believer, because we are all members together in the body of Christ. If you become angry, do not let your anger lead you into sin, and do not stay angry all day. Don't give the Devil a chance. The man who used to rob must stop robbing and start working, in order to earn an honest living for himself and to be able to help the poor. Do not use harmful words, but only helpful words, the kind that build up and provide what is needed, so that what you say will do good to those who hear you. And do not make God's Holy Spirit sad; for the Spirit is God's mark of ownership on you, a guarantee that the Day will come when God will set you free. Get rid of all bitterness, passion, and anger. No more shouting or insults, no more hateful feelings of any sort. Instead, be kind and tender-hearted to one another, and forgive one another, as God has forgiven you through Christ.

Those who find it difficult to keep working toward freedom can be encouraged by the fact that the Holy Spirit's presence with and in us is "a guarantee that the Day will come when God will set [us] free." God's working in us is exciting. But according to this passage and others, there is also a lot of work that we have to do if we are to enter fully into the freedom God has for us.

Hindrances to receiving healing. There are many hindrances to a person's being willing to work with God toward freedom from infected wounds. Fears of various kinds are common. *Fear of the past* is a major one. Frequently, the people we work with are ashamed of many of the things they did or participated in when they were younger. There is, then, very little they dread more than dredging up the memories of those things. See later in this chapter for suggestions as to how to deal with fear of the past.

A second hindrance is *unwillingness or inability to face the truth,* often coupled with *a fear of the truth.* As humans, we have a great capacity for denial. Often such denial is close enough to the surface that a person can easily be made aware of it. Many times though, people have been so badly mistreated that they seem to be incapable of admitting the truth even to themselves.

A forty-five-year-old woman I'll call Nancy is a case in point. Though her parents were satanists and had abused her in the most monstrous ways from birth, she, like all of us, feels an obligation to respect and honor them. Furthermore, she is bonded to them as their daughter. As I write, it is over eight years since she began dealing in earnest with the effects of her parents' abuse, including multiple personalities and demonization. In spite of lots of independent confirmation and her own intellectual agreement on what her parents did to her, in the deepest parts of herself she still continually questions and denies the truth. Perhaps she will someday be able to accept the truth. Or perhaps some part of her has been so damaged that she will never be able to bring herself to believe it.

GUIDELINES FOR MINISTRY

When ministering to those who may have infected wounds, there are several guidelines or rules that we need to be conscious of. (The reader should take note that here and in the following sections, there will be some repetition of material from earlier chapters since all deep-level healing—regardless of the root problem—involves common approaches to ministry.) Among these are the following:

1. Search the past for the roots of emotional and spiritual problems. This guideline should be quite obvious to us by now. Present problems usually have past roots. Our present life is punctuated with automatic, often irrational, reactions to present happenings. These reactions have, however, been learned earlier in life. We don't make them up on the spot. As Anderson states, "Unlike our day-to-day emotions which are the product of our day-to-day thought life, the emotional baggage from the past is always there. Years of exposure and experience in life have etched emotional grooves inside you which produce a decided reaction when a certain topic is introduced. In fact, as an adult, you aren't emotionally neutral about any topic."[4] Probing the past to discover how and when we learned these reactions is usually productive in seeking to gain control of them in order to change them.

2. Look for unforgiveness. This is at least as important as the first guideline. Jesus had a lot to say about the need to forgive. We have already dealt with this matter in detail in chapter seven.

3. Look for damaged emotions such as those listed in chapter three. Whether the problem is sin or abuse, the reactions to the problem and its effects tend to show up in emotional damage. Much of this book is devoted to dealing with such damaged emotions.

4. Lead counselees to discover and face the truth. Our God is a God of truth. And most of our battle with the Enemy is in one way or another a battle over truth. Whatever is there must be confronted and worked through if there is to be freedom. Ignoring or bypassing anything allows the Enemy to continue his harassment. When the issue is sin, every sin must be admitted, confronted, and confessed to God (1 Jn 1:9). When the issue is abuse, both the abuse and the reaction to it must be accepted as fact and worked through in the presence and power of Jesus.

Whether it is sin or emotional damage through abuse, we need to own our history and honestly deal with it. Our God does not allow us to skirt difficult events. The healing from infected wounds comes when we face another truth, the positive truth that Jesus was there when the difficult events happened to us. His protection of us in the past and his acceptance of us with our present burden are God's provision for our release to freedom.

5. Finally, it is very important to deal with the person's self-concept. As pointed out in chapter eight, the Enemy's heaviest artillery is often leveled at our self-image. He is desperately afraid that we will discover the truth about ourselves so he constantly feeds us lies about ourselves to keep us from being what God intends us to be and doing what God intends us to do. Learning and practicing the truth in this area is perhaps the most freeing part of deep-level healing.

FACING THE PAST WITH JESUS

The pain involved in recalling, "re-feeling" and dealing with infected memories is the pain of surgery, not the pain of further infection. As with physical surgery, it hurts. But we go through such surgery because we know that there is healing on the other side of it.

Though it is a fearful thought for survivors of abuse to have to face the past, the good news is that not every single memory has to be dealt with in the process. As many memories as possible would be ideal, but many times healing of one memory serves to apply healing balm to many others which are similar. John and Mark Sandford, in commenting on one session with a client, remark, "A traumatic memory is like a bushel of sour cherries.... By sampling only a few cherries, [people can] come to know their sticky texture and sour flavor. By sampling only a few memories, and their corresponding feelings, [a person can] step out of denial and experience the full bushel of God's comfort."[5]

I was ministering to a woman I'll call Jennifer who told me she had had a horrible childhood. I asked her which year was the worst. She replied, "Age twelve." I asked if she would be willing to go back and relive that year with Jesus. At that suggestion, her eyes opened wide and showed stark terror! The last thing Jennifer wanted to do was to have to relive that or several other years of her life.

After a discussion concerning how Jesus heals and how strong her motivation was to receive his healing, she consented. I instructed her to allow the Holy Spirit to bring back the memories of age twelve, to let her feel the hurts and to let her see Jesus in each event. This she did, sobbing freely, for nearly three quarters of an hour. Finally, through her tears, Jennifer smiled weakly and heaved a sigh of relief, happy that that was over. I let her catch her breath a bit, then asked her to go back through age twelve. Again, the look of terror came over Jennifer's face and she exclaimed, "Do I have to?"

"I'd like you to experience the difference," I said.

So she went through the same experiences again, this time in about five minutes, and came up smiling. I asked if there was any pain this time. "A little," she said, "but no fear!"

God is in favor of honesty and openness. Truthfulness demands that we admit and face the past as it really was. This is *our history* no matter how disagreeable. Denying or ignoring it doesn't heal it. In fact, denying and ignoring disagreeable experiences in the past make things worse, since such an approach buys into the lie that any damage done has been taken care of. God heals by facing and working *through* problems, not by circumventing them.

DEALING WITH PAINFUL MEMORIES

Though Jesus was there when a wounding event took place, we probably felt alone, dependent entirely on our own resources. We neither saw him nor felt his presence at that time. During ministry, however, Jesus graciously enables us to feel his presence and, usually, to see him in the event. Though he doesn't change the event itself, the awareness of his presence is usually sufficient to bring healing to even the most damaged memory.

The fact that Jesus takes most or all of the pain of such memories seems to fulfill the promise of Isaiah 53 where we read, "... he endured the suffering that should have been ours, the pain that we should have borne.... We are healed by the punishment he suffered, made whole by the blows he received" (vv. 4b-5b).

When Jesus takes the woundedness, he heals the reaction as well. The whole memory of the hurtful event is, therefore, transformed to focus not on the pain but on Jesus' presence. The damaged memories do not necessarily become pleasant ones, though for some even this happens. Usually, though, the memory remains unpleasant, yet the deep experience of Jesus' presence brings peace, freedom, and a tangible impression of the safety and security we have in him. It is healing for most to feel him fulfilling his promise, "I will never leave you; I will never abandon you" (Heb 13:5b). In this way they experience that this promise was just as true in the past as it will be in the future.

As stated earlier, it is important in ministry to *give the Holy Spirit complete freedom to run the session.* It is easy for us to step in to tell him what to do, which memories to handle first, and even how to go about healing them. When we let God work as he chooses, we find he typically brings forth the memories one at a time. He also usually starts with less traumatic ones, moving to the more difficult ones as the person gains more strength and confidence.

Sometimes God allows the memories to come in rapid succession, like a moving picture of a person's life. On several occasions I have found myself sitting quietly for long stretches of time as the memories have come to my counselee quite rapidly. The counselee, then, invites Jesus into each memory and feels the pain dissolve.

On occasion, a person may be convinced that the Holy Spirit wants to deal with events that happened at a certain time but has difficulty recalling them. When such is the case, it often helps to have the person begin to describe the physical surroundings in which the events took place. Detailed descriptions of such places as the room in which an event happened or the house and city in which the person lived are often sufficient to enable the person to recall the specific events God wants to heal.

Each painful event needs to be dealt with by experiencing Jesus in it. Counselees need to know beyond a doubt that Jesus was actually there. They are not simply imagining something that isn't true or trying to trick themselves into seeing something that isn't real. He really was there. But they didn't have eyes to see him at that time. They can, however, at this time, ask God to give them eyes to see where Jesus was and to accept his ministry to them.

They can now reinterpret events with Jesus there (Rom 8:28). When people can see Jesus in such painful events, healing, a new view of God, and a revitalization of their relationship with God naturally follow. People usually experience Jesus touching them physically, often hugging them as he releases them from their pain. Once people have been helped through a few events, they can often handle other problem areas. In fact, those who minister can assign people to deal with other problems as homework.

COUNSELING THE NEWLY FREED PERSON

At the close of the inner healing session, it is important that we send people out prepared to meet opposition. Satan undoubtedly will attempt to retake his "territory." Help counselees to know and use their authority to command Satan to leave them when they are tempted to fall back into old habits. Stress with them the importance of spending time with God and establishing an intimate relationship with him. Spending time in personal and corporate worship is crucial. Reading and studying the Bible will help continue to give the person a good foundation. Help them to understand that they have tasted something that the Enemy has kept them from for years: *freedom!* As they experience freedom in new ways, the Enemy will try his best to come in and knock them off course, stealing from them as much as possible the deep-level healing God has offered them.

Now we consider healing from the painful losses of death and divorce.

For Further Reading

John and Paula Sandford, *The Transformation of the Inner Man*, 41-70; *Healing the Wounded Spirit*, 163-202.

David A. Seamands, *Healing for Damaged Emotions*, 85-98; 125-48.

10

Healing the Loss of Death and Divorce

WE'D LIKE ANOTHER CHILD

Jim and Penny had a lovely little girl and wanted another. So far, though, their desire had been frustrated by two miscarriages. When I met them, they were very discouraged and fearful. They asked if I would pray with them over their situation.

What God led me to do was to deal with the miscarriages by using the exercise described in this chapter. As each of them held the babies they had lost, both Jim and Penny experienced tremendous release from the fear that had plagued them since the last miscarriage—fear that they would never be able to have another child. Penny also found release from the vague but tangible guilt she felt over the possibility that she had done something to cause the miscarriages. Without their knowing it, the Enemy had played games both with their minds and with their bodies to block the possibility of another conception.

Having worked through the emotional damage connected with the miscarriages, it was only a month or two before Penny was pregnant again. Now Jim and Penny have two more fine children, and Penny has suffered no further miscarriages.

THE ISSUES IN FACING DEATH OR SEPARATION

The death of or separation from a loved one is something that all of us will have to face eventually. Knowing this, however, does not decrease the pain and loss we will feel as a result of it. Among family members and close friends there is a spiritual bond, the breaking of which often leaves unfinished business for the living. Seamands comments, "Studies show that the two greatest stress-producing factors to body, mind, and emotions are the death of a spouse and divorce."[1] There are many types of deaths to be dealt with, each having its own issues. Miscarriages, abortions, infant death, death due to tragic accidents, serious illness, and the death of older persons all require healing. So does separation through divorce and the breakup of romantic or other close relationships.

Among the issues to be resolved in deep-level healing of the wounds caused by these kinds of separation are 1) agreeing with God that it is all right for this person to be gone, 2) dealing with guilt over past relationships or unfinished business with the person, 3) release from any bonding to the person, 4) coping with the pain of separation, and 5) allowing oneself to grieve.

As with all deep-level healing, it is important for people to acknowledge the truth of what happened, to allow themselves to feel the pain, to experience Jesus in the separation event, and to give their pain and damaged emotions to him. As we ask the Holy Spirit to guide in healing the damage, he usually brings to the person a picture of the separation event with Jesus present. The client is then free to talk with the other person and with Jesus in order to deal with any unfinished business. After this, the client is usually open to giving the other person to Jesus, signifying his or her agreement with Jesus' choice to allow the person to leave.

At the end of one of the sessions of a deep-level healing seminar, I noted a tall fellow I'll call Randy quietly weeping in the back of the room. I approached him and asked what was moving him so. His story was that of a badly hurting father who had watched his fourteen-year-old daughter waste away and die.

As I spoke about dealing with the separation of death, God took him back in a faith picture to the hospital room where he had counted his daughter's final breaths. Randy saw himself leaning over his daughter on one side of the bed and Jesus leaning over her on the other. As she breathed her last, Randy saw Jesus take her tenderly in his arms and carry her to heaven to be with him. At that moment, he felt all the pain, frustration, anger, and discouragement he had been carrying since his daughter's death drain away. His tears then became tears of joy and gratefulness to Jesus who had healed the damaged emotions within him.

THE LOSS OF A LOVED ONE—A SEVERED BOND AND A DEEP WOUND

There is a mystical bonding between human beings who are members of the same family. When that bonding is disrupted by death, the wounds can be very deep. Whether it is the death of a loved one as an adult or the death of a preborn child through miscarriage, there is emotional and spiritual disruption both internally for each person involved and externally between family members. Those who have lost parents, children, and others need ministry for their wounds. I have ministered to numerous mothers and fathers who, like Jenny and Jim, experienced wounds of which they often were not aware when a child was miscarried. Siblings of such miscarried babies also have needed ministry to deal with their wounds.

I believe it was God's intent when he created Adam and Eve that humans live forever. Death is an intruder into God's plan. We know that God created us like himself (Gn 1:26-27), higher than the angels and a little bit lower than himself (Ps 8:5). Satan, however, jealous of the high position God had given Adam and Eve, sought to thwart God's plan by destroying God's highest creatures. The Enemy's plan succeeded in part for when they ate the forbidden fruit, the curse of physical death fell upon them and on all of humanity to this day. There were curses on the earth, on physical labor, and on childbirth as well. But none of the problems raised by these has been nearly as disruptive as the parting caused by death.

Death is the ultimate goal of Satan and has been from the beginning. His intent has been "to steal, kill and destroy" (Jn 10:10b). He cannot carry out those purposes without God's permission, however, since his activities are strictly circumscribed by God's plans and power (for example, see Job 1:9-12). Yet, we are told in Hebrews 2:14b that Satan "*has* the power over death." Perhaps within the sovereignty of God, a part of the Enemy's responsibility is that he be the one who carries out death whenever God allows it to happen.

In the life, death, and resurrection of Jesus Christ, God came and made it possible for us to reconnect with him spiritually, defeating the Enemy who wanted to make spiritual death permanent. Though physical death continues, these events have sapped it of its terror, and we can look forward to the day when Jesus will return to abolish it completely. Jesus states in triumphant antithesis to the curse, "I am the resurrection and the life. Whoever believes in me will live, even though he dies; and whoever lives and believes in me will never die" (Jn 11:25b-26a).

Through Jesus, the terror of death has been broken forever, for those who believe. As the Apostle Paul reminds us, "[Jesus] has ended the power of death and through the gospel has revealed immortal life" (2 Tm 1:10b).

But many Christians are not yet experiencing the freedom from death's power that is our inheritance in Jesus Christ. And even for Christians, death and the fear of death are among the weapons Satan is able to use most effectively to imprison people. Though most of us Christians do not grieve as those with no hope (1 Thes 4:13), the pain we feel over the loss of a loved one can create deep wounds, wounds that God can heal through deep-level healing.

GOD'S PURPOSE IN HUMAN BONDING

As humans, we have a great capacity for bonding. I believe bonding is a spirit-to-spirit relationship entered into through birth or commitment. The commitment of marriage and the commitment of oneself to God are examples of the latter. As pointed out in chapter three, when people engage in sexual relationships, they are automatically bonded to each other. Close friendships also create a bond, as do relationships in which one person is under the domination of the other.

I believe the normal bondings between parent and child, between siblings, and between marriage partners are empowered by God. Abnormal and sinful aspects of these relationships may, however, enable the Enemy to empower part or all of the bonding. Adulterous and perverted sexual relationships allow satanically empowered bonding. So do relationships in which one person is dominated, even controlled, by another. Such relationships are sometimes referred to as "soul-ties." Soul-ties can occur between friends or relatives. Not infrequently, domination by one or both parents creates such satanically empowered ties between parent(s) and child.

When God-empowered bonding is disrupted by death, divorce, or some other breaking of a relationship, the wounding can be severe. When a person dies or leaves, the fabric of the relationship is abruptly torn in two. The tapestry of a relationship, once unified on many fronts, is now loose, jagged, and fraying from the wrenching of separation. The severity of the wounds accompanying the breaking of the bond varies with the closeness of the connection between the persons. The closer the relationship, the greater the painful effect that death or divorce or some other severing of the relationship has on the person. Something has died within that person, and there is now a need for deep-level healing.

Though God-empowered bonding needs to be blessed and strengthened while it is functioning, it can be very difficult to deal with when severed. A large number of those needing ministry come with wounds suffered from the severing of bonds that God has blessed. The ministry technique we most often use is like that described for Elsie in the section on adult deaths later in this chapter. If the loss is a miscarriage or abortion, see the following section.

When there is satanically empowered bonding, it needs to be broken. I have spoken in chapter three about the importance of dealing with sexual sin. The reason it is especially important to deal with sexual issues is because of the satanic bonding that is involved. I have outlined there how to go about breaking the bonding. Soul-tie bonding can be broken in the same way.

WOUNDS SUFFERED FROM MISCARRIAGES, ABORTIONS, AND INFANT DEATH

Miscarriage is seldom viewed by our society as a form of infant death. Since the child is usually not developed enough to live outside the womb, many see no reason to mourn or seek healing over a miscarriage. Yet any child conceived is a full-fledged human being, destined to live forever. From the very beginning the mother has a relationship with her developing child. By the fifth month the child usually can be felt growing and moving inside of her. Due to her changing physiology and the child's growth, both the mother's appetite and weight have begun to adjust. It becomes apparent that there is another living being growing within her. All of these factors and more contribute to the mother's sense of relationship with the child.

Though much of the relationship between mother and child is conscious, it is probable that much more is unconscious. When a miscarriage occurs, both the conscious and the unconscious parts of this relationship are severed. Deep within the mother, there is a rending of the close bonding with the child and a sense of loss. A miscarriage is not simply a loss of tissue, it is the severing of a bond, a death, leaving the mother in need of deep-level healing.

Abortion, however, is murder. Each of the 1.6 million babies aborted last year in the United States involved the taking of a life and the painful rending of a mother-child bond. It is interesting that every state in the United States treats the intentional death of an unborn child as murder, unless it comes in the form of abortion. That is, if a criminal shoots a pregnant woman in the abdomen, killing her child but not the mother, the criminal is tried for murder! The inconsistency in our laws at this point is astounding.

The rending of the bond between mother and child is a trauma that doesn't simply go away, in spite of "politically correct" rationalizations that ignore the spiritual reality of the bond between the mother (and, often, the father as well) and unborn child. The grief and mourning over separation by death are there, even if not recognized. They often emerge later in life in very troublesome ways. As Hayford points out, "Often we feel that if we've effectively pushed our emotions into some kind of submission that we've dealt with everything. Conquering feelings of pain or denying the reality of the depth of mourning through stoical denial of genuine human emotions can leave us emotionally desolate—or worse. And anger left undealt with can quickly turn into bitterness."[2] Though the sin of abortion needs to be dealt with through confession and the receiving of forgiveness, the emotional pain requires deep-level healing.

Dr. Susan Stanford, a professional counselor who herself had experienced an abortion and has written about it, reports:

> One of the most universal aftereffects of abortion is the feeling of guilt and loss. In my own practice some post-abortion women may deny feeling guilty and consequently avoid the topic of their abortions early in the counseling relationship. However, invariably the topic comes up, perhaps around the anniversary due date or death date. When I've asked my clients how they feel about it in retrospect more than 90 percent share they feel some level of guilt feelings. Other women, who perhaps have come to counseling with the presenting problem being the aftereffects of their abortion, define their feelings ranging from a pervasive dullness or depression to overempowering remorse and regret.[3]

The loss of an infant through illness or some other tragedy in its early stages of life outside the womb can also produce wounding that needs to be addressed in deep-level healing. Months of anticipation, sometimes years, if the parents have had trouble conceiving children, have passed in preparation for this little life to come into the world. The death of a child at any age is difficult, but the death of an infant is especially painful due to this increased anticipation.

One important set of difficulties is caused by the uniqueness of this time in the relationship between parent and child. No other time in their relationship is more dynamic in forming bonds than in these early stages. From conception on through childhood are the most formative years of development for the child. The parents are intensely devoted to this development. Deep bonding takes place between the parents and child. The death of an infant, therefore, can be expected to produce a high degree of wounding in both father and mother, but especially in the mother.

The loss of an infant, whether unintentionally through miscarriage or illness or accident, or by choice through abortion, is always traumatic. There is usually a great deal of questioning, confusion, and anger. Please see the references for further reading at the end of this chapter. They can be very helpful from both counseling and biblical perspectives. I recommend them highly both to the bereaved and to those who minister.

Something that is not ordinarily recognized in our individualistic society is the fact that siblings are also affected by miscarriages, abortions, and early infant death. As mentioned above, there is a spiritual bond between family members that gets ripped apart when there is death or separation. This is true even when the separated family member is preborn or an infant. In addition, the mother's emotions are often felt by any children conceived after the miscarriage or abortion.

A thirty-five-year-old man I'll call Bob described for me an intense feeling of guilt that he even existed. We found that the root of his guilt went back to the fact that his mother had miscarried a girl several months prior to Bob's conception. Her first child was a boy, followed by the miscarried girl, followed by Bob who inherited a double dose of emotional damage from his mother. Bob's mother passed on to him the deep hurt she felt over the loss of the girl and also the keen disappointment over the fact that he was a boy, rather than the girl she had hoped would replace the baby who was lost. So Bob lived with guilt over the loss of an older sister who died before he was conceived. Though Bob never knew that sister, he was bonded to her as well as to his mother whose reactions to the loss he shared.

With Bob, we went through the procedure detailed below for ministering to parents who have had miscarriages. It is good to minister to the siblings of children miscarried, aborted, or lost in infancy in the same way as to the parents.

MINISTRY TO THOSE WHO MOURN THE LOSS OF CHILDREN

In ministering to those who have lost children, men as well as women, there is a range of emotions that needs to be dealt with. People try to find reasons for such tragedies and will often assign blame where none really exists. Mothers think, "If only I had been more careful about my activities, I wouldn't have miscarried." "If only I had listened to my gut feelings instead of my boyfriend, I would not have gotten an abortion." "If only I had checked on the baby one more time before going to sleep." Sometimes fathers blame themselves for not having been there in time to do something to save the child.

Much of the difficulty in ministering to people in this category stems from the realization that we will often not receive an explanation for what happened. And most of the time, no amount of blaming will do the situation any good. It is important, however, for the person to feel the freedom to express any emotions, along with their anger toward God or others.

Once the venting of emotions has taken place, I've found it healing to have the parents ask Jesus to let them hold their child. The MacNutts give a helpful rationale for doing this: "Since [the mother] has no concrete image of the child to say goodbye to, she feels incomplete and a great emptiness. She is saying goodbye to a child she never held in her arms. For this reason, it may be helpful for the parents (if possible) to see and touch the miscarried child, to name... him and perhaps to hold a simple funeral."[4]

206/ Deep Wounds, Deep Healing

When asked, Jesus will usually give them a picture of the baby and show them whether the child was a boy or a girl. The parents can then give the baby a name. Next, they can imagine themselves either talking to Jesus concerning what they would like the child to know or talking directly with the child.

Some people are uncomfortable with the idea of picturing a conversation with someone who has passed away. It is best for these people to picture themselves talking to Jesus rather than to the child. Whether they picture themselves talking directly to the child or to Jesus, it is my custom to ask Jesus to have his way in conveying the messages to the dead person. Though the prohibition against speaking to the dead in Deuteronomy 18:11 does not refer to this kind of practice, I choose to be cautious. The prohibition there is against consulting the dead through divination to seek information concerning the future. I don't, however, want to encourage anyone to speak regularly to the dead for any purpose. Nor do I want any messages to get across the divide that are not specifically approved by Jesus.

In speaking to their child or to Jesus, the parents can express their love for the child and their sadness at not being able to raise her or him. They can also communicate other things such as the fact that the child will be in good hands with Jesus. In the case of an abortion, it is good for them to apologize to the child. When ready, the parents can then give the baby to Jesus, releasing him or her to the Lord and agreeing with his choice to allow the death of the child.

For those who have had abortions, there is a huge weight of guilt to be worked through. Seldom do they need us to tell them they have sinned. Usually they know this so well that they often do not believe forgiveness is even possible. We can help them to confess this to the Lord, then point out God's attitude toward sin that has been confessed and forgiven. It is removed as far from us as the East is from the West and forgotten (Ps 103:12). The hardest part is often to get them to forgive themselves. Talking to the baby or to Jesus in the way described above usually brings great freedom in this regard.

MINISTRY TO THOSE WHO MOURN
THE LOSS OF AN ADULT

Obviously, the two types of adult death that need deep-level healing are: death from tragedy (including untimely illness) and death of one who is old and "full of years." Each instance of death is unique and should be approached with its own particular set of circumstances in mind. Even when the person who dies is very old, we don't seem to be ready for it. How much less are we ready for a tragic death.

Tragedies are usually sudden. Hearing the news, therefore, usually results in shock. The door is open to large amounts of pain and guilt, eliciting cries such as: "I didn't even get a chance to say goodbye. We had been fighting all day. I thought I would see him again later to patch things up. If only I had told him that I loved him before he left that morning!" There are usually many unanswered questions, among them, "Why, God, did you let this happen?" Receiving no answer to that question usually brings anger which now combines with pain and guilt, causing the person to have outbursts of intense, unexplainable emotion.

It is important for those ministering to the bereaved to take both their loss and their emotions very seriously. Not infrequently, Christians will have gotten the impression somewhere that we are not allowed to be sad or to grieve. Though it is true that we are not to grieve as those who have no hope (1 Thes 4:13), we can certainly grieve as those who are hurting badly over the wresting away from us of a loved one. Indeed, we find that those who have not adequately grieved such a loss are sitting ducks for satanic attacks on damaged emotions. We need to encourage the honest expression of emotion by affirming people's need and right to grieve. Only when they honestly face and express their pain are they ready to receive freely the healing God has for them.

Have the bereaved visualize the situation in which the friend or loved one died. This may be a very difficult thing for people to do but help them to see its importance in the process of healing. Help them understand their need for a sense of closure in the relationship. Even though it may hurt somewhat now to "re-feel" this experience, the future benefits far outweigh the difficulties. The goal is to break free from the pain of the death and to be able to stop "holding onto" the loved one. Once this is done, they will have the freedom to live their own lives in wholeness and health.

Once the person has recalled the separation event, ask the Holy Spirit to guide the experience, including any picturing. Do not manipulate the experience by suggesting what is to be seen or experienced. What usually happens, though, is that the person sees him or herself, the loved one, and Jesus. He or she feels encouraged to talk to the loved one, settling anything that needs to be resolved. The person is then free to say goodbye to the deceased. Have the person renounce any unhealthy bonding that may have occurred with the deceased one. At the same time, you should take authority over it and break its power. The person then should commit the deceased to Jesus, telling Jesus in prayer that, even though they may not understand completely why the person was taken, they agree with his will to allow this to happen.

When an older adult dies, there is usually not the intense pain and shock that comes with a tragic death. Often the older adult has been sick for several months or even years. The obvious debilitation in the person's health has made the death process more gradual and easier to anticipate. The shock, though not entirely missing in many cases, is usually less. Nevertheless, the death of an older adult can cause painful wounding that needs the attention of deep-level healing, especially if there are unresolved issues.

We deal with this kind of death in the same way as suggested above. Be sure, however, to look for and deal with any trauma the person may have experienced in seeing the dying friend or family member in his or her last days. This is especially important if the death occurred after a lingering illness.

Elsie came to me with a number of problems. A major one was that her favorite elderly uncle had died quite unexpectedly, and Elsie felt she had not been able to say goodbye to him properly. Her uncle hadn't even been ill. Elsie had visited him the morning of his death but had no idea she would not get to see him again alive. And there was some unfinished business between them, so the Enemy used guilt over that unfinished business to gain a stranglehold on her.

When we committed the event of her uncle's sudden death to the Holy Spirit, he took Elsie back to her last visit with him. In her faith picture, she was able to talk the matter through with her uncle and to forgive both him and herself. She then could commit both him and the unfinished business to Jesus. As she saw Jesus take her uncle to be with him, she felt sure of two things: the matter between them was resolved, and she could agree with Jesus that it was all right for her uncle to die.

PRAYING FOR THE GRIEVING

Western society has made ministry to those who are grieving a difficult task. The belief that we should not show weakness in the face of difficulty has a tendency to keep many in bondage to the wounds and hurts suffered during the death of a close friend or family member. Our society, even our churches, have tended to frown on those who would say, "I'm not okay. I need help." Instead, we want to keep our grief and sorrow bottled up inside of us, thinking that repression is the best option. Such a custom is, however, very damaging. For we know that grief and sorrow are powerful emotions that, if suppressed, cause real damage. Those who have suppressed them usually suffer deeply until the damage is healed.

When ministering either to those suppressing grief or who are in the process of grieving, it is important to acknowledge the validity of grief. Those who have hidden grief need to feel the freedom to unlock the doors to the rooms they have kept shut, sometimes for years. People need the freedom to express their pain without fear of condemnation. In both cases, it may be helpful to make a distinction between grief and sorrow.

Here the Sandfords assert,

... grief may be quickly healed and banished by faith, whereas sorrow may return many times. Sorrow and tears are not marks of lack of faith. Sorrow is a healthy release of loss and hurt. For many months after grief is assuaged, tears may well up, especially at holidays or when some incident triggers a cherished memory. Such sorrow is not something to be done away with, nor banished as one would cast away a demon, nor healed too quickly. It is not something bad or evil. It is something to be endured and sweetened by. It is a mark of love's knowing the pain of loss. It will pass away naturally in time, when its work is done in the heart."[5]

Grief, then, is a poignant sense of loss. Sorrow implies the on-going yearning and loneliness that more naturally work themselves out in a person's heart.

In relating to a person's deep grief, we must respond with deep but firm compassion. Maybe they have never gotten over the death of the loved one or have repressed the emotion to the point of seeing it come out in harmful ways. Often repressed grief comes out as anger.

Sometimes, deep grief has regressed to the point of becoming a spiritual stronghold in the person's life. Grief can be so ingrained that it becomes a part of the person's normal personality. The initial wounding of death can provide the opening for the stronghold, while the person's refusal to let go of the grief may enable the stronghold to take root and develop.

Taking people back to "re-feel" the initial emotions is very important at this point. If their emotions have been repressed, this will enable them to get in touch with that pain again. If they have been wallowing in grief, going back to the scene can afford them opportunity to approach the grieving situation differently this time by setting some boundaries for its expression.

It is important now to break the stronghold of grief at the point of entry and allow the person to begin afresh the journey of dealing with the loved ones's death. Also, break any strong ties of bonding with the deceased person. Often it is important to have people renounce their connection with grief, asking God's forgiveness for holding on so long instead of giving their burden up to Jesus. They will then probably need to forgive themselves for holding onto the grief.

Once grief has been dealt with, sorrow can be addressed more readily. Sorrow is a less debilitating emotion than grief, but it can also have profound effects if a person wallows in it. As mentioned in the Sandford quotation above, sorrow can be appropriate and legitimate for a longer period of time than grief. Simply missing the person or feeling sad once in a while is more a testimony of love for the deceased than an indication of any dysfunction or need for deep-level healing. Nevertheless, it is a good idea to deal with sorrow by taking people back with Jesus to the death event or their reaction when they first heard about it in order to "re-feel" their emotions and receive healing.

FORGIVENESS OF THE DEAD

Often people are perplexed over what to do if they were holding something against a person at the time of that person's death. They may have been waiting for a reconciliation that never came and now it is too late. So they feel guilty over the fact that they didn't get the matter taken care of before the death. But forgiveness and reconciliation are quite different. To reconcile with a person, that person must agree and be present. Forgiving someone, however, does not require the presence of the one to be forgiven. It is an individual act of one who has been hurt and desires to be free.

Since the command to forgive is absolute, the first order of business is to help the person to forgive the deceased. Even if the person we need to forgive has passed away, we are required to release her or him from our unforgiveness. This, then, can be done in the normal way, as discussed earlier.

What is harder to deal with is the unforgiveness people often level at themselves for not dealing with a matter before the other person has died. To resolve such a situation, the negligence that resulted in the delay will probably need to be confessed as sin first. Having accepted God's forgiveness, the person then needs to forgive himself or herself. Often presenting the sin and guilt to Jesus visually and receiving his forgiving touch can bring powerful release.

DIVORCE, SUICIDE, AND OTHER SEPARATION FROM FAMILY MEMBERS

God in his wisdom has established the family as a group of people bonded together by blood and marriage. We should keep in mind that besides the traditional family of parents, children, grandparents, uncles, aunts, and cousins, today's families many times include step-relationships of all kinds, especially stepparents and stepsiblings. As we have said, this relationship between members of the same family is a mystical, spirit-to-spirit bonding. This produces social cohesion intended to provide much of the meaning we humans experience as we go through life.

This relational bondedness is so important to God that he uses the family as a model for the church (Eph 5:22-33). In the church, Christ is the Head with many members in his body. As with the human body, all of the members fit together with complementary functions. When one member hurts, all of the members hurt (1 Cor 12:12-31). There is a relational connectedness that is strong.

In the family, as in the church, God's intent was and is that he be the Head under whom the husband, wife, and children function. All are spiritually bonded to each other, then, and ideally each fulfills a special role in mutual submissiveness and obedience to each other and to God. The family is intended by God to be the basic social unit, a microcosm of what life on earth is supposed to be. Thus it has become a favorite target of the Enemy in his attempts to disrupt and destroy humanity.

Family and marriage are so important to God that we are given teaching on them several times in Scripture (for example, Eph 5:21-6:4; Col 3:18-21; 1 Pt 3:1-7). Among Jesus' teachings were the following words on marriage: "... in the beginning the Creator made people male and female. And God said, 'For this reason a man will leave his father and mother and unite with his wife, and the two will become one.' So they are no longer two, but one. Man must not separate, then, what God has joined together" (Mt 19:4b-6).

When there is separation from family—such as in divorce, suicide, or when a young adult chooses angrily to leave the family—

three painful things take place that contribute to the deep-level wounding of individuals. First, there is a severing of the relationship between family members. The spiritual bonding once firmly holding the family together has now been cut. As these ties are broken, each of the members experiences a wounding very like the kind that happens when a normal death occurs.

Second, divorce, suicide, or rebellious separation can wound a person even more than the normal death of a loved one since it involves the *choice* of a living person to abandon his or her family. "The death of a spouse, though painful, can be a clean wound. Divorce often leaves a dirty, infected wound, throbbing with pain."[6]

In addition to the pain of loss, then, comes the added pain of rejection. Those who have been left are constantly aware of the fact that it was by the choice of the person for whom they are grieving that they are no longer together. To the wounds of separation and rejection, then, is usually added a burden of guilt over how things might have gone differently.

Third, unlike normal death, with these kinds of separation there are underlying spiritual principles or laws of the universe that have been violated. Whether it is the death of a relationship or a family member who took his or her own life, the consequences of the sin of that event and those sins that led up to it must be dealt with thoroughly. Something that is specifically under God's lordship, whether it concerns the bond of marriage, a parent-child relationship, or a life he has created, has been wrested from his hands by humans. Forgiveness may be especially difficult.

The intensity of the wounds left by divorce, rebellion, and suicide make it very obvious that only the forgiving grace of God offered through Jesus Christ can heal. And this may take time. We who minister to people dealing with these issues, then, need to be very patient. We must allow the person a lot of freedom and space as they work through the various aspects of their situation.

With regard to divorce, we cannot realistically offer the wounded person hope that the separated one will return. There is usually more hope in the case of youngsters who have turned against their parents in rebellion. Prayer for the return of a rebellious youngster is appropriate, with advice such as, "Don't count the score at halftime," to encourage patience. In both situations, though, the immediate issue is to give the separated person to Jesus with no assurance that he or she will ever come back. Loss of a relationship through divorce or rebellion is a heavy load to carry and Jesus wants us to give it to him (1 Pt 5:7; Mt 11:28).

Suicide usually carries even more pain. It is so final. With suicide the decision to leave is irreversible. The act of suicide is inherently anti-relational and can produce gaping personal wounds.

"How could Daddy just leave us like that?" or "Didn't she love us anymore?" Unanswered questions like these abound in a post-suicide situation. In helping those who have gone through such an event, we are dealing with the most intense kind of anguish, wounding, and anger.

As with most other deep-level problems, it is usually helpful to allow the Holy Spirit to bring to mind faith pictures of various events. Help the person both to "re-feel" and to grieve again the loss in the presence of Jesus. Help the person to release to Jesus the pain of the memories and to turn over to the Lord the separated person. Even though it is difficult and painful, help the person to agree with Jesus in allowing what he allowed—that the person leave.

Both grieving and forgiving often take longer with these issues than with others. Self-forgiveness and forgiveness of God for allowing the events may be especially difficult. Several sessions may be required to work through all the issues completely, so be very patient and loving as you guide persons in dealing with these sorts of problems. There will frequently be a great amount of sorrow to deal with.

It is important to remember to deal with the bonding issue. Members of a family and also close friends are spiritually bonded to each other. We may picture this bonding as the connection between Siamese twins. All goes fairly well as long as the twins are moving in the same direction. When, however, one wants to go one way and the other another way, there is great difficulty. When death or divorce occur, it is as if the departed person is pulling the other in his or her direction with the person who remains exerting an equal pull to retain the relationship. As painful as it is for the latter to give up this bonding, it needs to be done if healing is to come. In the power of Christ, then, we sever this bonding as we do with the bonding between unmarried sexual partners (see chapter three). If in the case of divorce or a youngster leaving home, there should later be a reconciliation, the bonding can easily be reestablished.

HEALING THE TRAUMA OF MURDER

A distraught mother once came to me whose son was in prison because he had murdered someone. Though there are many complications, the process of dealing with the issues is the same as we have been recommending for less complicated matters. Repenting and receiving forgiveness from God is, of course, crucial. So is self-forgiveness. Repenting to the family of the one murdered is also very important in this instance.

Many ritual-abuse survivors have been forced to murder. Not atypical is the case of a man I'll call Mark. His parents were satanists and had made a practice of enticing vagrant women into a basement room where they would be forced to perform sexual acts. Mark's job as a young child was to slit the victim's throat, while she was in the act of sexual intercourse with one of the members of the cult. A cult member I'll call Esther was forced to entice men off the street, lead them to a secret place, and engage them in sex with herself. As they embraced, her job was to stab them to death. Another woman brought up in a satanist family was forced to murder her friend's baby soon after its birth with the threat that this was the only way to keep her friend from dying.

Each of these persons, and many others I've ministered to, were able to develop special personalities to perform these horrible acts (see chapter eleven). The host person, however, carries an enormous amount of guilt over knowing that he or she participated in murder, even though it was under extreme duress. The trauma of such events, plus the heavy load of guilt, have resulted in demonization, along with a multiple personality disorder.

Though the way to treat the emotional ills that have come to these people is the same as for others, the intensity of the clients' feelings is much greater. The amount of guilt, shame, self-condemnation, anger, and the like felt by these people is beyond estimation. Again, great patience and perseverence are required of the one ministering to them. It is often very difficult just to get them to believe that God could forgive them. Forgiving themselves may be an even greater problem. In addition, when there are multiple personalities, each personality has to be led through the same process.

Apparently, something deeply distressing and disruptive happens to people's inner being when they participate in wrongfully taking the life of another. In addition to the emotional wounds requiring healing, something like bonding between the one who lives and the one who has died needs to be broken.

DEMONS AND DEATH

"I should drive my car into that wall," Larry heard a voice say in his mind. "I wonder what it would be like to jump off this balcony?" another voice said on a different occasion. Larry was a Christian and had been getting closer to God in the last few years. Every now and then, though, he noticed subtle suggestions like these breaking in on his conscious thoughts. As Larry drove down the road, sometimes he would have the notion of killing himself in various ways using his car to ram a bridge or run off the road into a ditch. At other times, when in tall buildings, Larry would feel pressure to jump from the building and actually have flashes of what he would look like as he flew through the air.

Larry quickly put aside these thoughts. He had learned to take "captive every thought to make it obedient to Christ" (2 Cor 10:5b NIV). He knew Jesus did not want him to commit suicide or even to let the thought rest in his mind. He had no overt reasons in his life to contemplate the idea seriously. Yet from time to time he would have these urges, sometimes strongly. He wondered about the source of them.

Larry came for prayer and discovered that a generational spirit of death had been passed down to him from one of his parents. This spirit had tried to kill him when he was born but was unsuccessful. The spirit of death had invited in a spirit of suicide to aid in the attempt to destroy Larry's life. In the deep-level healing session, this was the spirit who confessed to be the one suggesting thoughts of suicide to Larry. Since Larry had been resisting these spirits for years and their only hold on him was generational, it was fairly easy to break their power and get them to leave. With the spirits gone, Larry is now free for the first time in his life from suggestions of suicide. See chapter twelve for more on dealing with demonization.

The aim of Satan and his minions is "to steal, kill and destroy" (Jn 10:10b). Demons are, therefore, active in seeking death. They hate life. They delight in abortions, murders, suicides, and the pain these cause. Often, in fact, it is demons who push people toward causing such deaths. In addition, demons are quick to take advantage of the pain people feel when someone close has died.

When doing deep-level healing, it is important to check with people to see if some of their problems could involve demons. While not all of them will, we find that where violent death is involved, demons are frequently involved.

Margaret seemed to be a fairly congenial person. From time to time, evidence of a hot temper emerged, but she never seemed to lose control of it. One day in a prayer session, Margaret, overwhelmed by several personal problems, blurted out between tears, "You know, sometimes I think I have demons." She was asked what she believed the names of the demons to be. She replied, "Suicide and murder."

Then Margaret recounted how often these themes recurred in her thought life. Outside she was pleasant, seemingly calm and mild, but inside she wanted to tear some people to pieces and had vivid thoughts of doing so. Her reactions to one family member in particular drove her to think such thoughts to the point of almost carrying them out at times.

Demons of suicide and murder, which usually come in pairs, were cast out and forbidden to return. A few days later, Margaret

218 / Deep Wounds, Deep Healing

remarked, "The strangest thing has happened. I can't find my anger anywhere. It's gone! And my hate for people is gone too." She said further, "I called up a friend of mine that I don't even like very much and told her I was sorry for all the mean things I said to her. That's not like me! What has happened?"

We explained to Margaret that her personality had been so affected by these spirits of suicide and murder that the violent thoughts had become habits. When the demons were cast out, the stimulus behind a lot of what she considered her normal behavior was now gone. Without them, she was learning new ways of relating to people in place of the pressure from the evil spirits.

One problem that we need to be aware of is that when a demonized person, especially a relative, dies, demons from that person sometimes attempt to inhabit other members of the family. Perhaps it is family bonding that makes this more possible within families than with other situations. Recently, I was asking a demon how he got into the man I was ministering to. He said it happened while the man was a boy when his grandmother died. As a boy, this man had had a close attachment to his grandmother. This attachment, plus his own ignorance, resulted in the entrance of the demon—an entrance that could have been prevented had he claimed the power of Christ to protect himself.

When there has been a death of a demonized person in a house, the demons will often stay and cause disruption to subsequent residents in that house. When this happens, the current residents need to take authority over the house and the land it is on. In the name of Jesus, they should break all previous authority over them that may have given the Enemy a right to be there.

Graveyards and mortuaries, being places of death, will also often have demons hanging around. For reasons I cannot explain, they frequently stay in places where the body they have inhabited once was, long after that body has left. I have even heard of a church that was badly disrupted by demons simply because they had been given a carpet once used in a mortuary. Apparently the demons came with the carpet. When the source of the carpet was taken seriously, and it was disposed of, the demonic disruption ceased.

Where there is or has been death, the Enemy often has an opportunity to work. We need to claim the protection of Jesus and, if possible, deal with whatever gives the Enemy permission to be there whenever we are in or near such places.

Now we turn to ways the Enemy cripples people from within.

For Further Reading

Bill and Sue Banks, *Abortion's Aftermath*.

Jack Hayford, *I'll Hold You in Heaven*.

Jeff Lane Hensley, *The Zero People*, 97-105; 203-207.

Charles H. Kraft, *Defeating Dark Angels*.

Francis and Judith MacNutt, *Praying for Your Unborn Child*, 129-42.

John and Paula Sandford, *Healing the Wounded Spirit*, 429-54.

Susan Stanford, *Will I Cry Tomorrow? Healing the Post-Abortion Trauma*.

11

Ministry to the Inner Family

A COMMON EXPERIENCE

I will call this person Gene, though he is a composite of several with whom I have worked. His reply to my opening question, "How can I help you?" was: "Part of me loves my wife, but part of me seems to be threatened by her, even to hate her. And part of me loves myself, but then there are voices within me that condemn me, especially when I do or think certain things. I can't even figure out whether I am totally committed to Christ since part of me seems to be committed, but other parts don't. What's wrong with me, anyway?"

What Gene was describing may be likened to an inner family made up of a variety of parts, subselves, or subpersonalities each with a different attitude and response to various persons and events in his life. This concept of the inner family is developed in a very helpful article by Richard Schwartz, a prominent family therapist, and in a book entitled *Subpersonalities* by another prominent therapist, John Rowan. Schwartz says in his article, "In my own work, I find it most useful to conceive of one's inner life as an internal family, in a loose, metaphorical sense. In this family, the Self is like the central executive of a loyal clan containing a wide range of members, from needy children to meddling older relatives. Indeed, if asked, most clients can conjure up an image of each part or sub-self... and the visages of the personified parts range from very young to old and haggard."[1]

Earlier in the article, Dr. Schwartz cites the findings of Michael Gazzaniga, a prominent researcher on the nature and workings of the brain. According to Gazzaniga, "The brain actually consists of an undetermined number of independently functioning units or 'modules' with specialized functions" that we access unconsciously at different times for various purposes as we go about the tasks of living. These modules shape both our cognitive and emotional functioning in such a way that our inner family can be seen to "consist of a group of 'modular selves,' clusters of related beliefs, feelings, and expectations about the world" that govern our everyday behavior.[2]

In his 1990 book, Rowan similarly defines a subpersonality as "a semi-permanent and semi-autonomous region of the personality capable of acting as a person."[3] Furthermore, Rowan traces the concept throughout psychological literature, making a good case for treating this theory as a well-attested psychological concept. A popular, though not fully developed, version of this theory was published by Eric Berne and labeled "Transactional Analysis" as early as 1961.[4] Since that date it has become common for many to speak of the "parent," "adult," or "child" parts of the human person. Similarly, Richard Dickinson refers to certain parts of the human person as the "inner child" and "inner parent."[5]

With this working knowledge of the inner family, we can see that Gene was identifying certain aspects of his own internal life and was puzzled by the conflicting attitudes embodied in the diverse parts of himself. Probably all of us can identify with him to some extent.

Rowan contends that the fact that we can experience such internal conflict indicates that we have more than a single subpersonality. These subpersonalities, then, form a continuum in the human person. "At one end of this continuum are fluctuations in mood, interpreted as a state of mind organized around a particular emotion.... Further along the continuum, but still well within the range of normal experience, are the roles and ego states and sub-personalities within which individuals perform state-specific tasks and life activities...."[6] Farther along the continuum, according to Rowan, are the subpersonality states that are not normal and require therapy. These will be our concern in this chapter.

If Rowan, Schwartz, Gazzaniga, and others who are analyzing human personality in this way are right, *all of us, whether normal or abnormal, are much more complicated than we usually think. "In a sense, we are all multiple personalities."*[7] According to this analysis, such abilities as talking to ourselves, holding differing opinions and attitudes at the same time, even of assuming a different persona as we adopt various roles in diverse settings, demonstrate the presence of subpersonalities within each of us.

Such an analysis rings true to me as I consider how I regularly conduct internal conversations with myself or, according to this theory, with my subpersonalities, especially during times of conflict. It also helps me explain differences in my behavior that occur when I am teaching as compared to playing with my grandchildren, when I relate to my wife as compared to talking with my students or counselees, and when I am worshiping as compared to playing softball.

I see such complexity as God-given, and this analysis as an insight into the way he has made us marvelous creatures as human beings. As we approach the question of bringing healing to those with deep-level dysfunction, then, we are not asking whether there are various internal parts in a person, but rather how those parts or subselves function, with the goal of integration and wholeness for the complete person. In ministering to people, we have found it possible to talk to subpersonalities other than the main Self in *nearly everyone.*

For example, I have frequently been able to talk to the six- or eight- or twelve-year-old part of a client to get information concerning how that person felt during a particularly traumatic episode of her or his life. But not all such subpersonalities I have talked to have been hurting. Some seem to have had rather normal experiences. Therefore, rather than treating the existence of such internal subpersonalities as pathological, as many have, we will here regard it as normal, given the complexity of the human personality.

Returning to Gene, he wanted to know whether the kind of internal conflict he was experiencing was normal. He suspected it was not and thought there was something radically wrong with himself. As we worked together, however, he came to see that the problem was not that there were so many parts to himself, but that some of these parts had sustained damage earlier in his life. His problems, then, could be handled under the power and guidance of the Holy Spirit by helping the damaged subselves toward functioning in a more integrated way with his relatively healthy and normal subpersonalities.

To help understand these subpersonalities better, we need to consider the term "inner child." This term is used in at least three different senses in inner healing and psychological literature. Some use it to refer to immature aspects of a person's personality (see Dickinson, *The Child in Each of Us*). Others, particularly those in the "recovery movement," see the inner child as "the sensitive, vulnerable part of ourselves" that should be discovered, healed, and then nurtured throughout our lives in order for us to achieve wholeness, emotional health, and our creative potential (for example, Lucia Cappachione, *Recovery of Your Inner Child*). Still others find the term a convenient label for one or more subselves created by persons as a kind of storehouse of reactions to negative experiences in their past, especially in their childhood (see Rita Bennett, *Making Peace With Your Inner Child*, and David A. Seamands, *Putting Away Childish Things*).

The concept as we are developing it here is most like the latter usage, though we see the existence of such internal parts as normal rather than pathological. The fact that some of these subselves sustain damage and, therefore, need to be ministered to makes the following discussion important in a treatment of deep-level healing.

Many have found that attitudes and behaviors of parents and other significant persons in their lives are often represented by the attitudes and behaviors of certain subpersonalities as well. These may be called "inner parents." In the inner family, then, the inner child or children of a particular person seem to encapsulate attitudes and behaviors reminiscent of their reactions to those significant others represented by inner parents—responses that may get triggered even in adult life when we encounter those people or others who remind us of them.

I have, for example, been fascinated and frequently disturbed by the immaturity of my own reactions as an adult to authority figures who remind me of my father. It helps me to think of a part of myself as embodying a "little boy" who responds unconsciously even now to such authority figures as a much younger "me" responded to my father. When this happens, the coordinator part of me, what Schwartz calls the "Self," has to take over and remind myself that I am now an adult and that the authority figure I am reacting to is not my father. I am no longer a little boy and do not have to respond unthinkingly in the dysfunctional way I did as a little boy in relating to my father.

DAMAGED SUBPERSONALITIES

Probably because they are more disturbing to us, we are more likely to be aware of our damaged parts or subselves than of those that are better adjusted. Take, for example, a person whose internal family includes a confident, well-adjusted subself, a tender, loving subself, a condemning subself, and a "poor me" subself. It is likely that that person will be more aware of and troubled by the latter two than by the first two. Those who interact with this person regularly will also be more troubled by the latter two. Seeing this person as a singular, uncomplicated being rather than as made up of several subselves, then, leads both to misjudgment and to confusion about the exact nature of the person's problems.

Gene, for example, found himself in the situation of one of Dr. Schwartz's examples: "If a husband says 'I hate you' to his wife in the midst of an argument, she is likely to think, even after his post-fight apologies, that down deep he really does hate her since 'he wouldn't have said it if he didn't mean it.' In other words, people tend to mistake the parts they activate in each other for the whole person... Similarly, if a sad, hopeless part of the wife is activated by her husband's anger and overwhelms her, she may conclude that that part is all she really is."[8]

Gene was helped considerably when he was able to see that different parts of himself could take control at different times and that only parts, not the whole, were dysfunctional. By working toward better cooperation between the parts under the direction of the Self, then, we made great progress toward helping him solve his personal problems.

To understand how our subselves can become damaged, it is helpful to realize that within each person, imprinted on the brain, is a lifetime record of experiences and that person's reactions to those experiences. Often, a subpersonality is built largely around one or more damaging experiences. This is particularly true in childhood when we are most vulnerable. Uncontrolled emotional responses that appear unwarranted in a current situation may indicate that there is such a subself or inner child within, responding out of pain from the past. It is these damaged parts, subselves, or inner children that need deep-level healing.

When there is damage, especially that of abuse, one of the functions of these subselves is to hide the memories from the conscious "overseer" Self. God has built into us the ability of certain parts of us to protect other parts. One may picture, then, an abused subself building walls inside to protect the coordinating or overseeing part of the total person from the traumatic memory, so the person is free to go on with life in as normal a manner as possible. When this happens, it may look on the surface as if the Self is in denial concerning the abuse. In reality, however, the Self may simply be protected from the memory by a subself.

UNDERSTANDING DISSOCIATION: A COPING MECHANISM FOR DAMAGED SUBPERSONALITIES

When such walls exist between subpersonalities and the self, psychologists have come to refer to the condition as dissociation. *The term dissociation is the technical label used by psychologists to des-*

ignate the very human ability to move away mentally from whatever is going on around us and to lose ourselves in something else. We all dissociate from real life from time to time. When we daydream to the point where we do not hear the phone ring or someone calling our name, we are dissociating. In itself, dissociation is not a negative thing. Indeed, it can be a useful mechanism that allows us to concentrate or relax when we need to.

There are, however, degrees of dissociation that far surpass daydreaming or getting lost in a movie or book. These extreme forms involve the building of walls between subselves and the Self and the producing of new subselves to encapsulate damage in such a way that few or none of the memories and feelings are shared with the conscious Self. Though these more extreme forms of dissociation serve the valuable purpose of enabling the total person to survive difficult, usually abusive, situations, they typically become problematic later in life. The person who dissociates to the extent of producing pathological multiple personalities or angry inner children will usually require deep-level healing at some point.

With an eye to these more extreme forms, we will define dissociation as *the human ability to separate off certain experiences from the mainstream of life and to encapsulate them in an alternate consciousness that functions to a greater or lesser extent separately from the main consciousness.*

We are concerned here, then, with the God-given ability to build mental and emotional "walls" around abusive experiences that keeps people from being consciously aware of, or even remembering those experiences. This degree of dissociation involves the separation of one or more internal subselves from the conscious Self to the extent that certain memories are encapsulated in the subselves. These memories are usually partially or even totally inaccessible by the Self until the subpersonalities agree to share them. When someone (usually a therapist) makes contact with one of these subselves, the person will usually exhibit the personality characteristics of a person at the age at which the trauma occurred and the subself dissociated. These dissociative subpersonalities, unlike the Self, are usually able to describe in detail the particular problem(s) that led to their being created.

The degree of dissociation in response to trauma seems to depend on at least two factors: the severity of the abuse and the creativity of the person. When the abuse is great and the person very creative, the walls between the various subselves and the coordinating part of the total person are built very high and thick. This results in Multiple Personality Disorder (MPD) in which there is, for many parts of the Self, a greater distinctness and completeness to each subself than in lesser forms of dissociation, such as inner children. When the abuse is less, though separation of subselves is a factor, the barriers between the subselves are not as difficult to take down. In both cases, though, we are dealing with dissociative reactions to trauma, not with the much milder and temporary dissociation of watching a movie or reading a book.

Although this will be viewed as controversial in certain circles, in my view, milder (inner child) and more severe dissociation (MPD) can be seen as at the opposite poles of a scale of trauma-induced dissociations. (See the scale below.) Within each, then, there is a range of variation. That is, there are weaker and stronger forms of inner child-type dissociations and weaker and stronger forms of multiple personality-type dissociations. Stronger forms of inner child dissociations, however, can be difficult to distinguish from weaker forms of multiple personality dissociations. For this reason we can view them as varieties of essentially the same phenomenon. *(Here it is very important that the reader remember the sense in which we are using the term "inner child." See page 224 for my earlier comments on this.)*

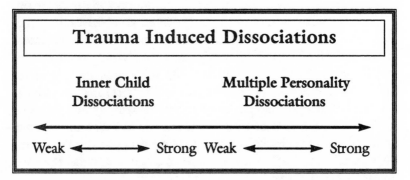

Trauma Induced Dissociations

Inner Child Dissociations	Multiple Personality Dissociations
Weak ←——→ Strong	Weak ←——→ Strong

There is a certain amount of inner healing literature dealing with inner children and a certain amount of psychological literature dealing with multiple personality disorder. Seldom, however, do these writings connect the two. Having worked with both, I find great similarities between them. Since the line between these conditions is a fuzzy one and not always distinguishable, I feel it best to conceptualize them as points on the same continuum. We will treat below first the milder forms of trauma-induced dissociations (inner child) and then Multiple Personality Disorder.

WARNING: Though in my experience mature lay counselors can be effective in working with mild (inner child) dissociation, I strongly recommend that any client who is a survivor of childhood trauma be advised to seek professional counseling. This is especially needed in dealing with MPD-level clients who require skill beyond that of any other issue we deal with in deep-level healing. Such clients should either be turned over to reputable, professional Christian counselors who specialize in MPD, or mature lay counselors should work under their direction.

For those who have experienced childhood trauma, Christian psychologist Dr. David King, who has counseled a number of people with dissociative disorders, recommends "great caution in applying these methods. For untrained and unsupervised [by professionals] lay counselors to apply these techniques could potentially cause considerable harm." Dr. King's point is that there is usually great psychological complexity in such cases. "Any person," King says, "who has been severely traumatized has built up a very large system of parts which protect the person from feeling certain feelings and re-experiencing various aspects of the original experience. Bringing a repressed memory too swiftly to awareness by wanton application of these powerful methods will almost certainly trigger strong reactions.... The consequences could range from episodes of self-loathing and shame to overeating, rage outbursts, self abuse, or even suicide."[9]

The reason for dealing with this subject at all, in spite of such a strong warning, is that as we work in prayer ministry, we are likely to come across such phenomena. We need, therefore, to be able to recognize such disorders and to take the necessary steps to obtain the right kind of help for the counselee. According to Dr. King, however, it can be very helpful for all involved in Christian counseling, whether on a professional or a lay basis, to employ both the inner family model summarized above and prayer ministry. He says, "In my experience the Schwartz model, adapted for Christians by allowing for Jesus' participation in the healing process, is by far the most powerful method of therapy that exists for certain kinds of problems, especially those resulting from deep trauma. I am glad to see these ideas being espoused by someone in the Christian literature. I think it will provide a foundation for others to build on."[10]

This being true, in dealing with trauma-induced dissociation, it is at least as important for professional counselors to engage the assistance of those experienced in deep-level, prayer-centered healing techniques as it is for deep-level healing specialists to call for professional assistance. Alternatively, professionals can learn the techniques of deep-level healing and employ them, in addition to those learned in their professional training.

MILD (INNER CHILD) DISSOCIATION: JERRY AND JENNY

Jerry, a career missionary in his mid-fifties, had been in therapy for some time when he came to my colleague, Mark White, for prayer counseling. Jerry had had a difficult childhood. Unlike many who have dissociative disorders, he could describe much of what had happened. However, he had no feelings attached to those experiences. As Mark worked with him using picturing techniques, Jerry was able to see Jesus in the childhood events, but found himself as a boy unable to turn and face the Lord. Recognizing that this indicated an emotional problem, Mark asked the Holy Spirit what to do.

The impression that Mark received was that he should try to find a "child" subself within Jerry. Without prompting or instruction to Jerry, Mark began speaking to him as if he was a little boy, asking about his feelings during the abusive situations in which he was involved. Immediately, Jerry's voice was that of a small child! In a little boy's voice, a subself spoke describing in detail his feelings as he experienced the abuse. Jerry was shocked by this development. Yet with the information supplied by this dissociative part of himself, he and Mark were able to pray, and with God's help, achieve an integration of this "child" part of himself, including the feelings, with the adult Self. The picture that came to Jerry, then, was of himself as a child who was no longer ashamed to face Jesus and who even allowed Jesus to embrace him.

Now let's turn to a more severe and complicated case than Jerry's to help us learn more about ministering to those with inner children. Jenny is a woman in her mid-thirties who came seeking help for confusion and pain stemming from memories of abuse as a young adult. During our discussion of these experiences, it became obvious that she also carried memories of abuse during her childhood. As the Holy Spirit began to help her recall these early memories, I noted that her voice often changed to that of a child when she recounted what had happened. It was, then, easy to interact with these subselves as if they were separate children living inside of her. In working with Jenny regularly over a period of months and then more sporadically for two years, we found a number of these mildly dissociated subselves, each encapsulating memories of difficult experiences and the emotions that go with them. Though these inner children had been keeping Jenny from remembering these experiences, they were not able to keep her present adult life free from turmoil.

With Jenny, I began the process by interacting with several of these inner children one by one. Jenny then continued the process on her own. In her case, it was helpful to identify each subself by age. Thus, we could label the inner child that encapsulated her six-year-old experiences, "Jenny-6;" the one who encapsulated her eight-year-old experiences, "Jenny-8;" and so on. We found that each inner subself had a series of difficult experiences to recount, most of which the adult Self could remember only in general, if at all. The inner children supplied her with detailed descriptions of traumatic events, though often they had to be coaxed to do so. The need for coaxing arose from the fact that most of these dissociated parts of herself saw their main purpose as the hiding of such facts from the adult Self.

So we dealt with each of the experiences in the ways described throughout this book. As the problems were first admitted to the adult Self, and then dealt with, each of the "children" forgave those who had hurt them. Strange as it may sound, several of them also needed to forgive Jenny for what they perceived as neglect. In addition, we sought to make sure that those subselves who were created prior to Jenny's decision to commit her life to Christ knew Jesus and were in agreement with this commitment.

Most of our interactions proceeded something as follows: once I had identified, say, Jenny-8, I would ask if eight-year-old Jenny would agree to talk to me. I would then describe myself as a friend of the adult Self who was trying to help her with some of her problems. An eight-year-old voice would respond, "Okay." After further conversation designed to build rapport, I would then ask if there was anything bothering her that I could help her with. I might suggest that Jenny had told me that her eighth year had been a difficult one, so we thought Jenny-8 might be able to fill us in on some of the details. Though sometimes shy and distrustful at first, Jenny-8 would eventually talk about the abuse that had taken place during that year and we would deal with forgiveness of the perpetrator(s), and her relationship to the adult Self and to Jesus. Our goals were to heal the pain, to take care of all reaction problems, such as unforgiveness, and to work toward integration of this dissociated part with the Self.

My first interaction with Jenny-13 was especially dramatic. Adult Jenny had been working through this process on her own. She had found it relatively easy to speak to the various subselves within herself without the need for me to be present. But one day she called me to ask for an appointment because her thirteen-year-old would not talk to her. In her picturing, adult Jenny could not even get Jenny-13 to face her. In fact, the picture she got was of

Jenny-13 running away whenever the adult Self tried to approach her.

When adult Jenny arrived at my office for help, I introduced myself to Jenny-13 and asked if she would talk to me. After awhile, she reluctantly agreed and I asked her what was bothering her. She confessed to me that she was ashamed to talk to the adult Self but would not tell me why. Our suspicion was that she was hiding some abusive event or series of events. I asked her then if she knew Jesus. She said she did, so I asked if she would agree to stop her running and to talk to adult Jenny if Jesus was present.

After some coaxing, she agreed. In that context, she eventually shared with adult Jenny the abusive events she had been hiding. Contrary to Jenny-13's fears, then, adult Jenny accepted her, assured her that she was not guilty, and they got to be friends. Soon after this event, Jenny was able to incorporate (technically "fuse") Jenny-13 into her main Self so that they are no longer separate.

HELPFUL TECHNIQUES FOR MINISTERING TO THOSE WITH INNER CHILDREN

Jenny's growing-up years involved a lot of sexual, physical, and verbal abuse. She grew up in an alcoholic family with a father given to long absences or drunken rages and a mother who was emotionally unavailable to her. Such childhood experiences frequently lead to the dissociation of one or more of a person's subpersonalities in order to enable the Self to survive.

In cases such as Jenny's, the predominant emotion hidden with the pain is likely to be anger. Those who grow up in other types of situations often carry inner children whose primary emotion is loneliness, fear, insecurity, the need to control, or some other negative emotion, accompanied by low self-esteem and self-rejection. As adults, then, such people will often find themselves reacting more like damaged children than mature adults, indicating the need for integration and deep-level healing. Yet they may go for many years without recognizing the source of the problem or what to do about it. This was Jenny's constant experience until we discovered the dissociative parts of her and dealt with their problems.

Those who minister deep-level healing will before long confront dissociative parts, subselves, or inner children in their clients. Unfortunately, this is a common phenomenon. But the positive aspect of this is that getting acquainted with inner children can help us identify our adult client's root problems and lead to effective ministry.

Though we have to regard as unproven theory our attempts to analyze exactly what is going on psychologically, it is my experience, as well as that of Drs. Rowan, Schwartz, and King, that these subselves are typically distinct enough for another person to communicate with them. Furthermore, these dissociative parts of a person are usually created as "containers" in which to hide disagreeable experiences and the emotions that go along with them. Working with these dissociative subselves, then, to bring healing to such deeply hidden experiences, needs to be an important concern of all of us involved in deep-level healing. Whatever arrangement such clients make with professional counselors, we must be concerned to see them dealt with under the power of God. For only then can freedom come at the deepest levels to damaged people.

For the most part, once contact is made with a subself, the lay counselor can follow the same patterns of inner healing discussed elsewhere in this volume. There are, however, a few specifics to keep in mind.

Making contact. The counselor has to discover or "make contact with" the damaged subself. If you suspect such a subself is present, first ask the Holy Spirit to enable you to find "him or her," then ask the adult Self for permission to talk with that part. You can then address the subself as you would a normal person of that age. If you are not sure whether a damaged subself is there, you may ask something like, "Is there a little boy [girl] here who would be willing to talk with me?" Often such hurt parts of the self, especially inner children, are fearful of being discovered lest they be treated as badly as they were in the past. They may, therefore, have to be coaxed and assured that they can trust the lay counselor and the adult Self.

Working on one's own. Much of the work with subselves can usually be done by clients on their own. Often, whether in the lay counselor's presence or on their own, they will be able to picture the subself at a specific age or stage of life. Guide them to note such things as posture, facial expression, and manner of speech. They may also notice or ask where the inner child is. The child may be hiding or in the dark for some reason. Often, important facts concerning the problems that need to be solved are indicated by what the person sees or hears concerning such matters.

Accepting Jesus. Dissociative subselves may not know Jesus as Savior, especially if they were created before the person accepted Christ. If so, they can be led to commit themselves to Jesus. I don't know what the theological implications of this are. All aspects of a person benefit, however, when subselves surrender to Jesus.

Forgiving the abuser(s). In my experience, it appears that forgiveness granted by a subself "at the age" at which the abuse occurred is often more complete and effective than if the adult Self simply grants the forgiveness. Granting forgiveness is difficult, especially for victims of abuse. Understandably, it is often a long-term process for adults. When an inner child forgives the abuser(s) for things that happened at the inner child's age, however, it is often quicker and less difficult.

Dealing with subselves at any age. As indicated, subselves can be any age. The fact that most of the abuse that leads to dissociation tends to happen to children, however, leads to the tendency to refer to these parts of the self as inner children.

Acceptance and love. It is essential that these parts of the Self be accepted and treated well both by the lay counselor and client.

Clients are sometimes so "freaked out" by the presence of dissociative subselves that they do not at first make them feel safe. This is one of the reasons why caution is in order in such ministry and why professional counseling should be sought by the client. These subselves usually remain hidden out of shame, anger, fear, guilt, or other negative emotions. They may have been badly hurt and are, therefore, unwilling to trust easily. Unless they are assured they will be accepted no matter what has happened to them or what they may have done, they will probably continue to hide. Further, as Dr. King points out, if inner healing is pursued too aggressively, it can trigger negative emotions in a way that is detrimental and possibly even dangerous to the client.[11] As we saw with Jenny above, if the inner child is reluctant to come out, it is often helpful to invite Jesus to be present to mediate between the Self and the subself. When Jesus is present, inner children will often be more willing to reveal to the one ministering and to the client what they are feeling and needing.

In communicating love and acceptance to the inner child, it is usually helpful for the adult Self to apologize for not acknowledging the existence of this inner part earlier on. While this may sound bizarre to many readers, it is important to realize that the inner child typically feels that the way the Self has apparently ignored it indicates something is badly wrong with it. To overcome this problem, the Self usually needs to spend time with this inner part, supplying the safety, acceptance, and love it felt deprived of.

Reparenting. Disaffected inner children usually need nurturing and "reparenting." This term refers to the ability of adults to commit themselves to be parents to parts of themselves more adequately than their own parents were as they were growing up. This often requires the adult to spend a good bit of time with the inner child or children. This can usually be done by clients on their own once the major issues have been addressed and worked through. Eventually, the child and adult may decide to fuse or integrate. This often happens automatically once enough inner healing has taken place.

When inner children are discovered, either the lay counselor or the client can converse with them as would be appropriate with any real child of that age. It may be helpful to use a nickname the child had, as long as it did not hold negative connotations. Such dissociative subselves will need to be listened to, comforted, and befriended. Allow them to express the emotions they have been holding, then encourage them to give their hurts to Jesus for healing. To some extent the lay counselor, but mostly the client and Jesus, can supply what was lacking in acceptance, nurture, and love. With Jesus we can supply such things as comfort in distress, a trusting relationship in loneliness, love and acceptance in place of rejection, freedom to cry or grieve, attention to remedy neglect, hope and forgiveness in place of hopelessness and self-condemnation.

The goal of integration and wholeness. When damaged subselves experience healing, there comes a time when they want to integrate with the Self. Though this time should not be rushed, the lay counselor should watch for it and welcome it. When both parties are ready, I simply ask Jesus to fuse them. After each such integration, the Self begins to move toward a degree of wholeness and emotional maturity that he or she has never known previously. Though this wholeness does not happen overnight, learning to live in an integrated way usually begins to pay large dividends right from the start. The immature emotional reactions that used to characterize the person's life no longer happen so frequently. There is a new sense of freedom, even though the process of integration has just started.

One pitfall in seeking integration and wholeness is that, as mentioned earlier, the material revealed by inner subselves may be surprising or alarming to the conscious Self. (Once again, this is why professional counseling can be so helpful, in addition to long-term prayer ministry.) We need to be alert to this possibility and help clients to accept such information so they, in turn, can communicate acceptance and support to the subself. Integration should not be sought until both the Self and subself are in full agreement about being joined. In addition, it is important for the client to thank the damaged part for his or her hard work in holding the painful feelings and hiding the traumatic experiences for so long. Often both the conscious Self and the inner subself need to ask forgiveness of each other—the Self for not paying attention to the hurting subself, the latter for causing overreactions in many situations.

A commitment on the part of the Self to pay attention to the subselves from now on goes a long way toward healing and integration. Before integration takes place, the knowledge of life experiences (especially the good things) that have happened since the inner children were created can profitably be communicated to the subselves, providing them with a good deal of hope. Those things that build the inner child's faith to the level of the conscious Self are particularly helpful. In this transition from dissociation to cooperation and integration, the Self can be nearly an ideal parent for inner children, providing opportunities (often through picturing) that the person never had as a child, as well as the appropriate discipline in love that may have been lacking. Let Jesus and the Self reparent the child inside and many exciting changes can occur.

UNDERSTANDING MULTIPLE PERSONALITY DISORDER

As I have indicated, when the inner parts, subselves, or inner children we have been discussing are hurt, they often move into dissociation. The kind of dissociation discussed above is, however, mild compared to what psychologists call Multiple Personality Disorder (MPD). Though treatment of MPD should *always be directed by trained and experienced professional therapists*, it is not unlikely that readers of this book who launch into inner healing will find themselves faced with it from time to time. We need, then, to be able to recognize the problem, if for no other reason than to refer the client to the right kind of professional. As we have seen, though, prayer ministry can make a valuable contribution of its own to the total therapeutic process in dealing with dissociative disorders.

The psychological establishment seems to be coming to the conclusion that MPD is much more common than previously believed, especially among those who have experienced ritual abuse and incest. And since ritual abuse usually has a spiritual dimension to it, when people coming out of such a background seek healing, they often turn to prayer ministry. This increases the chances that those of us engaged in deep-level healing through prayer will be faced with people suffering from MPD. This has certainly been the experience of the lay counseling group I'm a part of.

The following is designed to assist us to understand enough of the problem so we can refer people to professionals and assist them in the therapeutic process. Those with MPD (as well as those with other problems) usually profit greatly from receiving both prayer ministry and professional counseling on a regular basis.

Professional Christian counselors, therefore, are likely to encourage their people to continue working with those who are seasoned and tested in deep-level healing and willing to make a long-term commitment to the client. As I write, I am involved regularly with four clients who have MPD. This brings me into a relationship with three professional Christian therapists, each of whom seems to highly value my role in the process of helping our clients to freedom. And I certainly value their professional expertise and insight.

MPD involves a high level of dissociation. Virtually impenetrable walls are built between subselves and the Self to protect the latter from the devastation of being conscious of abusive experiences. With such experiences segmented off into distinct alternate consciousnesses, the Self can often lead a fairly normal life, as if the abusive events had never occurred. There usually comes a time, though, when the surfacing of disturbing memories or some other mental or emotional dysfunction alerts persons who have been protected in this way to the reality that all is not well at the deep levels of their being. They then become prime candidates for deep-level healing.

As with the inner-child kind of dissociation but with greater intensity, the dissociation of MPDs is a defense mechanism, usually employed unconsciously, against the kind of psychological disintegration that could occur if the person retained a consciousness of the abuse. Like the weaker forms of dissociation, the consciousnesses that get split off can be memories (of specific events or whole periods of time), feelings (such as those thought to be wrong, dangerous, or shameful), or even bodily sensations that relate to abusive events. When children are forced to cope with circumstances beyond their ability, this form of defense can enable them to escape destruction from the immediate trauma. This method of coping may, however, result in deep trauma later in life when the subselves seem to weaken in their ability to protect the Self from the memories.

At the MPD end of our scale are full-blown alternate personalities (called "alters") who have identities, memories, and emotions that often differ completely from those of the host or core personality (the personality most often in control or "out"). In the milder form of dissociation (inner children) described above, the Self usually had at least a general knowledge of the events known in detail by the dissociative subselves. Sometimes, the adult Self will have rather detailed knowledge of the events but, because of the existence of the inner child, be disconnected from the emotions he or she felt when the abuse happened. With MPD, however, the encapsulation of knowledge of the events and of the emotions associated with them is usually much more complete.

As an example, I will produce a typical case and call her Abby. She came with no awareness that she was a multiple. This is the usual situation, since it is the job of alters to hide all information concerning the hurtful events, including the fact that they are hiding it, from the "host" or "core" personality. As Abby described the fact that she could not recall certain parts of her life, however, and that sometimes there were short periods of time even in the present that she could not account for, I began to suspect that we were dealing with MPD.

We spent our first few sessions, before we were certain that Abby was a multiple, dealing with the usual inner healing matters.

There were events she could remember in which she was hurt, so we dealt with these and turned over to Jesus any anger and unforgiveness. As is usual with abused persons, there were also a few demons to deal with in her core personality, so we weakened and cast them out in the way described in chapter twelve. To attempt to get at the gaps in her memory, I then began to probe to see if there were any more personalities there.

I asked Abby if she had ever been called by any other names. She said, "Yes, my dad used to call me 'Sweetie' and an uncle called me 'Pudge' because I was a bit heavy when I was younger." Often other personalities in a multiple will be called by names used by the abusers or even by others close to the person during childhood. When a name is uncomplimentary, it is advisable to get the personality to agree to change it. In this case, I asked if there was a person named "Sweetie" there who would agree to talk to me. Without waiting for an answer, I introduced myself and stated that I was there to see if I could help with some of the wounds she had experienced. I mentioned that Abby had invited me and asked if Sweetie knew Abby.

Soon, a youthful voice replied that she was Sweetie. I asked how old she was. "Eleven," she replied. Sweetie did know Abby, but was angry at her for not paying any attention to her. She was also angry at men in general and her father and uncle in particular for the way they treated her—and again at Abby for not at least comforting her. I tried to explain that Abby didn't know Sweetie was there but that I was sure she would treat her better now that she knew. I asked if there were any others there. Sweetie knew of a three-year-old named Cathy as well as another child, age unknown, named Joey. But she couldn't tell me if there were any others.

In such cases, the first order of business for me is to ascertain that the alter knows Jesus. So I asked Sweetie this question. She said she didn't know him herself, but she did know that Abby had a relationship with him. "Would you like to know Jesus," I asked. She replied in the affirmative. So I led her to the Savior.

Next, I probed to see if there were any demons present. Experience has shown that abused alters are almost always demonized. So

I asked Sweetie if she was aware of any beings that came around and tried to get her to do bad things. She asked, "Do you mean those black things?" I said I thought they might be the ones I was referring to and asked her for permission to talk with them. She gave me permission, and I prayed silently for the Holy Spirit to show me what to do. The word "abuse" came into my mind. So, looking into Abby's face, I commanded any spirit of abuse to come to attention. Within a few minutes, this spirit answered that he was indeed there, so I began getting information from him concerning what rights he and any others had to live in this alter. The demon told me that Sweetie was angry at the men who had misused her sexually.

Disengaging from the demon, then, I asked Sweetie if she would agree to forgive the men who had hurt her. After some discussion as to what this meant and how to do it, she consented and forgave them. I then recalled the demon. He was now considerably weaker because Sweetie had forgiven the men who had abused her. So, using the procedures in chapter twelve and in my book *Defeating Dark Angels*, I was able to bundle several (hopefully all) of the demons together and cast them out. Sweetie remarked that she felt much different, much lighter and less fearful, after that. As we have continued to work with the "family" of alters inside of Abby, Sweetie has proven to be a delightful little girl.

This is how we got started with Abby. Since it was clear that she (and we) needed professional assistance, we contacted a therapist who is experienced in dealing with MPD. Together, we and the therapist have continued to work with Abby and the several alters we have so far discovered within her.

God has apparently built into humans, especially in our childhood years, an ability to defend ourselves by dissociating whole chunks of our experience into compartments quite separate from the core personality. Christian psychologist James Friesen, a specialist in dealing with multiple personalities, tells us, "Dissociation is the most wonderful protection against pain that any child could ever develop. There could be no more effective defense—the child pretends the traumatic event happened to somebody else, and then ... Poof!... COMPLETELY forgets about it. It is gone."[12] This fact enables many to continue to function under very difficult circumstances.

A common scenario is for a child to respond to abuse during the first few years of life by walling off separate alters designed to contain the memories of abusive events, either singly or in groups. Perhaps some of these alters are made from subselves already in existence, while some are created specially to contain the memories. This strategy, then, becomes the person's primary way of dealing with trauma and is resorted to quite unconsciously whenever the trauma of an event is too great. Severely abused children often get into the habit of dealing with even relatively minor crises by splitting off alternate personalities. Friesen states, "MPD usually begins in childhood in response to stress and abuse. The child encapsulates and organizes each part of herself, the resultant splits becoming personalities, each with its own life, history, feelings, and behaviors. Their various personalities may also have verifiable differences in physiology, neurology, and immune system characteristics, which can be proven when the multiple switches."[13]

The Diagnostic and Statistical Manual of Mental Disorders (DSM-III) offers a clinical definition of MPD with three components: 1) The existence within an individual of two or more distinct personalities, each of which is dominant at a particular time; 2) the personality that is dominant at any particular time determines the individual's behavior at that time; 3) each individual personality is complex and integrated with its own unique behavior patterns and social relationships.

Friesen lists four factors contributing to the development of MPD. First, a biological factor allows about 25 percent of all children to dissociate—splitting off parts of their memory and personality. Second, for this 25 percent severe early childhood abuse can trigger MPD. About 85 percent of MPDs, usually women, have been sexually abused at a very young age. Third, if a pattern of continuous abuse and lack of nurture continues, this unsafe environment encourages the child to continue to use this severe form of dissociation as a defense mechanism. Fourth, these children are highly creative and intelligent, with the creative ability to develop such a rich and complicated inner life.[14]

MINISTERING TO THOSE WITH MPD

Following are several important points to remember in ministering to those with MPD:

Like working with several clients. Ministry to those with MPD follows the same pattern as that outlined for any other deep-level healing. In this case, however, it is as if we are dealing with several distinct clients all in the same body. That is, each alter must be treated as a separate individual. MPD personalities, more so than subselves with milder dissociation, are usually quite complete personalities, each with different memories and emotions, likes and dislikes, and even habits. Friesen says, "Every alter is a real personality with real problems. Each has real feelings to work through and real needs that must be attended to.... Every alter is important. Any alter can sabotage treatment if it is not given the same respect as the others. Be careful not to let any alter convince you it is bad—it may be contaminated because of cruelty and it may have spiritual problems, but it is not inherently bad. It belongs to the system, and has an important job to do for the system.[15]

It is important to recognize that each alter has been created out of a specific need. Some have been incredibly traumatized, while others appear not to have a care in the world and serve to keep things organized or perform certain tasks. Get to know them as they appear. Find out their stories one by one—but do not push for more than they want to share. Just like any other person who has been injured, they need the healing touch of Jesus in their lives and will benefit greatly from acceptance, love, and prayer.

Further, since the abuse suffered by MPDs tends to be greater than that of those with inner children, it is often more difficult to deal with issues such as unforgiveness, anger, and hate. So those who minister need to exercise great patience in helping them work through those issues.

The alters will be organized into a family. When starting to work with a multiple, there is usually no way of knowing how many alters there will be. There may be a handful, tens, or, in rare cases, many more—all organized to more or less keep internal order. In this internal system, Bryant, Kessler, and Shirar observe, "You can be certain that ages will vary and roles differ... just as they do in any family system."[16] Though this fact will seem strange to the inexperienced, as in a family, one or more of the personalities will usually be of the opposite sex from the core personality.

Those with MPD "lose time." When an alter other than the core personality is out, the core person is spoken of as "losing time." That is, since the person cannot account for what may have happened during the time the alter was in charge, the time is "lost" to the host. Though such an experience seems weird to most of us, as Friesen says, "People who have grown up with MPD are accustomed to losing time, and think it is the way everybody lives."[17]

Alters are often "frozen" in time. Alters, like inner children, often lack information about the host person's current life situation. But it often is much more difficult to bring them up to date. Time has stopped for many of them, and they frequently live as if they are still back in the abusive situation. When dealing with memories of abuse, they may believe it is still happening when, in fact, it was several years earlier. Thus, they may be feeling abused and unsafe even in your presence. Helping them to feel safe and in the present, then, becomes an important priority in working with multiples. So does the need to bring about greater communication between the alters and the core personality and between them and the counselor.

One aspect of the time problem is the way in which alters recall events. Often, the mere mention of the abuser or the event will trigger what is called an *abreaction* in which the person experiences all of the sensations of an abusive event as if it were taking place right now. Often the best thing to do when this happens is to simply wait, providing comfort and safety until the abreaction is over. Being there, helping them with time and safety before, during, and after such events is most important and the basis on which whatever else we do is built. If it seems best to bring them out of the abreaction, the switching chairs exercise described in chapter six usually works well. Whether or not you bring them out of the experience, you need to encourage them to tell you what happened, while you continue to show them that it is a memory and not actually a present event. Again, invite Jesus to come and heal the pain—physical and emotional.

Providing safety, support, and affirmation. Bryant, Kessler, and Shirar point to four things anyone attempting to help a multiple needs to supply. Multiples need 1) to know they are believed; 2) to know they are safe and supported; 3) to be gently helped toward the truth that the abuse was the fault of the abusers, not something they deserved; and 4) to affirm that it is all right to feel as they do about the abuse.[18] Once their right to feel angry and resentful toward their abusers is affirmed, then we need to carefully and lovingly lead them to forgive.

Working in tandem with a professional therapist. Since there are more complications with MPDs than with other types of clients, it is imperative that the client also work with a professional psychologist. Not all therapists understand MPD, however. The client should, therefore, be careful about whom he or she chooses to work with. Since Satanic Ritual Abuse and other types of abuse seem to be on the rise, it is important that we who work in deep-level healing attempt to find reputable Christian psychologists who have experience with MPDs, so we can recommend them to our clients. An increasing number of helpful books dealing with MPD are coming out. Though written from a non-Christian point of view, the one by Bryant, Kessler, and Shirar is an excellent clinical treatment. Friesen's *Uncovering the Mystery of MPD* is, in my opinion, the most helpful from a Christian perspective.

Integrating or Fusing Personalities. As with milder forms of dissociation, the ultimate goal for those with MPD is to become one whole person. While there are some who do not agree with this or think it is not possible for every multiple, studies by specialists such as Richard Kluft and Frank Putnum have shown that non-integrated multiples do not attain the highest level of functioning and continue to be triggered by outside stimuli or internal emotional cues (see Kluft and Putnam's books listed in the bibliography).

Fusion, the process of uniting the personalities, occurs as healing takes place. Sharing of information, memories, and feelings, as well as breaking down the amnesic barriers that often exist between alters, are steps in the process of integration. Friesen tells us, "*Fusion* is the point at which two or more alters actually become one. Fusions can occur spontaneously in places other than therapy, but it seems safer and more predictable if they are accomplished during the therapy session. The use of imagery facilitates the process nicely. Imagery is the tool, but the alters need to be willing to make it happen. (*Joining* is a good synonym.)"[19]

When the various alters become significantly healed from their trauma, they may or may not wish to join with the host person and become one. There might be fear that fusion means the "death" or obliteration of one in favor of the other. What it actually brings, however, is the blending of all of the qualities and characteristics of both into a normal Self-subself relationship. Thus, the core person gains all of the memories (good and bad), emotions (pleasant and unpleasant), and strengths and weaknesses of the alter who joined. Given that all that is gained is not necessarily positive, it is imperative that each alter (along with the Self) be in full agreement with the process and that all of the trauma be worked through first to insure successful fusion. When personalities are fused prematurely, they will usually split again.

When alters are ready to unite with the host person, I normally ask Jesus to come and do it. The person often reports a picture or various sensations. In one fusion, the core person reported seeing herself standing facing the alter. Both of them were mostly transparent, like transparent fish, allowing her to see the complementarity of the parts she contained and those of the alter. Then she saw Jesus place one hand on her shoulder and one on that of the alter.

As he drew them together into one, she saw both her inner parts and outer body come together to form a single person. Though this was a unique moment for both my client and myself, it has not been repeated in subsequent fusions. We need to recognize that each host person, as well as each alter, is unique and the way the process of joining was accomplished once will likely never repeat itself exactly. Flexibility is important, and the characteristic creativity of such persons is often seen in the fusion process.

After such integration has taken place, it will take a while for all segments of the new combination to get used to the newly fused person. We, and they, dare not assume that fusion solves all the person's problems. It does resolve some, but raises others the person has never dealt with before as he or she struggles to cope with new feelings, attitudes, and abilities. But usually the person reports enhanced functioning soon after.

DEMONIZED ALTERS

The same kind of abuse that produces multiple personalities, often results in demonization. This is not hard to understand, since the conditions that push people to this level of dissociation are the same as those that allow demons in. I have found that approximately 75 percent of the alters of MPD clients I have worked with are demonized. Alters usually carry their own demons and have to be dealt with as separate demonized persons in keeping with the principles outlined in the following chapter and articulated in greater detail in *Defeating Dark Angels*. Here are some tips for those working with demonized alters.

Alters may not know Jesus. As illustrated above, alters often need to be won to Christ first. Then the demons need to be cleaned out of them before we work at getting them to cooperate and eventually fuse with the core personality. For some, it is quite distressing to learn that there may be parts of themselves who either do not know Christ or actively reject him. They need to recognize, however, that these parts have had only limited and largely negative life experiences. They may not have heard or understood the gospel previously, since they probably were not aware of what was going on when the core person made this decision.

A thirty-year-old woman I'll call Diane had a six-year-old alter who didn't know Jesus. She suffered from deep feelings of rejection, inadequacy, distrust, and guilt stemming from some very difficult life experiences. Since at age six, Diane had not yet turned to Christ, however, this alter had been "left behind." As I interacted with the six-year-old, showing her love and acceptance she had not experienced previously, she came to trust me. I was then able to lead her to Christ and get her to forgive her parents who had hurt her deeply. With her permission, then, I was able to cast out a group of demons whose job it was to reinforce the above emotional problems. Soon after this session, six-year-old Diane was ready to fuse with the thirty-year-old core personality.

Victims of Satanic Ritual Abuse (SRA). Those who have been victims of SRA often encounter special difficulties in accepting Jesus because of the lies they have been told about him. Satanic Ritual Abuse abusers often deliberately contaminate references to Christian beliefs by claiming they are doing things in Jesus' name or by mocking Christian claims that God will help in time of need. Thus, the very mention of God or Christ may be terrifying to some of the alters. Also the person may have been coerced into some sort of ritual of dedication to Satan and believe it is irrevocable. Many survivors of SRA have been used in various rituals and often purposely demonized. It is very important to refer to Jesus as "the true Jesus," or "the Jesus who lives in the light," or simply as "the Authority we work under" with these victims.

Sally is a woman in her forties who experienced years of the most horrible kinds of abuse as a part of satanic rituals. She, her therapist, and those of us who minister deep-level healing to her now have to deal with several dozen alters, many of whom are quite hostile and most of whom are heavily demonized. Since the leader of one of the cult groups in which she participated called himself "Jesus," several of her alters consider Jesus to be an abuser. Because such alters are reluctant to accept Christ, so far we have been unable to employ the power of the Holy Spirit from within her as we can with persons and alters who know the Lord.

Some demons have authority over demons in other alters. Though ordinarily demons seem to be assigned to a single alter, some head demons have authority over demons in other alters. When I am working on a head demon in one alter, then, I will command it to tell me if it has demons in any of the other alters. If it does, I command them to be bound to the head spirit so they can be cast out all at once. While this is not always possible, it frequently proves effective in freeing a number of alters from a host of evil spirits at once.

In working with a man I'll call Herb, we found this approach to work well. He came to me with the report that one of his alters was very violent. Though I have had good success in keeping demons from getting violent, I did not want to have to deal with a violent alter if it could be avoided. So I began working with the demons in Herb's core personality. To my delight, I found that the head demons in Herb had authority over the demons in the violent alter. By commanding the demons in the alter as well as those in the core personality to be bound together, I was able to rid the violent alter of his demons at the same time as we cast out those in the core personality. When I met the (formerly) violent alter, his comment was, "Something's changed. I'm not angry anymore!"

Demons may switch alters on the counselor. A common trick demons will play in multiples is to switch alters just when you are getting somewhere with the demons in the one you are working with. When this happens you may suddenly find yourself speaking to a very confused personality who has been unaware of what has been going on, but unexpectedly is forced to come out! To prevent this, I forbid the demons to switch alters during deliverance. This usually keeps them from playing this trick on us. Before I learned this, the more powerful demons in Sally pulled such switches on me several times.

Freeing an alter from demons often brings dramatic change. I have found that, once freed from demons, even totally hostile, depressed, or uncooperative alters usually become much more willing to work together with the one ministering as well as to cooperate with the other alters and the core personality.

In working with a woman I'll call Irene, we came upon a very angry 19-year-old alter. She was especially angry at Irene for ignoring her. As I gained rapport with that alter, I asked her if I could explore the possibility of demonic spirits in her. With her permission, then, I found some and cast them out. To our complete surprise, the 19-year-old alter immediately asked to unite with the host personality. After ascertaining that this was indeed her will, we asked Jesus to join them and he did.

STRONG WARNING: never treat an alter as a demon. Key in dealing with multiples who may be demonized is to *take extreme caution that alters not be treated as demons.* When an alter is mistaken for a demon it can lead to further damage and set the healing process back. While demons may pose as alters and vice versa, they are actually quite different and, with practice, can readily be distinguished from one another. Demons never evoke the kind of sympathetic response that personalities can. Though they speak, act, and have a good deal of information, demons are in some ways more two-dimensional and flat than personalities. While every alter may not be likeable, especially those created to perform evil tasks, they are considerably more developed and well-rounded than demons. With a little experience, you will seldom mistake the one for the other. Friesen provides a helpful (though not infallible) chart suggesting certain of the differences between alters and demons. (See the following chart.)

Discerning Alter Personalities From Demons[20]

Alter Personality	Demon
1. Most alters, even "persecutor" alters, can become strong allies. There is a definite sense of relationship with them, even if it starts out negative.	1. Demons are arrogant, and there is no sense of relationship with them.
2. Alters initially seem [out of sync] with the person but that changes to [in sync] over time.	2. Demons remain ego-alien—"outside of me."
3. Confusion and fear subside with appropriate therapy when only alters are present.	3. Confusion, fear, and lust persist despite therapy when demons are present.
4. Alters tend to conform to surroundings.	4. Demons force unwanted behavior, then blame a personality.
5. Alters have personalities with accompanying voices.	5. Demons have a negative voice which has no corresponding personality.
6. Irritation, discontent, and rivalry abound among alters.	6. Hatred and bitterness are the most common feelings among demons.
7. Images of alters are human in form and remain consistent during imagery.	7. The imagery of demons changes between human and non-human forms, with many variations.

For more on dealing with demons, see the next chapter, which explains more about how demons operate and how to oppose them in praying for deep-level healing.

For Further Reading

Rita Bennett, *Making Peace with Your Inner Child.*

Doris Bryant, Judy Kessler, and Lynda Shirar, *The Family Inside,* 1-41; 44-69; 218-43.

James Friesen, *Uncovering the Mystery of MPD,* 41-67; 69-102; 205-23.

Charles H. Kraft, *Defeating Dark Angels.*

John Rowan, *Subpersonalities.*

Richard Schwartz, "Our Multiple Selves," *The Family Therapy Networker.*

David A. Seamands, *Putting Away Childish Things.*

12

Demonization and Deep-Level Healing

ALLYSON'S STORY

A few years ago a student came into my office for an appointment. She wasn't one of my students and seemed rather nervous, so I asked if she was embarrassed. "Of course, I am," she said, "I don't even know why I'm here." "Don't worry," I told her, "we'll figure it out." After that we talked for about twenty minutes, in which time I got a history of major family dysfunction, divorce, drug use, and lots of bizarre, inexplicable activities going on in her apartment and her life in general since her move to California for school. When I asked her to come back the next week so we could talk more about her family, she was quite surprised and told me, "There's nothing to tell, they're all Catholic." But she agreed to come back.

By the next week, things had changed dramatically. Allyson had begun to hear demonic voices in her head very clearly telling her not to come to see me. They told her that I would not stick with her. I would stop in the middle of the process and leave her to them. This was an effective lie in her case, since she had a history of people abandoning her. Previously, the demonic activity had been more clandestine. Now, however, the demons seemed to see the possibility of Allyson being set free and, in panic, began to escalate their activity to get her to stop seeking help. Demons often overplay their hand like this when they feel threatened. As in this case, they begin to act in ways that allow people to distinguish their own thoughts and actions from demonically-motivated ones.

During the intervening week, the demons had tried their best to get Allyson to capitulate to them. They fed her quite a number of lies. They attempted to convince her to move back home, away from this interference, and even attempted to get her to commit suicide. Their behavior made it obvious, at least to me, that they were desperate to keep her from coming back for ministry. They even tried to entice her to stay with them by offering to enhance certain abilities she had to predict the future through dreams and to know things about other people that she had no natural way of knowing. All she had to do was to agree to never see me again, they told her.

With all of this and more opposition, Allyson just barely got to my office the next time. Although she was Pentecostal and believed in demons, she had been taught that demons could not reside in Christians. So what seemed clearly to be demonic opposition coming from inside of her was a big surprise. Not knowing the demons were there, Allyson had never been able to distinguish their voices from her own thoughts. They played on her ignorance of their presence to get her to believe that all of their deceits were her own thoughts. Hearing them so distinctly was quite a shock.

She also saw manifestations of spirits in her bedroom at night. A demon would appear to Allyson in the form of a beautiful woman, but when asked to name itself, would turn into a horribly ugly figure. The night before our second meeting, God had shown her numerous objects in her possession that had been given to her by an aunt who was a self-proclaimed witch. Though her family had always made a joke of this claim, Allyson was now beginning to take it seriously. She collected all the objects, including a ring she had worn for six years and was still wearing, along with some other objects she just felt suspicious about, and brought them to my office.

She told me where the objects came from and what had gone on during the week. A colleague of mine who is gifted in discernment came in to help. He had not heard the explanation of the objects, so I asked him to come take a look at them. Within a few moments, he had discerned the very objects that she had reported were from her aunt, the witch, from all the other ones. As we prayed together over them to break their power, there was a noticeable reaction in Allyson, who began to shake, especially as we prayed over the ring.

As is my usual objective, I wanted to work on some inner healing issues because, though I knew there were demons present, I wanted to substantially weaken them before tackling them. We talked for awhile, then I prayed and asked her to report whatever memory or issue the Lord had brought up for us to work on in prayer. Once I prayed, she opened her eyes and said she couldn't concentrate on the prayer, felt dizzy, and all she could see was a huge hand inside pushing everything down. Again I asked her to close her eyes, so we could try something else. At that point I addressed a spirit of death within her. Instantly, her eyes flew open and she said, "This can't be happening! I'm a Christian." The demons had responded in her head quite clearly.

After a discussion of demonization in Christians, she was willing to allow me to speak to the demons. That was the first of many deliverance sessions with Allyson in which we discovered inherited demons, familiar spirits, spirits that came through witchcraft and dedication, and those that were attached to emotional wounds.

Now after many sessions, she is substantially cleaned out, though she continues to work on emotional issues. Probably the most gratifying moment was when she told me that for the first time in her life she no longer heard voices in her head.

RATS AND GARBAGE

In the course of a deep-level healing ministry, we very frequently have to deal with demons. In my book, *Defeating Dark*

Angels, I cover in detail the topic of deliverance from demons. I recommend that that volume be used in conjunction with this for a well-rounded approach. Here, we will briefly look at the interface of inner healing and deliverance from demons. That interface is very important since *demons are like rats and rats go for "garbage,"* the kind of inner emotional and spiritual damage to which deep-level healing seeks to bring health. If there are demons, then, there automatically is deep-level damage that needs to be healed. And it is this garbage, not any "rats" attached, that is the major problem.

Because people are integrated beings, whatever spiritual, emotional, and physical problems may be present all interact with each other. In seeking to bring healing, we must deal with all of them. We cannot deal with any in isolation from the others if we want the person to get well. Among the spiritual problems we need to treat is the problem of demonization.

By *demonization* we mean that a person is inhabited by a demon. Unfortunately, many of our Bible translations have used the term "demon possession." This is an unwarranted translation of the two Greek expressions used in the New Testament, each of which means simply "to have a demon." The translation "demon possession" is not only inaccurate, it is dangerous, since it gives the impression that the Enemy has more control over a demonized person than he usually does. The fact is that demons inside a person may be quite strong or very weak (see below), but they never have complete control of a person 100 percent of the time. More often, whether weak or strong, a demon will exert considerable control on some occasions and virtually none at other times. It is best, then, to use a term that does not give the impression of complete control.

The satanic kingdom is sterile and cannot create something from nothing. Demons can only take advantage of conditions that already exist. When they find such conditions, they exert pressure to get the person to cooperate with them. They specialize in finding weaknesses that they can make worse or strengths that they can get people to exaggerate. They like to work, as in Allyson above, while keeping people ignorant of their presence, so they can tempt and deceive—pushing people to fear, anger, bitterness, rejection, self-hate, unforgiveness, lust, shame, guilt, perversions, and com-pulsions of various kinds. When people submit, then demons like to get them to blame themselves, as if they made their mistake unaided.

In short, any of the garbage we seek to deal with through deep-level healing can be infested by demons. Not that everyone who has such problems has demons. There are plenty of people who need deep-level healing who have no demons. But demonic rats may well inhabit people who harbor such garbage. Without the garbage, demons typically have no foothold to exploit. As Jesus said, the Enemy could find nothing in him (Jn 14:30).

DEMONIZED CHRISTIANS?

Usually when we mention demonization, the question arises as to whether or not Christians can have demons. Unfortunately, in spite of the myth that demons cannot inhabit people in whom the Holy Spirit lives, the experience of each of us who have had to deal with demonized people is that we have had to cast demons out of many Christians. In the seven years since I was involved in my first deliverance session, I have dealt with approximately three hundred demonized Christians, including Allyson above, a committed Pen-tecostal Christian. The vast majority of the demons we have found in Christians have, however, entered them before they accepted Christ.

The fact that Christians can be demonized does not call into question the believer's salvation. What we have found is that a demon cannot live in a Christian's spirit ("heart"). If people are demonized before they accept Christ, the Holy Spirit comes to live within their spirit and the demons have to leave that part of them. Demons can, however, continue to inhabit their mind, emotions, body, and will. I have asked hundreds of demons if they live in the Christian's spirit. They always say something like, "No, Jesus lives there. We can't get in." "Did you ever live in his (her) spirit?" I sometimes ask. "Yes," they say, "until he (she) accepted Christ. Then we had to get out."

It appears that the spirit part of us, that part of us that died when Adam sinned, can be the home of the Enemy only until we give ourselves to Jesus. When we come to Christ, he moves into our spirit and we become alive with his life in that innermost part of us. If Enemy spirits live there before we come to Christ, they have to leave. Just as after salvation we still have to deal with sin in other parts of us, as Christians, we also need to deal with any grip the Enemy may have gotten on us through demonization. Though all of us have the sin problem to deal with, not all of us have to deal with demons living within us.

Since demonization is a reality for many Christians, that is what we have to deal with. For an in-depth study of demonization in Christians, see C. Fred Dickason's excellent book, *Demon Possession and the Christian.*

HOW AND WHY DEMONS ENTER

During the course of ministry, it is not uncommon to run up against strongholds in the person's life that are empowered by demons or at least influenced by them. Sometimes this becomes evident while trying to do faith picturing. Either counselees are blocked from getting any images when normally they can, or the picture suddenly goes black. Confusion, disorientation, sudden unwarranted fear or pain, or other bizarre behaviors might indicate the presence of demons. Internal voices can also indicate demonic presences, though be cautious to distinguish between these and the possible presence of alternate personalities.

Demons most often enter a person's life in one of four ways: 1) by invitation of the person or someone in authority over the person, 2) by inheritance, 3) through wrong reaction to emotional hurts, and 4) through sin. In dealing with demons, we are dealing with laws that God has placed in the universe, laws that operate whether or not we know or believe in them. Our ignorance of these laws as Westerners puts us at a serious disadvantage in understanding and dealing with them. As I have said in *Defeating Dark Angels:*

Laws and principles in the spiritual realm are every bit as binding as those that operate in the physical realm. Even an unconscious invitation for demons to enter has the same effect as an unconscious breaking of the law of gravity. If we stumble, no matter how unconsciously, we fall because we are subject to the law of gravity. Or if we consciously declare that we don't believe in the law of gravity and defy it, we soon find we are subject to it whether we want to be or not. The same is true of spiritual laws. *Invite a demon, consciously or unconsciously, and you get a demon, whether or not you know what you are doing or even believe in demons.*"[1]

1. Inviting demons to enter before accepting Christ. Many Christians have in their pre-Christian days consciously or, usually, unconsciously invited demons to enter them. Some have belonged to occult organizations such as the New Age, Freemasonry, Scientology, Mormonism, or even certain college fraternities and sororities. In joining such organizations, usually without their knowing it, they invited the demons attached to the organization to come live within them. Others—by getting involved with certain rock groups and their music, playing with ouija boards, attending seances, playing computer games such as Dungeons and Dragons, going to fortune tellers, or playing mirror games such as Bloody Mary—have unconsciously invited the demons attached to certain games and activities to come in. Some have quite consciously invited demons in by seeking New Age spirit guides or, sometimes, simply by crying out for help in abusive situations. John and Mark Sandford tell us,

> It can take only a moment to become demonized—for example, just one seance. The first commandment is, "You shall have no other gods before me" (Ex 20:3). Deuteronomy 18:10-11 forbids consulting occultic sources. One who does so calls on a power other than God. Rest assured that if anyone from the darkside is nearby, it will answer that call for more than we bargained for!
> Or we need commit only one act of sexual perversion. If

there happens to be a demon specializing in sexual sin anywhere in the vicinity (most likely in the sexual partner), it will probably enter. The prostitute Mary Magdalene was delivered of seven demons (Mk 16:9).[2]

In addition to demonization through a person's own invitation, we find demonization by invitation of someone in authority over the person. In one of my sessions with Allyson, we were dealing with a demon who had an especially strong grip on her. I asked what right the demon had to be there. It said, "Her mother gave her to me." Apparently, when Allyson was very young, her mother had dedicated her to that demon. Since Allyson is an adult and has given herself to Christ, we simply asserted her and Jesus' authority to break the authority of her mother and were able to cast the demon out with ease.

In dealing with a man I'll call Nate, we found a demon who had a right to live in him because of a babysitter. Nate and his parents had lived in a Latin American country when he was small and his parents regularly turned him over to a native babysitter. The babysitter, either because she consciously wanted to infect his family or because she didn't know any other way to help Nate when he got ill, gave him to the spirit. Since she had been given authority over the child by his parents, her authority was sufficient to get him demonized. Again, we were able to take that authority away from the demon and to free Nate. The satanic world takes such authority very seriously and is able to infect many through it.

People from many non-Western societies are routinely dedicated to their clan or tribal gods and spirits before or at birth. It is customary for Chinese parents and grandparents to take a written record of the date and time of the birth of a newborn to a temple, so the baby can be blessed and dedicated to a god. In doing this, the relatives believe they are gaining protection and blessing for the child but actually they are putting him or her under the authority of evil spirits.

2. Inherited demons. Unfortunately, one of the laws of the universe is that demons can be inherited. The book of Exodus (20:5) tells us that the sins of the fathers get passed on to the following generations. This has been an ongoing point of personal struggle for me when I encounter people who have been severely damaged by inherited demons. While it does not seem fair to us that a baby can enter the world already demonized, this is what we encounter. We who minister to such people must continually give our questions, confusion, and anger over to the Lord.

People who have themselves become demonized through belonging to occult organizations often pass these demons on to their offspring. Freemasons, for example, curse themselves and their families, allowing demonic infestation that can be passed from generation to generation. Some of the strongest demons I've met have been inherited by the children of men involved in this evil organization. We have found that almost every type of demon can be passed on through inheritance. Frequently, when people manifest the negative emotional characteristics or even the physical illnesses of their parents, these have been passed on demonically. We have found inherited spirits of fear, death, pornography, rejection, hate, rage, homosexuality, cancer, and diabetes.

3. When people wallow in negative reactions to emotional wounds, they often get demonized. When we are injured, it is a natural response to be hurt. Our second response, our reaction to the hurt, however, is the one that can bring trouble. Apparently, retaining reactions to abuse such as anger, bitterness, unforgiveness, and self-rejection weaken our systems to such an extent that demons are able to enter. When Paul cautioned us, "... do not stay angry all day [lest we] give the Devil a chance" (Eph 4:26b-27), I believe he was warning us against harboring the type of feelings that give the Enemy a foothold.

All of the issues we have discussed as reasons for needing deep healing can also give demons opportunities to attach themselves to us. Again, the key element is dealing with the garbage so that the Enemy cannot find a place to attach to us. Over and over I have dealt with people who, in response to verbal, sexual, or physical abuse have reacted in anger, resentment, and unforgiveness. They have held onto these emotions and gotten demonized. Though they were the victims rather than the perpetrators, they got demonized. I don't like the rule in the universe that allows this, but I have to recognize it and work with the victims toward freedom.

4. Unconfessed sin can also lead to demonization. Whether it is an obvious sin such as adultery or abortion, or a less recognized sin like unforgiveness or anger, when we hide sin we are in grave danger of becoming demonized. Apparently, hidden, unconfessed sin gives the Enemy the right to enter and live within.

If we trace the issues that give the Enemy rights to inhabit us, sin would probably underlie every one of them, simply because of the fallen world we live in and our fallen nature. The satanic kingdom, however, specializes in accusing people and getting them to blame themselves for much that is not their fault. Undeserved guilt, then, becomes a major avenue for demonization. And one of the spinoffs of this is the self-blame that many feel for being demonized. We must, therefore, be very careful when we are dealing with hurting people who often live under a load of condemnation lest we unwittingly add to their guilt and thus to the grip the Enemy has on them.

Especially with demonized people, remember that *if it is not loving, it is not God's way.* Jesus gave us a prime example of this when he forgave the woman who was about to be stoned (Jn 8). He knew, and she knew, that she was living a sinful life. He did not need to tell her that. What she needed was forgiveness and encouragement to adopt a new lifestyle. While we may see sinful patterns in people's lives, it is likely that they already know that and, for some reason, are unable to overcome it on their own. Jesus never condemned anyone for being demonized or ill.

WHAT ALLOWS DEMONS TO STAY?

If, as we have been contending, Christians often carry demons, what is it that allows them to stay? Why don't we become aware of this excess baggage early in our Christian lives and do something about it? These are legitimate questions, but there are several reasons for the lack of freedom many Christians experience.

1. Our Western worldview is a major contributor to the ability of demons to stay with their hosts. The whole subject of spiritual beings has been relegated by Western societies to the realm of superstition and make-believe. We laugh when we hear stories of gremlins, ghosts, and goblins on the prowl at Halloween. We regard fairy stories as flights of imagination suitable only for children. When missionaries come back to tell us of strange beliefs and events in other lands, most people listen with the assumption that there must be rational explanations not yet discovered for such beliefs and events.

We even have theological systems, preached faithfully from orthodox pulpits, that explain away most of the types of activities of invisible spiritual beings recorded in Scripture. Many Christians have assumed that Jesus took care of demons once and for all. Others believe that, though demons may be active in other societies, our Christian society is at least mostly clean. Many pastors, Bible school and seminary professors, and even whole denominations teach that Christians cannot be demonized. And if they believe in demonization, many Christians consider the whole prospect of trying to get rid of them terrifying.

Furthermore, our churches and training institutions have been infected with Western assumptions such as, "If you can't see it, it either doesn't exist or can't be very important," and "If a thing can be explained scientifically, neither God nor Satan is involved." Unfortunately, many non-Westerners, having been taught such Western worldview assumptions in school, have come to believe them too.

Peter Wagner in *The Third Wave of the Holy Spirit*, writes concerning these naturalistic assumptions,

> In my opinion, [they] stem mainly from our traditional Anglo-American worldview which is increasingly materialistic and naturalistic. Secular materialism has penetrated our Christian institutions to a surprising degree. This is not to say we have an *atheistic* worldview. No. A large majority of Americans believe there is a God, and many of them know him personally through Jesus Christ. But our worldview is heavily influenced by secular

science. We are taught to believe that almost everything which happens in daily life has causes and effects which are governed by scientific laws.[3]

When people have understandings like these, the emissaries of Satan can work freely right under our noses with the assurance that whatever they do, we will either not notice it or will explain it some other way. So demons can do pretty much whatever they have a legal right to do in Western societies without being discovered.

2. Our ignorance of evil spirits. A related reason is our own ignorance concerning the ways in which the Enemy does his job. Satan's primary strategy is to keep us ignorant. Even when our worldview allows us to believe that demons exist and are active, we are usually ignorant of how they work. Thus, many harbor demons without ever knowing they are there. They interpret the pressure put on them by demons as that of their own natural desires and their difficulties in opposing such pressures as their own weakness. And then they get discouraged.

3. Our failure to deal with internal garbage. Whether because of ignorance, unwillingness, or laziness, a certain number of people never deal with their internal garbage. Often they feel that's just the way things are for them. They don't seem to know that God can give freedom. Since they don't deal with the garbage, they continue to harbor any demons attached to it. Lest we be too hard on these people, it is often very hard work to resolve deep-level issues. Many start to work on them but get very discouraged over the amount of effort required. So they give up.

4. Some, of course, suspect they have demons but are unable to get help. This problem speaks of the discouraging inability of our churches to deal with demonization. It also is a function of the fact that those who do know how to deal with them are very over-worked.

5. Some who have demons choose to keep them. Often these are people who have been given special power by demons to know certain things or control certain situations. They have been told they also have special protection. If they consider getting rid of the demons, they hear lies such as, "If you get rid of me, you will have no more ability to control your life or to know things others don't know. You will lose all your protection if you abandon me." Out of fear of losing such advantages, they hang onto the demons.

Whatever the reasons may be, it is a sad thing when people allow the intruders to stay. Often, it is a major part of the task of those who minister to help such people understand that there is freedom from demons and to keep encouraging them toward it.

DEMONIC ATTACHMENT AND STRENGTH

Demons vary in the amount of influence they can have on their hosts. Some demons are very strong; others, very weak. For example, occult demons tend to be stronger than those that go by the names of functions or emotions. Among the latter, however, spirits of death, rage, hatred, rejection, abuse, destruction, darkness, and rebellion tend to be stronger than those of lust, fear, confusion, skepticism and the like.

We usually find that the major variable lies in whatever it is that gives the demons the legal right to be there. When first contact is made with a demon, it is important to find out why he has a right to be there. Demons cannot live in a person without such a legal right. We have focused largely on the right that emotional garbage gives them to inhabit a person. They gain permission also through inheritance, vows, curses, and dedications. These are issues based on authority given either by the persons themselves or by someone over them.

If there is unforgiveness in the person's life, or if there are traumatic events that have not been worked through, these will enable any demons that may be present to retain their grip. If the demons have been invited in by the person, they are likely to have quite a strong grip until that person renounces the invitation and cancels all authority given to them. If there is a lot of unforgiveness, anger, bitterness, and the like, or if the person has been deeply involved in such things as sexual abuse and pornography, the demons will be strong. If a person continues to practice these attitudes and behaviors, then, the demons gain strength.

On the other hand, when people grow spiritually and emotionally, demons attached to their garbage lose much of their power. I have talked to many very frustrated demons who couldn't do what they wanted to do because the person was "too close to Jesus." Or, as I heard from one demon of lust, "I can't get him to look! Whenever I bring a pretty girl across his path, he turns his head!"

We can talk of demonic strength of attachment on a scale of one to ten, ten being strongest. We'll call weak-attachment levels 1-3, medium-attachment levels 4-7, and strong-attachment levels 8-10. Since the amount of garbage the demons are attached to is the variable that predicts the strength of attachment, then, when we get that garbage taken care of, the strength of the demons decreases. This is why *we see deliverance from demons as a subcategory of deep-level healing.* See my book, *Defeating Dark Angels* for more on the strength of demons, as well as on the other subjects raised in this chapter.

Even weak demons can harass, confuse, engender guilt, and contribute to many other annoying problems. Stronger demons, on the other hand, can exert quite a bit of pressure even on Christians who appear to have things pretty well together. People seem to have differing levels of tolerance to demonic pressures, however. Some people seem to be strong enough to endure quite a lot of pressure without buckling. Others seem to nearly collapse at the slightest pressure.

FINDING AND EVEN USING DEMONS IN DEEP-LEVEL HEALING

Often when helping people toward healing at a deep level, it appears that there may be demons attached to the problems we are dealing with. Usually I will continue to do the most important job, the inner healing, reserving the casting out of the demons for later when they are very weak. But not infrequently it is helpful to call up a demon to get information from him concerning what to tackle next in the process of getting the person healed.

Working with a man I'll call Ollie, I decided to seek more information from the demons I suspected were there. Ollie was a typical American male, not very well in touch with either his emotions or his pain. We had been dealing with his anger, especially toward his father. I suspected there were parts of his relationship with his father that we weren't able to deal with because Ollie wasn't admitting them. So I asked his permission to see if there might be a demon present. I let Ollie know I would keep things under control and he agreed.

So I looked straight into Ollie's face and said, "If there's a spirit of anger here, I command you in the name of Jesus Christ to come to attention. I forbid you to hide. I forbid you to remain silent. I forbid you to cause any violence, any throwing up, or any other theatrics. I also forbid you to receive any help either from higher-level demons outside or from any others inside. Anger, are you there?"

After challenging this demon and others I suspected might be there and getting no verbal response, I asked Ollie if he was feeling anything. He replied that he was experiencing a tightness in his chest when I challenged anger and rejection. So I challenged anger again. This time Ollie got the impression the demon was admitting that he was there. This came as words in his mind, "Okay, okay, I'm here." Though Ollie's natural resistance to something as strange as having another being talk through him kept us from finding the demon immediately, we now had direct contact. The spirit of anger turned out to be at about a level three, not really strong but strong enough to bring about a good bit of disruption in Ollie's life.

So I asked the demon when he got in. He replied by bringing to Ollie's memory an event when his father was beating him. He was about five years old at the time. This information led me to turn aside from dealing with the demon and to address myself to a five-year-old inner child I suspected was there. The five-year-old replied that he was indeed there, feeling lonely and hurt over his father's beatings and the fact that the adult Ollie was neglecting him.

During the next few minutes, five-year-old Ollie was able to forgive his father, taking that grip away from the demon.

By using additional insights revealed to us by the spirit of anger and several other demons, we were able to deal with a number of other events Ollie had forgotten about. In this way, we were able to use the demons to assist in getting at the garbage. When the garbage was dealt with, the demons were weakened to the point that they were easy to banish. This is a typical way in which we discover, come in contact with, and then use demons to help us deal with deep-level issues.

Demons like nothing better than to disrupt ministry times by causing physical pain, scaring the person, or by attempting to take over. Whatever their tactics, we need to assert our authority, letting them know who's in charge and commanding them to stop. As indicated above, it is best to deal with as many of the inner-healing issues as possible before dealing with the demons. This weakens the demons and reduces the possibility of their being able to interfere. If they are reasonably strong, however, they may interfere with the process of dealing with the garbage. If they do, confront them, get information from them, and use that information to do the inner healing.

Prayer ministry such as this, in which we focus on both deep-level healing and freeing the person from demons, often requires a number of sessions before the person is totally free. Those who simply do deliverance can often complete their job in a shorter amount of time. But a person is seldom completely well who has only been delivered of the demons. And getting rid of demons without dealing with the garbage often entails a big fight. We are not to be discouraged, then, if such ministry takes many sessions with a particular person. Working through the layers of the person's problems is simply part of the process.

GETTING DEMONS OUT

Usually, as with Ollie, there are several demons. They work in groups with one at the head of each group. In the above case, anger turned out to be the head demon with spirits of fear, abuse, hurt, pain, and several others working under him. Though not infrequently there is more than one cluster, in Ollie's case, this was the only one. Once I made contact with the spirit of anger and took some ground from him, I set about binding the lesser spirits to the head spirit. This is done by commanding that all spirits under the authority of the head spirit be bound to him.

Next, we check to see if there are any that have not been bound to the head spirit. This is done by simply commanding the head spirit to tell us the names of any that are not bound to him. If, for example, the spirit of fear is still loose, it is usually because the person has not yet taken care of whatever that spirit is attached to. So we go back to the person and deal with the root of his or her fear problem through inner healing techniques. When that is finished, we recall the spirit of fear to find out if he is now bound to the head spirit. If not, command him to be and it will usually happen. If this doesn't do it, more deep-level healing needs to be done to gain full authority over this and any other spirits that are not yet bound to the head spirit.

When we are pretty certain all the spirits are bound together, we can do one of three additional things. We can send the whole group to Jesus' feet immediately, we can pump them for additional information, or, as an additional check on them, we can "put" them into a locked box until we are ready to send them away. This latter approach is a helpful thing to do if we suspect that there might be other clusters of demons that need to be gathered before we send them all away. It also provides us with an additional way of checking to make sure they are all together, since we can command them to tell us if all the demons are in the box. Often at this point we discover that some have eluded us and still need to be rounded up.

Whether they are simply bound together or collected in a locked box, we can still talk to them. Frequently, by pumping them for more information at this time, we can learn more about the kinds of things that need to be dealt with through inner healing. We can often also find out at this time whether or not there are additional clusters of demons to be dealt with.

When we're finished getting information from them, we send

them to the feet of Jesus and ask Jesus to dispose of them. At this point, it is my habit to say something like, "I command you to the feet of Jesus and separate you from (name of person) as far as the East is from the West. I place the cross of Jesus and his empty tomb between (name of person) and these spirits, and forbid them to ever return or ever to send any other spirits."

Once the demons are taken to the feet of Jesus, the person being delivered can usually see what the Lord does with them. Often he crushes them or throws them away. At this point, the person usually feels a great release. Some have reported to me that they feel empty or light. Most speak of the freedom they feel. Once the demons are gone, I like to "seal all that Jesus has done" for the person and then to call down upon him or her blessings that are just the opposite of the problems that have been dealt with. For example, in place of anger we may speak blessings of peace, patience, and love; in place of fear, hope, confidence, and boldness; in place of rejection, self-love and the ability to feel that the person is a child of the King.

POST-DELIVERANCE COUNSELING

If people are to retain the freedom God has brought them during our sessions, we need to counsel them concerning what to expect next and what to do about it. For example, demons will often try to harass their former hosts and to convince them that nothing has changed. With the authority we have in Christ, however, the freed person can simply command them to be gone. And it usually works. I recommend that people say something like, "If this is the Enemy, stop it!" Or, simply, "Get away from me!"

Our counselees need to know that they have the same Holy Spirit and the same authority we do. All of us, especially the newly freed, need to obey James' command to "Resist the Devil, and he will flee from you" (Jas 4:7 NIV). Knowing their authority (Lk 9:1) should be accompanied with the assertion of their position in Christ. They have probably heard the Enemy lie to them about who they are. They can, however, assert on the authority of the Word of God that they are Jesus' children (Rom 8:14-17; Gal 4:4-7; 1 Jn 3:1-3), set apart to become like Jesus (Rom 8:29), called and chosen by Jesus to be his friends (Jn 15:15-16). The right we have to assert such truths concerning who we are is a powerful weapon for defeating the Enemy when he comes around.

Clients should, of course be advised strongly against allowing themselves to slide back into the same kinds of patterns and sins the demons had attached themselves to. There will probably be many habits to be broken, habits of anger, unforgiveness, lust, and the like. Though habits can be difficult to break, they are much easier when the person is free from demonic rats who spent their time and energy enforcing them. There may also be friendships to break, places to refrain from going to, and other changes of attitude and behavior.

In addition, counselees should be advised to become part of a support group, to spend time worshiping, memorizing worship songs, and listening to worship tapes. The Enemy does not like it when we glorify Jesus and when we associate with God's people. When we do any of these activities, not to mention regular Sunday worship, we make a statement to the whole universe concerning our allegiance.

For Further Reading

Neil Anderson, *Victory Over the Darkness*, 155-73; *The Bondage Breaker*.

James Friesen, *Uncovering the Mystery of MPD*, 243-69.

Charles H. Kraft, *Defeating Dark Angels*.

John and Mark Sandford, *A Comprehensive Guide to Deliverance and Inner Healing*, 127-57; 275-303; 355-59.

John and Paula Sandford, *Healing the Wounded Spirit*, 309-42.

Conclusion

Seeking Intimacy

FREEDOM LEADS TO INTIMACY

We started with a discussion of freedom. We proceeded to present deep-level healing as a method of bringing the freedom God intended to his people. But the payoff is not simply in the freedom. *It is when that freedom to be open to God enables us to experience the intimacy with him that we were made for.*

A forty-one-year-old woman I'll call Joy expressed it well in a series of letters she wrote to me soon after my wife and I had ministered to her at a seminar. Joy is married with three children and seems to everyone to be a happy, committed Christian, very active in ministering to others. She had, however, been badly abused sexually and in several other ways as a youngster. In spite of years of professional therapy, she was still carrying a considerable load of hurt inside herself. Yet Joy says, "When I got set free on February seventh, it was the most life-changing thing that's ever happened to me." In an earlier letter, she recorded some of her feelings at the time of ministry as follows:

"Thank you" doesn't seem adequate... but it will have to do. The Holy Spirit keeps reminding me of your words to go slowly, but it is not easy. I have been *healed* of a "condition" that I have lived with my whole life! I have a peace and freedom inside, and

276 / *Deep Wounds, Deep Healing*

it is undescribable! I'm so grateful to God and to you and Meg....

"Toward the end of our time together when you asked me if I wanted a hug from Jesus, I *fully* expected *you* to put your arms around me. Then you asked me if I saw Him. Boy, did I!!! I will never forget, as long as I live, how real Jesus was and is as He held me in His lap!"

What Joy experienced was intimacy with Jesus. It is this that she and all of us were made for. It is this intimacy that Adam squandered in the Garden. It is this intimacy that Jesus modeled for us. And *since he modeled it for us within the limitations of his human nature, his example is not completely out of reach for us.*

MINISTRY LEADS TO INTIMACY IN TWO WAYS

Since intimacy with God is what we are made for, it needs to be the aim both of those who minister and of those who receive ministry. We who minister in Jesus' name need to start with intimacy. Our aim is to lead those who receive ministry into freedom so they can experience that same intimacy.

The object of deep-level healing is freedom. The reason we need freedom is so that we can experience what we are made for, intimacy with God and others. Deep-level healing functions in two ways to bring this intimacy: 1) when we hurt from deep wounds, prayer ministry brings healing of the hurts so that we can relate properly to self, others, and God; and 2) when we assist others to come to this freedom, prayer ministry bonds us to God in ways we never dreamed possible.

1. Intimacy for those who hurt. For those who hurt, this book is an attempt to instruct them and those who help them concerning how to work with the Holy Spirit to gain more freedom. Though the book is not intended to be a self-help book, many will find it possible to use it to help themselves with the kinds of problems that are referred to. Others will find it a useful guide in their attempts to bring freedom to people who are in captivity to their hurts.

2. Intimacy for those who minister. Those who minister can also use this book to discover intimacy. All of us who minister in this way to hurting people soon find we are receiving an incredible bonus as we spend time and energy with God involved in doing things we cannot do in our own strength. As we pray with people, the presence of the Holy Spirit is real and tangible. The guidance we receive and the changes that happen as we apply his power to human hurts keep us constantly aware that we do not work alone.

Seeing people move from the tenseness and pain of captivity to the release of freedom never gets old. As often as I've seen this process take place, I never get tired of it. And it sends my spirit soaring to realize that it was God *and me!* The God part is easy to understand. When God appears, marvelous things happen. It's the *and me* part that challenges my self-concept and draws me ever closer into the intimacy with God that I was made for. Renewal for me, then, is my constant portion.

OUR CHARGE TO MINISTER HEALING

We are called to minister as Jesus did. Like him, we minister freedom. Both the authority to minister freedom and the aim of that freedom lie in intimacy with God, something that Jesus demonstrated continually. At the end of his career on earth, he promised his followers that they would do as he did (Jn 14:12) and commissioned them, saying "As the Father sent me, so I send you" (Jn 20:21b). To minister effectively, we can do no better than to imitate him.

Jesus, our model, limited himself to saying and doing what he heard the Father saying and saw the Father doing (Jn 5:17; 8:26-29). To maintain this standard, he received empowerment from the Holy Spirit (Lk 3:21-22) and continuously maintained an intimate relationship with the Father. These should be our aims in seeking to minister deep-level healing.

I bless each reader with the ability to follow Jesus' example in intimacy, empowerment, love, and skill in ministering so that you may be able to claim with Jesus:

> The Spirit of the Lord is upon me, because he has chosen me to bring good news to [victims]. He has sent me to proclaim liberty to the captives and recovery of sight to the blind, to set free the oppressed and announce that the time has come when the Lord will [rescue] his people. **Luke 4:18-19**

References for Further Reading

Oswald Chambers, *My Utmost for His Highest*.

Henri J.M. Nouwen, *The Way of the Heart*.

J. Oswald Sanders, *Enjoying Intimacy with God*.

A.W. Tozer, *The Pursuit of God*.

Notes

INTRODUCTION

1. Charles H. Kraft, *Christianity with Power* (Ann Arbor, Mich.: Servant, 1989), 211.
2. Gary Collins, *Innovative Approaches to Counseling* (Waco, Tex.: Word, 1986), 73.
3. Siang-Yang Tan, *Lay Counseling: Equipping Christians for a Helping Ministry* (Grand Rapids, Mich.: Zondervan, 1991), 14.

ONE
It's about Freedom

1. David A. Seamands, *Healing of Memories* (Wheaton, Ill.: Victor, 1985), 54.
2. John and Paula Sandford, *The Transformation of the Inner Man* (South Plainfield, N.J.: Bridge, 1982), 261.
3. Kraft, *Christianity with Power*, 77-90.
4. Kraft, *Christianity with Power*, 1-9.
5. George Eldon Ladd, *The Gospel of the Kingdom* (Grand Rapids, Mich.: Eerdmans, 1959), 48.
6. David A. Seamands, *Putting Away Childish Things* (Wheaton, Ill.: Victor, 1982), 138.
7. David A. Seamands, *Healing for Damaged Emotions* (Wheaton, Ill.: Victor, 1981), 52-57.
8. John and Paula Sandford, *Healing the Wounded Spirit* (Tulsa, Okla.: Victory House, 1985), 14.

TWO
What Is Deep-Level Healing?

1. Seamands, *Healing of Memories,* 24.
2. Betty Tapscott, *Inner Healing through Healing of Memories* (Kingwood, Tex.: Hunter Publishing, 1975, 1987), 13.
3. Charles H. Kraft, *Defeating Dark Angels* (Ann Arbor, Mich.: Servant, 1992), 141.
4. David A. Seamands, *Healing Grace* (Wheaton, Ill.: Victor, 1988), 7.
5. Rita Bennett, *Making Peace with your Inner Child* (Old Tappen; N.J.: Fleming H. Revell, 1987), 174.
6. Tan, *Lay Counseling.*
7. Seamands, *Healing of Memories,* 139.
8. Seamands, *Healing of Memories,* 181.

THREE
Who Needs Deep-Level Healing?

1. Sandford, *Healing the Wounded Spirit,* 126.
2. Neil Anderson, *Victory over the Darkness* (Ventura, Calif.: Regal, 1990), 77.
3. Sandford, *The Transformation of the Inner Man,* 90.
4. Sandford, *Healing the Wounded Spirit,* 91.
5. Rich Buhler, *Pain and Pretending* (Nashville, Tenn.: Thomas Nelson, 1991), 35.
6. Seamands, *Putting Away Childish Things,* 9.
7. Buhler, *Pain and Pretending,* 101-2.
8. Buhler, *Pain and Pretending,* 76-77.
9. Seamands, *Healing Grace,* 155.
10. Buhler, *Pain and Pretending,* 124-25.

FOUR
An Orientation for the One Who Ministers

1. Seamands, *Healing of Memories,* 165.
2. Seamands, *Healing of Memories,* 133.
3. Seamands, *Healing of Memories,* 44.

FIVE
How to Do Deep-Level Healing

1. C. Peter Wagner, *Prayer Shield* (Ventura, Calif.: Regal, 1992), 119ff.
2. Wagner, *Prayer Shield,* 161.
3. Seamands, *Healing of Memories,* 109.
4. Seamands, *Putting Away Childish Things,* 114.
5. Anderson, *Victory over the Darkness,* 43.

6. Anderson, *Victory over the Darkness*, 34.

7. John Wimber, *Power Healing* (San Francisco: Harper & Row, 1987), 198-235. Kraft, *Christianity with Power*, 150-57.

SIX
Helpful Techniques in Ministering

1. Buhler, *Pain and Pretending*, 159.
2. Seamands, *Healing of Memories*, 38.
3. Fred Littauer, *The Promise of Restoration* (San Bernardino, Calif.: Here's Life Publishers, 1990), 185.
4. Littauer, *The Promise of Restoration*, 192.
5. Fred Littauer, *The Promise of Restoration Workshop Manual* (San Bernardino, Calif.: Here's Life Publishers, 1990), 7-8.
6. Gary Smalley and John Trent, *The Language of Love* (Pomona, Calif.: Focus on the Family, 1988), 24.
7. Seamands, *Putting Away Childish Things*, 28.
8. John and Mark Sandford, *A Comprehensive Guide to Deliverance and Inner Healing* (Grand Rapids, Mich.: Chosen, 1992), 52.
9. Sandford, *Healing the Wounded Spirit*, 47.
10. Seamands, *Healing of Memories*, 39.

SEVEN
Our Reactions Are Usually the Main Problem

1. John T. Noonan, "The Experience of Pain by the Newborn," in Jeff Lane Hensley, *The Zero People* (Ann Arbor, Mich.: Servant, 1983), 141-56.
2. Thomas Verny, M.D. with John Kelly, *The Secret Life of the Unborn Child* (New York: Dell Books, 1982). The quote was taken from Francis and Judith MacNutt, *Praying for Your Unborn Child* (New York: Doubleday, 1988), 3.
3. Seamands, *Healing of Memories*, 21.
4. Sandford, *Healing the Wounded Spirit*, 40-42.
5. Sandford, *Healing the Wounded Spirit*, 34-37.
6. Sandford, *Healing the Wounded Spirit*, 42-43.
7. Sandford, *Healing the Wounded Spirit*, 44.
8. Sandford, *Healing the Wounded Spirit*, 44.
9. Seamands, *Putting Away Childish Things*, 11.
10. Seamands, *Putting Away Childish Things*, 138.
11. Seamands, *Putting Away Childish Things*, 138.
12. Buhler, *Pain and Pretending*, 62.
13. Seamands, *Putting Away Childish Things*, 116.
14. Buhler, *Pain and Pretending*, 196.
15. Seamands, *Putting Away Childish Things*, 46.

EIGHT

Healing Our Wounded Self-Image

1. Seamands, *Healing for Damaged Emotions*, 52-57.
2. John Bradshaw, *Healing the Shame that Binds You* (Deerfield Beach, Fla.: Health Communications, 1988), 143.
3. Bradshaw, *Healing the Shame that Binds You*, 66.
4. Sandra Wilson, *Released from Shame* (Downers Grove, Ill.: InterVarsity, 1990), 67-68.
5. Wilson, *Released from Shame*, 67-68.
6. Seamands, *Healing for Damaged Emotions*, 49.
7. Seamands, *Healing for Damaged Emotions*, 120.
8. Anderson, *Victory over the Darkness*, 43-44.
9. Colin Brown, ed., *Dictionary of New Testament Theology* (Grand Rapids, Mich.: Zondervan, 1976), vol. 2, 821-22.
10. Anderson, *Victory over the Darkness*, 34.
11. Bradshaw, *Healing the Shame that Binds You*, 201-2.

NINE

Healing from Infected Wounds in Our Past

1. Seamands, *Healing for Damaged Emotions*, 106.
2. Sandford, *A Comprehensive Guide to Deliverance and Inner Healing*, 295.
3. Sandford, *A Comprehensive Guide to Deliverance and Inner Healing*, 296.
4. Anderson, *Victory over the Darkness*, 194.
5. Sandford, *A Comprehensive Guide to Deliverance and Inner Healing*, 117.

TEN

Healing the Loss of Death and Divorce

1. Seamands, *Healing for Damaged Emotions*, 44.
2. Jack Hayford, *I'll Hold You in Heaven* (Ventura, Calif.: Regal, 1986, 1990), 84.
3. Susan Stanford, *Will I Cry Tomorrow? Healing the Post-Abortion Trauma* (Old Tappan, N.J.: Revell, 1987), 135.
4. MacNutt, *Praying for Your Unborn Child*, 133.
5. Sandford, *Healing the Wounded Spirit*, 442.
6. Seamands, *Healing for Damaged Emotions*, 44.

ELEVEN

Ministry to the Inner Family

1. Richard Schwartz, "Our Multiple Selves," *The Family Therapy Networker* (Washington, D.C.: The Family Therapy Network, Inc.) March/April 1987, 80.

2. Schwartz, "Our Multiple Selves," *Networker*, 26.
3. John Rowan, *Subpersonalities* (New York: Routledge, 1990), 8.
4. See Eric Berne, *Transactional Analysis in Psychotherapy* (New York: Grove Press, 1961).
5. Richard W. Dickinson and Carole Gift Page, *The Child in Each of Us* (Wheaton, Ill.: Victor, 1989).
6. Rowan, *Subpersonalities*, 9.
7. Schwartz, "Our Multiple Selves," *Networker*, 27.
8. Schwartz, "Our Multiple Selves," *Networker*, 20-29.
9. Remarks of Dr. David W. King, a Christian psychologist in private practice in Ann Arbor, Michigan, who has extensive experience in counseling clients with dissociative disorders. From a personal communication of August 9, 1993.
10. King, personal communication, August 9, 1993.
11. King, personal communication, August 9, 1993.
12. James Friesen, *Uncovering the Mystery of MPD* (San Bernardino, Calif: Here's Life, 1991), 114.
13. Friesen, *Uncovering the Mystery of MPD*, 31.
14. Friesen, *Uncovering the Mystery of MPD*, 42.
15. Friesen, *Uncovering the Mystery of MPD*, 164.
16. Doris Bryant, Judy Kessler, and Lynda Shirar, *The Family Inside* (New York: W.W. Norton, 1992), 71.
17. Friesen, *Uncovering the Mystery of MPD*, 54.
18. Bryant, Kessler, and Shirar, *The Family Inside*, 158-59.
19. Friesen, *Uncovering the Mystery of MPD*, 178.
20. Friesen, *Uncovering the Mystery of MPD*, 222.

TWELVE
Demonization and Deep-Level Healing

1. Kraft, *Defeating Dark Angels*, 70.
2. Sandford, *A Comprehensive Guide to Deliverance and Inner Healing*, 112.
3. C. Peter Wagner, *The Third Wave of the Holy Spirit* (Ann Arbor, Mich.: Servant, 1988), 76.

Bibliography

American Psychiatric Association. *The Diagnostic and Statistical Manual of Mental Disorders* (Washington, D.C.: American Psychiatric Association, 1987),3rd ed.

Anderson, Neil. *Victory over the Darkness* (Ventura, Calif.: Regal, 1990). *The Bondage Breaker* (Eugene, Oreg.: Harvest House, 1990).

Baars, Conrad. *Feeling and Healing Your Emotions* (Plainfield, N.J.: Bridge Publishing, 1979).

Banks, Bill and Sue. *Abortion's Aftermath* (Kirkwood, Mo.: Impact Books, 1982).

Bennett, Rita. *Emotionally Free* (Old Tappan, NJ: Fleming H. Revell, 1982). *How to Pray for Inner Healing* (Old Tappan, N.J.: Fleming H. Revell, 1984). *Making Peace With Your Inner Child* (Old Tappan, N.J.: Fleming H. Revell, 1987).

Berne, Eric. *Transactional Analysis in Psychotherapy* (New York: Grove Press, 1961).

Blue, Ken. *Authority to Heal* (Downer's Grove, Ill.: InterVarsity Press, 1987).

Bobgan, Martin and Deidre. *Psychoheresy: The Psychological Seduction of Christianity* (Santa Barbara, Calif.: Eastgate Publishers, 1987).

Bowlby, J. *The Making and Breaking of Affectional Bonds* (London: Tavistock Publications, 1979).

Bradshaw, John. *Healing the Shame that Binds You* (Deerfield Beach, Fla.: Health Communications, 1988).

Brown, Colin (ed.). *Dictionary of New Testament Theology* (Grand Rapids, Mich.: Zondervan, 1976).

Bryant, Doris; Judy Kessler; and Linda Shirar, *The Family Inside* (New York: W.W. Norton, 1992).

Buhler, Rich. *Pain and Pretending* (Nashville, Tenn.: Thomas Nelson, 1991).

Capacchione, Lucia. *Recovery of Your Inner Child* (New York: Simon and Schuster, 1991).

Chambers, Oswald. *My Utmost for His Highest* (New York: Dodd, Mead and Company, 1935).

Cole, Star. "What is Memory Retrieval Like?" Based on material distributed privately by author. (Anaheim, Calif.: Hope and Restoration Ministries, 1992).

Collins, Gary. *Innovative Approaches to Counseling* (Waco, Tex.: Word, 1986).

Crabb, Lawrence J. *Effective Biblical Counseling* (Grand Rapids, Mich.: Zondervan, 1977).

Dickason, C. Fred. *Demon Possession and the Christian* (Chicago: Moody Press, 1987).

Dickinson, Richard W., and Carole Gift Page. *The Child in Each of Us* (Wheaton, Ill.: Victor, 1989).

Dobson, Theodore E. *How to Pray for Spiritual Growth* (Mahwah, N.J.: Paulist Press, 1982).

Flynn, Mike. *Holy Vulnerability* (Old Tappan, N.J.: Fleming H. Revell, 1990).

Friesen, James. *Uncovering the Mystery of MPD* (San Bernardino, Calif.: Here's Life, 1991).

Gazzaniga, Michael. *The Social Brain* (New York: Basic Books, 1985).

Gibson, Noel and Phyllis. *Evicting Demonic Squatters and Breaking Bondages* (Drummoyne, NSW, Australia: Freedom In Christ Ministries, 1987).

Hammond, Frank D. *Overcoming Rejection* (Plainview, Tex.: The Children's Bread Ministries, 1987).

Harper, Michael. *Spiritual Warfare* (Ann Arbor, Mich.: Servant, 1984).

Hayford, Jack. *I'll Hold You In Heaven* (Ventura, Calif.: Regal, 1986, 1990).

Hensley, Jeff Lane. *The Zero People* (Ann Arbor, Mich.: Servant, 1983).

Hunt, Dave, and T.A. McMahon. *The Seduction of Christianity* (Eugene, Oreg.: Harvest House, 1985).

Hurding, Roger. *Roots and Shoots* (London: Hodder and Stoughton, 1985).

Jacobs, Michael. *The Presenting Past* (New York: Harper and Row, 1985).

Kelly, Bernard. *The Seven Gifts* (London: Sheed and Ward, 1941).

Kelsey, Morton. *Healing and Christianity* (New York: Harper and Row, 1973).

Kluft, Richard P. (ed.). *Childhood Antecedents of Multiple Personality* (Washington, D.C.: American Psychiatric Press, 1985).

Kraft, Charles H. *Christianity with Power* (Ann Arbor, Mich.: Servant, 1989). *Defeating Dark Angels* (Ann Arbor, Mich.: Servant, 1992). *Inner Healing and Deliverance Tapes* (Intercultural Renewal Ministries, Box 2363, Pasadena, CA 91102).

Ladd, George Eldon. *The Gospel of the Kingdom* (Grand Rapids, Mich.: Eerdmans, 1959).

Linn, Dennis and Matthew. *Healing Of Memories* (New York: Paulist Press, 1974, 1984). *Healing Life's Hurts* (New York: Paulist Press, 1979). *Deliverance Prayer* (New York: Paulist Press, 1981). *Healing the Greatest*

Hurt (New York: Paulist Press, 1985).

Littauer, Florence. *It Takes So Little to Be Above Average* (Eugene, Oreg.: Harvest House, 1983).

Littauer, Fred. *The Promise of Restoration* (San Bernardino, Calif.: Here's Life Publishers, 1990). *Promise of Restoration Workshop Manual* (San Bernardino, Calif.: Here's Life Publishers, 1990).

Littauer, Fred and Florence. *Freeing Your Mind from Memories that Bind* (San Bernardino, Calif.: Here's Life Publishers, 1988).

MacNutt, Francis. *The Prayer That Heals* (Notre Dame, Ind.: Ave Maria Press, 1981).

MacNutt, Francis and Judith. *Praying for Your Unborn Child* (New York: Doubleday, 1988).

Martin, Ralph. *Husbands, Wives, Parents, Children* (Ann Arbor, Mich.: Servant, 1978).

Matzat, Don. *Inner Healing, Deliverance or Deception?* (Eugene, Oreg.: Harvest House, 1987).

McCall, Kenneth. *Healing the Family Tree* (London: Sheldon Press, 1982).

McDonald, Dr. Robert L. *Memory Healing* (Atlanta, Ga.: RLM Ministries, Inc., 1981).

Murphy, Ed. *Handbook for Spiritual Warfare* (Nashville, Tenn.: Nelson, 1992). *Spiritual Warfare.* A tape series with workbook. (Milpitas, Calif.: Overseas Crusades, 1988). "From My Experience: My Daughter Demonized?" in *Equipping the Saints* (Vol. 4, No. 1, Winter 1990, 27-29).

Noonan, John T. "The Experience of Pain by the Newborn," in Jeff Lane Hensley, *The Zero People* (Ann Arbor, Mich.: Servant, 1983), 141-56.

Nouwen, Henri J.M. *The Way of the Heart* (New York: Ballantine, 1981).

Payne, Leanne. *The Broken Image* (Westchester, Ill.: Crossway, 1981). *The Healing Presence* (Westchester, Ill.: Crossway, 1989).

Powell, John, S.J. *Why Am I Afraid To Love?* (Niles, Ill.: Argus Communications, 1975).

Putnam, Frank W. *Diagnosis and Treatment of Multiple Personality Disorder* (New York.: The Guilford Press, 1989).

Pytches, Mary. *Set My People Free* (London: Hodder and Stoughton, 1987). *A Healing Fellowship* (London: Hodder and Stoughton, 1988). *Yesterday's Child* (London: Hodder and Stoughton, 1990). *A Child No More* (London: Hodder and Stoughton, 1991).

Reed, William S. *Healing of the Whole Man—Mind, Body, Spirit* (Old Tappan, N.J.: Spire Books, 1979).

Rentzel, Lori. *Emotional Dependency* (Downers Grove, Ill.: InterVarsity Press, 1990).

Rowan, John. *Subpersonalities* (New York.: Routledge, 1990).

Sanders, J. Oswald. *Enjoying Intimacy With God* (Chicago, Ill.: Moody, 1980).

Sandford, John and Mark. *A Comprehensive Guide to Deliverance and Inner Healing* (Grand Rapids, Mich.: Chosen, 1992).

Sandford, John and Paula. *The Transformation of the Inner Man* (South Plainfield, N.J.: Bridge, 1982). *Healing the Wounded Spirit* (Tulsa, Okla.: Victory House, 1985).

Sandford, Loren. *Wounded Warriors—Surviving Seasons of Stress* (Tulsa, Okla.: Victory House, 1987).

Sandford, Paula. *Healing Victims of Sexual Abuse* (Tulsa, Okla.: Victory House, 1988).

Sanford, Agnes. *The Healing Gifts of the Spirit* (Old Tappan, N.J.: Revell, 1966).

Scanlan, Michael. *Inner Healing* (New York.: Paulist Press, 1974).

Schwartz, Richard. "Our Multiple Selves," in *The Family Therapy Networker* (Washington, D.C.: The Family Therapy Network, Inc.), March-April 1987, 25-31; 80-83.

Seamands, David A. *Healing for Damaged Emotions* (Wheaton, Ill.: Victor, 1981). *Putting Away Childish Things* (Wheaton, Ill.: Victor, 1982). *Healing of Memories* (Wheaton, Ill.: Victor, 1985). *Healing Grace* (Wheaton, Ill.: Victor, 1988).

Smalley, Gary and John Trent. *The Language of Love* (Pomona, Calif.: Focus on the Family, 1988).

Smedes, Lewis B. *Forgive and Forget* (San Francisco: Harper and Row, 1984). *Caring and Commitment* (San Francisco: Harper and Row, 1988).

Spenser, J. *Suffer the Child* (New York: Pocket Books, 1989).

Stapleton, Ruth. *The Gift of Inner Healing* (Waco, Tex.: Word, 1976). *The Experience of Inner Healing* (Waco, Tex.: Word, 1977).

Stanford, Susan. *Will I Cry Tomorrow? Healing the Post-Abortion Trauma* (Old Tappan, N.J.: Revell, 1987).

Tan, Siang-Yang. *Lay Counseling: Equipping Christians for a Helping Ministry* (Grand Rapids, Mich.: Zondervan, 1991).

Tapscott, Betty. *Inner Healing through Healing of Memories* (Kingwood, Tex.: Hunter Publishing, 1975, 1987). *Ministering Inner Healing Biblically* (Houston, Tex.: Tapscott Ministries, 1987).

Tozer, A. W. *The Pursuit of God* (India: Alliance Publications, 1967).

Verny, Thomas, M.D., with John Kelly. *The Secret Life of the Unborn Child* (New York: Dell Books, 1982).

Wagner, C. Peter. *The Third Wave of the Holy Spirit* (Ann Arbor, Mich.: Servant, 1988). *Prayer Shield* (Ventura, Calif.: Regal, 1992).

White, Thomas B. *The Believer's Guide to Spiritual Warfare* (Ann Arbor, Mich.: Servant, 1990).

Whitfield, Charles L. *Healing the Child Within* (Deerfield Beach, Fla.: Health Communictions Inc., 1987).

Wilson, Sandra. *Released from Shame* (Downers Grove, Ill.: InterVarsity Press, 1990).

Wimber, John. *Power Healing* (San Francisco: Harper and Row, 1987).

Index